new york real estate sales

REVIEW CRAMMER™

3rd edition

HONDROS LEARNING™

HONDROS LEARNING™
4140 Executive Parkway
Westerville, Ohio 43081
www.hondroslearning.com

14 13 12 11 10   1 2 3 4 5
978-1-59844-163-5

For more information on, or to purchase, our products, please call 1-866-84LEARN or visit www.hondroslearning.com

TABLE OF CONTENTS

NEW YORK REAL ESTATE SALES—REVIEW CRAMMER™

You have completed your real estate pre-licensing coursework. Now what? It is time to begin preparation for the real estate licensing exam. New York Real Estate Sales— Review Crammer focuses on the concepts, subjects, and topics you must know to pass the New York State Real Estate Licensing Exam.

A thorough review of the information presented here along with the knowledge you gained from your 75 hours of pre-licensing education are what you need to pass the exam and begin a rewarding career in real estate.

Crammer highlights include:

- Test-taking techniques to help reduce anxiety by fully preparing you for exam day
- Detailed key terms listings to reinforce the terms that form the basis of many exam questions
- Chapter quizzes on key points to immediately apply what you learned to help you retain the information more easily
- Math review includes concepts for a solid knowledge base and exam success

USING THE CRAMMER

This text was designed to give you the information you need to successfully pass the New York State Real Estate Licensing Exam. Contained here is a **complete review of important topics included on the exam**.

You will find the information presented in a clear and concise manner. Extensive key terms listings, chapter summaries, and chapter quizzes reinforce the concepts presented throughout each chapter.

ADDITIONAL EXAM PREPARATION PRODUCTS FROM HONDROS LEARNING

- New York Real Estate Sales CompuCram® Exam Prep Software
- Real Estate Vocab Crammer Audio CD and Dictionary
- Real Estate Vocab Crammer Flash Cards
- Real Estate Math Practice CompuCram
- Real Estate Sales National Crammer Course (textbook included)

INTRODUCTION

New York Examination

Before you can apply and be seated for your sales examination, you must complete all requirements for prelicensing. The New York Department of State (www.dos.state.ny.us) provides exam procedures, policies, score reporting, and information about the exam.

Through this site, you will also be able to access a user-friendly online Occupational Licensing Management System called **eAccessNY** from which you can:

- Schedule your state licensing examination
- View the results of your licensing examination
- Submit your real estate license application
- Renew your license

To use eAccessNY, you must first register and set up a user account. After completing the online form, you'll receive an email with a temporary password. Then, when you log into eAccessNY, you can then change your password and complete your desired tasks. If you have already registered on eAccessNY, you simply need to log in with your user ID and password to complete the tasks listed above.

New York Exam Policies

Test moderators enforce the regulations closely. When you schedule your examination, you will be given specific requirements about what you can bring into the examination room and what you cannot bring. Pay attention to the guidelines and follow them closely. Don't fail your exam because of a simple technicality.

Calculators are permitted if they are battery or solar powered, silent, nonprinting, and do not contain an alphabetic keyboard.

◊ **Caution:** Your calculator may not function properly, just when you need it most. Be sure you take two calculators with new and extra batteries.

The following items are *not* permitted:

- PDAs
- Dictionaries, books, other reference materials, large bags
- Eating, drinking, or smoking
- Visitors, guests, and children

Cellular phones, beepers, and any other electronic devices must be turned off during the exam.

Most important, any person found using notes, books, or other aids; giving or receiving help; removing examination materials or notes from the exam site; causing a disturbance or engaging in practices contrary to the rules of proper examination conduct will be dismissed from the exam site. Any decisions regarding disciplinary measures will be made by the Exam Supervisor at the Department of State.

About the Exam

The written exam includes all multiple choice questions and is based on the 75-hour pre-licensing curriculum. You will be allowed **1 1/2 hours** to complete the test.

You must correctly answer at least **70 percent** of the questions to pass the exam. Exam results are reported as either passed or failed; you will not receive a numerical score.

Exam results will be available online by utilizing your account in eAccessNY. The exam results will be available as soon as possible after they are received by the Exam Unit and scored. If you pass the exam, you should apply online utilizing your account in eAccessNY. If you fail the exam, you can schedule another exam by utilizing your account in eAccessNY.

Passed exam results are only valid for a period of **two years**. Results will not be given over the phone, so please do not call Licensing Services for them.

Basic Test Taking Techniques

Since it may have been a while since you've taken an exam, let's start with a review of some basic test-taking techniques. The licensing exam focuses on concepts, definitions, calculations, and techniques. Definitions of real estate language and terms represent one of the largest parts of the exam. These techniques can easily add 10 to 15 points to your score:

1. *Read the question. Read the question. Read the question.* Read the question at least **three times** before you look at the answers, and then read the answers at least two times before selecting the best one. People tend to read the questions quickly. Don't do this since you'll often read it so fast you will fall into the "sounds alike" trap and confuse words, (e.g., grantor versus grantee, gross income versus net income). When reading a question, do not jump to quick conclusions. Before you choose an answer, be sure you have read the entire question and all answer choices.

2. *Answer questions that you know first, then go back to the other questions.* Do not spend a lot of time on one question. Go through the exam and answer only those questions that you ***know*** are correct. If you're in doubt about an answer, skip the question and go to the next one. It's best to move through the questions you can answer as quickly as possible and return to the others later, if you have time. If you are in doubt about a question, "mark" it, skip it, and move on. At the end of the test, after answering the questions you know, go back and review all marked questions, if you have time. Sometimes other questions in the exam will help you answer a question with which you are struggling.

3. *Relax and keep calm.* Maintain your concentration. Sometimes, you may lose your train of thought because a question appears to be poorly written, make no sense, or have more than one correct answer. Getting caught on one of these questions can throw you off for a series of questions to follow. When this happens, relax your mind and your muscles—and skip the question. There may be three or four of these questions on the exam. If, by chance, you miss them because you had to guess, you will not fail. What causes you to fail the exam is becoming so frustrated that you miss the second, third, or fourth question after that. Keep your composure. Remember, even if you miss these and no others, you will still pass.

4. *Look for the best answer.* If a question on the exam appears to have more than one correct answer, look for the best answer based on the supplied information— not your assumptions.

5. *Answer all questions, even if you have to guess.* Two of the four answers are often not even worth considering. Narrow your choices by process of elimination—weeding out the obviously incorrect answers, or answers you know are wrong. Pick one of the remaining answers when guessing.

6. *Don't change your answers.* Your first answer is usually the right one. Don't change it unless you're sure.

7. *Eliminate answers with absolutes.* Answers with absolutes such as must, always, greatest, never, and has to be are generally not the correct ones.

8. *Be careful of "except" questions.* You tend to read these questions too fast and even though you know the correct answer, you will choose the opposite.

> **All are required to be included in any ad placed by a broker except the broker's**
> A. identification as a broker.
> B. license number.
> C. name.
> D. phone number or address.

The best way to answer these questions is to cover the word except or not when reading the question, and then decide which choice does not belong. '

9. *Watch your time and use it wisely.* Watch your time to ensure you budget it wisely, but remember time is **not** your enemy. You'll have plenty of time to complete the exam as long as you work consistently. Do not spend 15 minutes on one question to get one point, when you could have answered 10 questions for 10 points.

   If you try to answer every question the first time through, you may end up wasting valuable time on the questions you are not sure of. This will only increase your anxiety level. If you see this happening, make a concerted effort to answer only the questions you know and can complete quickly. After you've regained your sense of balance, go back and answer the difficult questions. If you have used your time well on the review exam, you will be prepared for the real exam.

10. *Double check your math and don't be thrown off if your calculation is slightly off.* Double-check your math answers by reversing the process, if time permits. Also, it's possible that different calculators round answers differently. Since this is the case, don't let small differences in math worry you. Close counts! Pick the closest answer and move on. Do not waste 10 minutes looking for 10 cents in your answer.

11. *When coming back to skipped questions, read them carefully and completely.* If you have the time to review the questions you skipped, take time to **read them again completely**. Then, dissect the question into parts (clauses and prepositional phrases). This will help you understand what the question is really asking. This is even true for math questions. When you cannot determine the answer, and before you guess, ask yourself, "What concept is this question trying to make sure I know?"

    Ask yourself which answer best illustrates that concept. Keep in mind that the purpose of the exam is to make sure you have the minimum amount of knowledge needed to function in the real estate industry.

12. *Above all—don't panic!* During the exam, you may lose your train of thought. When this occurs, stop and take a moment to relax. Take a deep breath, let your shoulders drop; relax your muscles and your mind before proceeding. Recall what you have studied. You know more than you think you do—just relax enough to let it become clear.

13. *Be positive and have confidence.* Starting today, say to anyone who will listen, "I'm going to pass the exam," and mean it!

Most importantly, though, you need to be relaxed. If you study and prepare, you'll do fine. Telling your family, friends, and colleagues you are taking the exam creates pressure on you by setting expectations. Constant worrying about everyone's expectations for success may have the opposite effect on your ability to comfortably and successfully complete the exam. Go back and tell everyone you have decided to wait a month before taking the exam. Their expectations will disappear, and the sense of pressure will be gone. Try it—it works!

Using the Review Crammer™

Remember there's only one sure-fire way to pass the exam—study. This Review Crammer™ has been developed with that in mind. To create your best chance for success on the New York Real Estate Sales Exam, once you have completed your pre-licensing course(s), immediately begin studying for the state exam by reading this Review Crammer™ in its entirety and doing the following:

1. Put the test taking techniques we just discussed into practice as you take the sample quizzes at the end of each chapter. Learn the techniques so they become second nature.

2. Memorize the key terms in every chapter. When you read the key terms the first time, mark the terms you don't know. Read them a second time, focusing on the marked terms. Highlight terms you still don't know the second time and repeat this review process. There's an added benefit to knowing all the key terms: **If you do not know what a word means in a test answer, then it is probably NOT the right answer.**

3. As you read all sections of this Review Crammer™ book the first time, mark the concepts you don't know. Read the Review Crammer™ a second time, focusing only on the marked parts. Highlight concepts you don't know on the second reading and repeat this review process. **Read, review, and focus on these areas!**

4. Review the basic math formulas in the Math Review chapter. Follow the steps in each example that illustrate the formula. Then, do the sample problems to be sure you understand the concept. These formulas have been broken down to the most basic steps. If you can do these, you can do almost all the math on the exam. If there are one or two formulas you can't get, don't worry too much because you should only see these in a few questions on the exam—not enough to cause you to fail.

Golden Rules

If you have studied all the material in this Review Crammer™ and followed our advice for test-taking techniques and how to study, you should do well on your exam. Remember to:

1. Read the question. Read the question. Read the question! Read all of the answers, too, before you make a choice.

2. Answer all questions, even if you have to guess.

3. Your first answer is usually the right one. So, don't change it unless you're sure.

4. Answers with absolutes such as must, always, greatest, never, and has to be are generally *not* the correct choices.

5. Know definitions! Study the key terms in this book—if you don't, you are doing yourself a disservice.

6. For math questions, at least know the circle formula and tax formula.

7. For math questions, when in doubt, DIVIDE (÷).

8. If you're not sure of a math question, you can always try plugging in each of the given answers.

9. For math questions, close counts on the exam—don't waste time trying to get an exact match, since rounding may be different.

10. Double-check your math answers by reversing the process, if time permits.

In conclusion, if you do it once, do it right, and do it as outlined in this book, you'll never have to do it again—and you'll be on the road to success in your real estate career!

The Real Estate Profession

A real estate license and affiliation with a broker are necessary to act as an agent for someone who wants to buy or sell real estate. In New York, a real estate license also covers who wish to become:

- Commercial agents
- Property managers
- Rental agents who negotiate leases with residential and/or commercial tenants

There are six exceptions to New York's real estate license requirements, including:

1. Attorneys licensed to practice in New York.
2. Building supervisors and maintenance workers.
3. Persons acting in any capacity under the judgment of the court.
4. Property owners.
5. Public officers.
6. Tenants' associations and nonprofit corporations.

Careers in Real Estate

In addition to the brokerage and sales side of the real estate business, many careers exist within the field, including in:

- Finance
- Appraisal
- Property management
- Development
- Title work
- Trade association work
- Education
- Government work
- Urban planning

Personal Considerations

After confirming your preference for a real estate sales career over a career in another aspect of real estate, you must then select a broker with whom to work. When choosing a broker, consider:

- The level of training offered

- The office support staff available to you
- The compensation plans offered

Like any career, there are advantages and disadvantages to real estate sales.

Advantages

- Compensation is based on commissions, so earnings are only limited by your knowledge, experience, desire, activity, and hard work
- You control your time
- Office time is kept to a minimum, as contact with people is the primary means of soliciting listings, showing properties, and making sales
- Owning your own brokerage is possible

Disadvantages

- Since compensation is based on commissions, your income may not be steady, especially in the early stages
- Real estate sales are affected by seasonal and cyclical swings
- Most successful people in real estate need to work at least some evenings and weekends

Specializations within Real Estate

Within residential and commercial real estate, there are a number of specialties:

- Single-family residential properties
- Multi-family residential properties
- Condominiums and cooperatives
- Commercial properties
- Property management
- Industrial properties
- Farm properties

Professional Organizations

Real estate licensees may choose to join one or more of many national, state, and local professional organizations. Some important organizations are:

- **National Association of REALTORS®** (NAR®). Only those who join the National Association of REALTORS® may use the term REALTOR® because it is a registered trademark of NAR®. A primary benefit of NAR® membership is participation in the Multiple Listing Service (MLS), a service whereby local member brokers agree to share listings, and agree to share commissions on properties sold jointly.
- **New York State Association of REALTORS®** (NYSAR®). A not-for-profit trade organization representing more than 54,000 of New York State's real estate professionals, providing a variety of benefits including legislative and legal representation, educational programs, publications such as the New York State REALTOR, and a code of professional standards.
- **National Association of Real Estate Brokers®** (NAREB®). Comprised mostly of minority brokers, members of NAREB® use the term Realtist.
- **Women's Council of REALTORS®** (WCR®). Committed to addressing the issues, needs, and concerns of women in the real estate profession.

Real Estate License Law

Key Terms

Administrative Discipline The New York Department of State's enforcement of license laws through reprimand and denial as well as the suspension and revocation of licenses.

Apartment Sharing Agent An individual licensed by the New York Department of State who, for compensation, arranges, conducts, or coordinates meetings between a customer and the current owner or occupant of legally occupied real property.

Article 12-A Article of New York Real Property Law, which contains most of the laws relevant to real estate brokers and salespeople.

Article 78 Proceeding Refers to an article of the Civil Practice Law and Rules that allows aggrieved persons to bring an action against a government body or officer.

Associate Broker A real estate broker who works for another broker.

Blind Ad An ad in which a broker attempts to advertise a property for sale without disclosing the fact she is a licensed real estate broker or when a broker attempts to mislead the public into believing a property is for sale by owner. Blind ads are illegal in New York.

Broker One who is licensed to represent one of the parties in a real estate transaction, for compensation.

Commingling Illegally mixing money held in trust on behalf of a client with personal funds.

Continuing Education In order to renew a real estate license and keep up to date on real estate knowledge and trends, licensees must complete 22.5 hours of continuing education courses in the two years prior to renewal. Coursework must provide at least three hours of instruction on fair housing or discrimination in the sale or rental of property. These courses must be approved by the Department of State.

Dual Licensure When real estate licensees hold more than one license at a time.

Escrow System in which things of value (e.g., money or documents) are held on behalf of parties to a transaction by a disinterested third party (escrow agent), until specific conditions have been satisfied. *Also called*: **In Escrow**.

Exemption Provision holding that a law or rule does not apply to a particular person, entity, or group (e.g., a company with a property tax exemption does not have to pay property taxes).

(continued on next page)

The New York Department of State

- The purpose of license law is to protect the public by ensuring a consistent level of competence, ethics, and professionalism.
- New York license law is found in **Article 12-A** of Real Property Law, Licensing of Real Estate Brokers and Real Estate Salespersons of the New York Administrative Code.
- In New York, the state agency that issues real estate licenses to qualified applicants is the **Department of State, Division of Licensing Services**.

Secretary of State

The Secretary of State is responsible for the administration of licensing, examination, education, and compliance provisions of Article 12-A, the rules of the Board, and the rules of the Secretary of State. The Secretary has specific authority to adopt rules and regulations as well as the authority to:

- Enforce the provisions of Article 12-A upon complaint by any person or upon the secretary's own initiative.
- Investigate any violation.
- Investigate the business, business practices, and business methods of any person applying for or holding a license as a real estate broker or salesperson.

Key Terms - continued

Irrevocable Consent A form out-of-state licensees must sign, which subjects them to the jurisdiction of the courts of the state of New York.

Kickback Paying part of the proceeds to a sale to another party that helped secure the sale, but is unlicensed.

Misdemeanor A misdeed that may be tried in a court of special sessions.

Mortgage Banker An individual or entity licensed by the New York Banking Department to engage in the business of making residential mortgage loans.

Multiple Listing Service® (MLS®) A service whereby local member brokers agree to share listings, and further agree to share commissions on properties sold jointly. The MLS® generally consists of online computer services. A book published regularly, and updated to include new listings, may also be available in some areas.

Net Listing Agreement A listing agreement in which the seller sets a net amount acceptable for a property; if the actual selling price exceeds that amount, the broker is entitled to keep the excess as commission; illegal in New York.

Office Manager A licensed associate real estate broker who by choice elects to work as an office manager under the name and supervision of an individual broker or another broker who is licensed under a partnership, trade name, limited liability company, or corporation.

Pocket Card Contains a photo ID, name, business address of the licensee, and for salespersons, a name and address of the affiliated broker. These are prepared, issued, and delivered by the Department of State, in cooperation with the Department of Motor Vehicles.

Real Estate Appraiser A person licensed by the Department of State who is specially trained to offer an unbiased value of real property.

Reciprocity When states agree to allow licensees from other states to sell real estate in their own, by accepting the licensee's out-of-state course credits or license level.

Revocation A real estate agent's license being permanently withdrawn; may apply for reinstatement after one year, however.

Salesperson A person performing any of the acts included in the definition of real estate broker while associated with and supervised by a broker.

Sponsoring Broker The broker for whom a licensee works.

Suspension A real estate agent's license being temporarily withdrawn. Usually, reactivation is automatic the day after the suspension is lifted.

Violation An action which goes against specific rules or regulations set by national, state or local government and those set by specific governing bodies of a trade or profession. Such as when a licensee goes against any Act set forth in Article 12-A.

- Approve or deny license applications and renewals.

- Suspend or revoke a license or impose a fine or reprimand, for violations of Article 12-A.

New York State Board of Real Estate

The New York State Board of Real Estate consists of 15 members who oversee **all activities** that require a real estate license. The Board is responsible for:

- Setting rules and regulations that impact brokers and salespeople.

- Administering and enforcing Article 12-A.

- Deciding content for courses of study and advising the Secretary of State on exam administration.

- Establishing rules and regulations on continuing education.

- Making recommendations regarding legislation.

- Filing an annual report to the assembly and judiciary committees that contains the types of complaints received, the status of cases, and the length of time from complaint to final disposition.

Activities Requiring Licensure

In New York, it is illegal to act in real estate on behalf of another for a fee or valuable consideration without first being licensed or registered (unless specifically exempted). According to the New York law, these activities require a broker's license:

1. Listing or attempting to list real estate for sale

2. Selling or attempting to sell real estate or an interest in real estate

3. Negotiating or attempting to negotiate the purchase of real estate or an interest in real estate

4. Negotiating or attempting to negotiate the resale of a condominium or cooperative

5. Selling or purchasing a lot or parcel of land at auction

6. Negotiating or attempting to negotiate the exchange of real estate

7. Selling or negotiating the sale of lots or parcels of subdivided land

8. Negotiating or attempting to negotiate a lease for the rental of real estate

9. Negotiating or attempting to negotiate a commercial mortgage (requires registration as a mortgage broker if for one- to four-family residences)

10. Relocating a commercial or residential tenant

11. Collecting or attempting to collect rent for more than one client

12. Selling a business that has more than half its value in real estate

Licensing

License Categories

Broker

A broker is licensed to represent buyers, sellers, landlords, or tenants within the State of New York with no restrictions on the type of real estate involved or the brokerage activities. A broker may:

- Be an individual or a legal entity such as a corporation, partnership, or association
- Manage real estate
- Supervise and direct a real estate office
- Employ other licensees
- Be multi-licensed

Types of Broker Licenses

- Individual Broker (Class 35)
- Associate Broker (Class 30)
- Trade Name Broker (Class 37)
- Partnership Broker (Class 32)
- Corporate Broker (Class 31)
- Limited Liability Company (LLC) or Partnership (LLP) (Class 49)

Associate Broker

- Someone who has met the requirements to be a broker but chooses to work under the name and supervision of another broker
- May also serve as an office manager for a real estate office
- May not be a principal in the brokerage firm nor own voting stock in a licensed brokerage corporation

Office Manager

A licensed associate broker could choose to work as an office manager under the name and supervision of an individual broker or another broker who is licensed under a partnership, trade name, limited liability company (LLC), or corporation. The office manager retains his license as a real estate associate broker, but operates under the provisions of a salesperson. He may elect to retain a separate broker's license under an individual, partnership, trade name, LLC, or corporation.

Salesperson

A real estate salesperson is an individual who is licensed to engage in real estate brokerage activities on behalf of his or her employing broker with no restrictions (unless imposed by the employing broker). A real estate salesperson must:

- Work only under the name and supervision of a sponsoring licensed broker.
- Be compensated only by the employing broker.

A real estate salesperson may **not**:

- Employ other licensees.
- Be multi-licensed.
- Manage property.

- Receive compensation from anyone other than the employing broker.
- Manage a real estate office.
- Be a principal in the brokerage firm nor own voting stock in a licensed brokerage corporation.

Dual Licensure

- A real estate licensee who holds more than one license at a time (not to be confused with dual agency)
- May occur when a broker wishes to also be an associate broker with another firm or when a salesperson or associate broker wishes to work with more than one broker
- Associate brokers and salespersons required to obtain a statement from each sponsoring broker acknowledging each licensure

Licensing Qualifications

Salesperson applicants must:

- Be at least 18 years old.
- Successfully complete 75 hours of approved real estate pre-licensing coursework (or apply for a waiver for comparable college-level education).
- Pass the New York State licensing exam.
- Be a U.S. citizen or lawfully admitted permanent resident of the U.S.
- Have a basic understanding of the English language.
- Never have been convicted of a felony, though there are some exceptions.
- Be in compliance with child support laws as outlined in the 3-503 General Obligation Law.
- Complete the license application and pay the required fees.
- Have a sponsoring broker.

Broker and associate broker applicants must meet all of the salespersons' qualifications and also must:

- Be at least 20 years old.
- Successfully complete 120 hours of approved real estate pre-licensing coursework.
- Provide proof of experience, as established by the Department of State's point system:
  - Two full years and 3,500 points earned as a licensed salesperson, or
  - Three full years and 5,250 points earned for equivalent real estate experience
- Pass the state broker's license examination and pay the required fees.

POCKET CARDS

- Issued by DOS, in cooperation with the New York State Department of Motor Vehicles
- Contain photo ID as well as the licensee's name and business address
- Must be carried whenever engaging in real estate activities and shown on demand
- Violators may be subject to reprimand or suspension

Licensing Exemptions

The following categories of individuals and entities are excluded from needing a real estate license in New York State:

- Attorneys admitted to practice in New York courts
- Building supervisors and maintenance workers
- Persons acting in any capacity under the judgment of a court
- Property owners
- Employees of an owner who perform tasks on the owner's behalf, such as collecting rent or showing apartments
- Public officers
- Tenant associations and nonprofit corporations

New York City also exempts tenant associations and not-for-profit corporations responsible for enforcing housing maintenance codes to manage residential property owned or managed by the City.

Nonresidents and Reciprocity

Reciprocity allows a license in one jurisdiction to be valid in another jurisdiction. All applicants for a reciprocal license must:

- Have current certification, dated within six months, from the Real Estate Commission in the state with a reciprocal agreement with New York.
- Be sponsored by their home-state broker who must hold a current New York State broker's license.
- Submit a completed application.
- Submit an irrevocable consent form.
- Pay the appropriate fee.

Operating a Brokerage in New York

Brokers must maintain a physical place of business within the State of New York. The office must include:

- Permanent signage identifying name and license of broker in conspicuous place
- Broker license displayed in conspicuous place
- Space for maintenance of agency records and files
- Supplemental branch office license (as appropriate)

An **unlicensed assistant** may handle general office administration tasks.

Broker Supervision

New York law states that every real estate office must be under the direction and supervision of a broker, or in the case of a branch office, an office manager.

According to New York State law, broker supervision of a licensee includes providing the following:

- Guidance
- Oversight
- Management

- Orientation
- Instruction

Broker Responsibilities

- Brokers have **vicarious liability** for affiliated salespersons and associated brokers.
- Brokers cannot write contracts with a licensee that diminish supervisory obligations.

General Business Practices

Compensation

- Salespeople receive the agreed upon share of the commission from their sponsoring brokers and only from them.
- To receive compensation, a salesperson must be duly licensed at the time of the transaction.
- RESPA prohibits licensees from kickbacks from service companies involved in a transaction.

Disclosure of Interest and Unlicensed Practice of Law

- Licensees must disclose any interest they may have in the property.
- Anyone not licensed as an attorney is prohibited from giving legal advice.

Handling Funds and Records

- Once earnest money has been presented, it must be placed into an escrow account as promptly as is practical to protect the interests of all parties and prevent **commingling**.
- Agreements related to sale or lease transactions must be in writing, and each party should receive a duplicate.
- Copies of all contracts and records should be retained for at least **three years** after the transaction closes.

Advertising

Broker Advertising

- All advertisements to buy, sell, exchange, rent, lease, or mortgage real estate must include:
  - The business name of the broker exactly as it appears on the license.
  - The telephone number associated with the brokerage.
  - Clear indication that person is licensed broker.
- Ads that do not include the broker's name (blind ads) are illegal in New York.

Licensee Advertising

- Must be done in the name of and under the supervision of the employing broker
- Salesperson's name cannot be larger than the name of the broker(waived when a licensee is advertising his own property for sale or lease in their own name, however, they must disclose their license status)

Untruthful or Misleading Information

- Any advertisement for property placed by a licensed real estate professional should be truthful and should not mislead a potential customer in an attempt to lure them into looking at a property.
- A broker may not use a trademarked or copyrighted term or symbol in any ad without authorization.

Permission to Advertise

New York State law prohibits placing a sale or lease sign on any property without the express consent of the owner of the property.

Contests and Lotteries

Licensed brokers in New York cannot promote or sell real estate through any plan or scheme involving any game of chance or gambling device, such as a lottery, contest, prize, or drawing.

No Discriminatory Advertising

Ads indicating a preference for or against someone based on race, creed, color, national origin, age, sex, disability, marital status, or familial status are prohibited in New York State for sale or rental of residential or commercial property.

Maintaining a Real Estate License

Renewal Cycles and CE Requirements

- All real estate licenses are renewed on a staggered **two-year** license renewal cycle.
- Real estate broker, associate broker, and salesperson licensees must complete **22.5** hours of continuing education during every license renewal cycle with these exceptions:
  - Attorneys who hold a license and are admitted to the New York State bar
  - Brokers with more than **15 years** of consecutive licensure *before* **July 2008** and who are actively engaged in the real estate business

License Transfer

In order to transfer a real estate license to another brokerage:

- The original sponsoring broker must file a termination of association notice with the Department of State and pay a small termination fee.
- The new sponsoring broker must file a new record of association with the Department of State and also pay a small fee.

Administrative Discipline

The Department of State investigates every complaint filed against a licensee. DOS must notify licensee of disciplinary charges *in writing* at least 10 days prior to hearing date. If there is evidence of a violation of the Acts of Article 12-A, the Department of State will hear the case and impose penalties, which may include:

- Refusal to issue a license or to renew a license

- A reprimand
- License suspension
- License revocation
- A fine of up to **$1,000** per offense

Licensees have the right to appeal any DOS decision to the Supreme Court of New York State through an **Article 78 proceeding**.

Suspension and Revocation of Licenses

- If a broker's license is suspended (temporary withdrawn until conditions are met) or revoked (may apply to DOS for reinstatement after one year, otherwise permanent), then all salespeople working for him are suspended as well.
- If a salesperson or employee of a broker violates regulations, the broker cannot be held responsible and will not have his license revoked, unless the broker had knowledge of or benefits from the violation.

Criminal Penalties

License law violations are **misdemeanors**, which may be punishable by:

- A fine of up to $1,000 and/or
- Imprisonment of up to one year

Required Disclosures

- Article 14 of the New York Property Law requires sellers of one- to four-family residential properties to provide a **Property Condition Disclosure Statement** to a buyer or buyer's agent prior to entering into a sales agreement. Licensees must inform their seller clients of their obligation to complete this form, but are not required to complete any part of the form themselves,
- A seller's agent has a duty to disclose to buyers any **material defects** related to the property that could influence the client's judgment in the transaction.

QUIZ

1. *From whom may a salesperson accept commission?*
   - A. employing broker only
   - B. employing broker or buyer
   - C. employing broker or listing broker
   - D. employing broker or seller

2. *Salesperson candidates are required to complete ____ hours of state-approved education and have ____ years of experience.*
   - A. 75 hours / no years
   - B. 75 hours / three years
   - C. 120 hours / two years
   - D. 120 hours / three years

3. *John has an associate broker's license. He can also have*
   - A. a commercial associate broker's license.
   - B. a real estate broker's license.
   - C. a real estate salesperson's license.
   - D. no other professional licenses.

4. *Sophie just renewed her real estate salesperson's license for the first time. How many hours of approved continuing education is Sophie required to complete before she renews her license again?*
   - A. 15.5 hours
   - B. 14 hours
   - C. 22.5 hours
   - D. 25 hours

5. *Salesperson Greg works for Tom Ace, owner of Ace Realty. He decides to spend his own money to take out an extra ad for a home he's really eager to sell. Which statement about this ad is true?*
   - A. Greg must include his name, phone number, and license status.
   - B. Only Greg's broker is allowed to place an ad.
   - C. Since Greg is paying for the ad, he can put whatever he wants on it.
   - D. The sign must include Ace Realty and the office phone number.

6. *Harry and his wife buy a small apartment building in Watertown and they're ready to hire resources to help run it. Who would need to have a real estate license?*
   - A. Ella, Harry's otherwise unemployed neighbor whom he hires to collect rents from the tenants
   - B. Joe, an employee of Ace Property Management
   - C. Kyle, who works for Joe as a plumber and general handyman
   - D. Harry's wife when she decides to sell the property as a FSBO

7. *All four of the real estate licensees who work for Joe Wilson, owner of Wilson Realty Inc., have passed the New York real estate broker's exam and have received their licenses. How many broker licenses must be hanging on the wall at Wilson Realty?*
   - A. 1
   - B. 2
   - C. 4
   - D. 5

8. *Olivia is the office manager for a branch office of Hitch Real Estate Inc. What license does Olivia have?*
   - A. associate broker
   - B. corporate broker
   - C. individual broker
   - D. office manager

9. *Phil Smith's brokerage is licensed under the name Smith and Sons Realty LLC. His children have since left the business, and since Phil believes in truthful advertising, he wants to make sure his ads and signs reflect reality. What can Phil put on the sign he's placing in his sister Julia's yard when he sells her house?*
   - A. FSBO
   - B. Phil Smith Realty
   - C. Smith and Sons Realty LLC
   - D. Smith Realty LLC

10. *Which action would NOT be a violation of New York license law?*
   - A. a broker accepting a referral fee from a title company without permission of the client
   - B. a broker commingling money of principal
   - C. a broker depositing earnest money in an escrow account two days after he receives it
   - D. a broker entering into a net listing agreement

Law of Agency 1
Relationships with Sellers, Buyers, Tenants, and Landlords

Key Terms

Accountability In an agency relationship, the agent's fiduciary duty to account to the principal.

Actual Fraud Intentional misrepresentation or concealment of a material fact; when a person actively conceals material information or makes statements known to be false or misleading. *Also called*: **Deceit**.

Agency Relationship of trust created when one person (principal) gives another person (agent) the right to represent the principal in dealings with third parties.

Agency Relationship The representation of a party in a real estate transaction.

Broker's Agent Engaged and works directly for the broker—a broker's agent is not a subagent of the seller or buyer. Still owes the same fiduciary duty to the broker's seller or buyer as the broker does.

Buyer Broker Contract A written agency contract between a buyer and a real estate broker stipulating the broker will be paid a commission when the buyer purchases real estate.

Buyer's Agency Represents and owes all loyalty to the buyer in a real estate transaction.

Client Person who employs a broker, lawyer, or other professional. Real estate clients can be sellers, buyers, or both. *See*: **Fiduciary**.

Confidentiality Any information learned during the course of the agency relationship can never be revealed or used later against the principal, even after the transaction is closed.

Constructive Fraud A negligent misrepresentation or concealment of a material fact; when a person carelessly fails to disclose material information, or makes false or misleading statements. *Also called*: **Negligent Misrepresentation**.

Customer A party in a transaction to whom an agent does not have a fiduciary duty or relationship, but to whom an agent must still be fair and honest.

Designated Agency When two licensees within a single brokerage represent their individual clients fully.

Disclosures Points or facts in a real estate transaction that must be revealed.

Dual Agency Occurs when a broker or salesperson represents both parties (buyer and seller) in a transaction; most states require written consent from both parties before this can occur.

(continued on next page)

Key Terms - continued

Estoppel Legal doctrine that prevents a person from asserting rights or facts inconsistent with earlier actions or statements.

Expressed Agency Agency relationship based on an expressed agreement, either written or oral.

Fiduciary Person in a position of trust, held by law to high standards of good faith and loyalty.

Fiduciary Duties What is owed to all clients in an agency relationship—obedience, loyalty, disclosure, confidentiality, accountability, and reasonable care.

Fiduciary Relationship A relationship of trust and confidence, in which one party owes the other (or both parties owe each other) loyalty and a higher standard of good faith than is owed to third parties.

Fraud Intentional or negligent misrepresentation or concealment of a material fact; making statements that a person knows, or should realize, are false or misleading.

General Agent A person authorized to handle a principal's affairs in one area or in specified areas.

Implied Agency Agency relationship created through the behavior (actions or words) of one or both parties.

Listing Agreement A written agency contract between a seller and a real estate broker, stating the broker will be paid a commission for finding (or attempting to find) a buyer for the seller's real property.

Loyalty An agent must put the principal's interests above all others', including the agent's own.

Meeting of the Minds Occurs when the parties agree on price, down payment, financing method and other essential terms.

Misrepresentation A false or misleading statement.

Negligence Conduct that falls below the standard of care a reasonable person would exercise under the circumstances; an unintentional breach of a legal duty resulting from carelessness, recklessness, or incompetence.

Obedience An agent must follow the (legal) instructions of the principal, obey the parameters of the agency relationship, and not stray beyond the scope of authority.

Ostensible Agency Occurs when an agent is perceived as the principal's fiduciary by a third party and the principal does not declare otherwise.

Principal 1. A person who grants another person (an agent) authority to represent him or her in dealings with third parties. 2. One of the parties to a transaction (such as a buyer or seller), as opposed to those who are involved as agents or employees (such as a broker or escrow agent). 3. With regard to a loan, the amount originally borrowed, as opposed to the interest.

Puffing Superlative statements about the quality of a property that should not be considered assertions of fact.

Ratification Confirmation or approval of an act not authorized when it was performed.

Renunciation When someone who has been granted something or has accepted something later gives it up or rejects it; as when an agent withdraws from the agency relationship.

Revocation When someone who granted or offered something withdraws it, as when a principal withdraws the authority granted to the agent, an offeror withdraws the offer.

Self-Dealing When a real estate agent buys the principal's property (or sells it to a relative, friend, etc., or to a business the agent has an interest in), without disclosing that fact to principal, then sells it for a profit.

Seller's Agent The agent who is representing only the seller in a transaction and owes, all loyalty to that seller/client.

Special Agent An agent with limited authority to act on behalf of the principal.

Subagent An agent of an agent; a person that an agent has delegated authority, so the subagent can assist in carrying out the principal's orders.

Undisclosed Dual Agency Occurs when both principal parties in the same transaction are represented by a fiduciary without full disclosure to and approval from all parties in the transaction.

Undivided Loyalty This is given up by the buyer and seller when they consent to dual agency.

Universal Agent An agent authorized to do everything that can be lawfully delegated to a representative.

Vicarious Liability When one person is responsible for the actions of another.

Broker-Client Agency Relationship

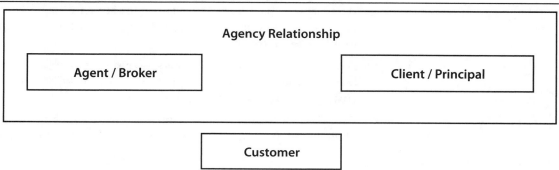

A **broker** (**agent**) enters into contract to represent the **client** (**principal**). The third party in the transaction is referred to as the **customer**. No agency relationship exists between the agent and the customer or between the client and the customer.

A **fiduciary relationship** is one between an agent and a principal that is a relationship of trust and confidence in which one party owes the other (or both parties owe each other) loyalty and a higher standard of good faith than they owe to third parties or customers.

Fiduciary Duties Owed to a Principal

Licensees owe fiduciary duties **only to their clients**, either the buyer or the seller as the case may be, but an agent is *not* a fiduciary in relation to a third party, such as a customer in real estate transaction. The basic fiduciary duties include:

- **Obedience** – an agent must follow the (legal) directions of the principal, obey the restrictions of the agency relationship, and not stray beyond the scope of his or her authority.

- **Loyalty** – an agent must put the principal's interests above all others, including the agent's own.

- **Disclosure** – an agent must make a complete disclosure of all material information, including defects, and not conceal anything from their client, including:
  - True property value
  - All offers to purchase
  - Financial condition of the prospective buyer, if known
  - Disclosure of interest (arm's length transaction)
  - Licensee status
  - Compensation
  - Any relationship between the buyer and the broker

- **Confidentiality** – is perpetual; confidential information learned during the course of the agency relationship can never be revealed or used later against the principal, even after the transaction is closed.

- **Accountability** – recognizes that money received in an agency relationship belongs to the principal, not the agent.

- **Reasonable Care** – reasonable care and skill must always be used by an agent when acting on behalf of a client; agents should always be working in their clients' best interest.

Agent's Duties to Other Parties

- **Honesty** – being honest with a customer does not require disclosing information deemed confidential in the agent-client relationship, but it does require an agent to **disclose material facts**.
- **Disclosure of material defects** – one that may affect the desirability, and probably the value, of the property; when it is known, it must be disclosed to customers and other third parties.
- **Fair dealing** – involves obeying the law; disclosing information that one is obligated to disclose and avoiding misrepresentation or fraud.

Fraud and Misrepresentation

- **Fraud** – an intentional or negligent misrepresentation or concealment of a material fact
- **Actual fraud** – an **intentional** misrepresentation or concealment of a material fact or information, or making statements known to be false or misleading
- **Constructive fraud** – a **negligent** or unintentional misrepresentation or concealment of a material fact
- **Misrepresentation** – can be intentional or unintentional (negligent) and is simply a false or misleading statement

Agency Creation

- **Expressed** – based on an expressed agreement, either written or oral, and, therefore, most enforceable
- **Implied** – is created through the behavior (actions or words) of one or both parties
    - **Agency by estoppel** – estoppel prevents a person from asserting rights or facts that are inconsistent with earlier actions or statements when he failed to object to those actions; in agency by estoppel, it is the action of the principal that infers the relationship
    - **Agency by ratification** – occurs when a later action confirms an implied agency relationship
    - **Ostensible agency** – occurs when an agent is perceived as the principal's fiduciary by a third party and the principal does not declare otherwise; also known as **apparent agency**

Types of Agents

- **Universal** – authorized to do anything and everything that can be lawfully delegated to a representative
- **General** – authorized to represent the principal in a broad range of matters as specified, usually as part of a long-term relationship
- **Special** – also called a limited agent; has limited authority to do a specific task or conduct a specific transaction

◊ *Note:* **Unauthorized Practice of Law**—Agents should never give legal advice or perform any acts that require a lawyer's expertise.

Single or Principal Agency

One agent signs an employment agreement to represent just one party in a specific transaction.

- **Seller's Agency** – an agency relationship between a seller and a licensee in a real estate transaction; created with a written document referred to as a **listing agreement**
- **Buyer's Agency** – an agency relationship between a buyer and a licensee in a real estate transaction; created with a written document such as a **buyer broker contract**

In a traditional principal agency, **all** affiliated licensees are considered to have the **same agency relationship** as the broker, and therefore, the same fiduciary obligations to the broker's clients.

Subagency

- A **subagent** is created when someone is given authority by an agent to assist in carrying out the principal's instruction, for example, when a cooperating broker is given authority by the listing broker to help a seller find a buyer.
  - The cooperating broker is an agent of the listing broker.
  - The cooperating broker is a subagent of the client.
  - All affiliated licensees are agents of their employing brokers.
- The client has **vicarious liability** for any subagent.

Broker's Agent

- A broker's agent cooperates with the listing broker or buyer broker, owes all fiduciary duties to that broker and to the client.
- The client has **no vicarious liability** for the broker's agent.
- This relationship must be offered in the MLS (with client's consent).

Dual Agency

- One agency representing **both** parties – buyer and seller – in a single transaction (known as an **in-house transaction**)
- Creates an inherent **conflict of interest** as each client gives up **undivided loyalty**
- A dual agent must remain **neutral** at all times
- Must have the informed written consent of both parties
- All affiliated licensees have the same relationship with the broker's clients as the broker

Dual Agency with Designated Agents

- Created in response to problems with dual agency
- Allows supervising broker to assume the role of dual agent
- Designated licensees represent only their clients, but cannot provide **undivided loyalty**
- Affiliated licensees are dual agents of both clients
- Some brokers are considered designated agencies and require every in-house transaction to have a designated seller's agent and a designated buyer's agent

Termination of Agency

- **Accomplishment of Purpose** – most common reason for termination of an agency relationship; agency relationship between a client a real estate broker ends when the reason for the agency relationship ends

- **Expiration** – agency ends automatically when the term of the agreement expires

- **Operation of Law** – ends automatically, as a matter of law, if certain events occur:
  - The broker or the client dies or becomes incapacitated
  - The broker or the client goes bankrupt
  - The property that's the subject of the agency is destroyed or condemned
  - The broker loses his or her license

- **Mutual Agreement** – both the principal and the agent voluntarily agree to terminate without liability

- **Renunciation** – the grantee (agent) rejects the agreement; could be considered breach of contract if renounced prior to termination date of the contract

- **Revocation** – the grantor (principal) withdraws the contract; could be considered breach of contract if done after the offer was accepted by the agent

QUIZ

1. **Broker Dave knew that his listed property had a leaky roof, but in his eagerness to close the deal, he decided not to tell the buyer. This might be considered an example of**
   A. actual fraud.
   B. constructive fraud.
   C. opinion.
   D. puffing.

2. **An affiliated licensee of the listing agent in a brokerage practicing traditional agency will have what agency relationship with the seller?**
   A. buyer's agent
   B. dual agent
   C. seller's agent
   D. universal agent

3. **Howard walks through a home listed by Owen's agency during an open house. Howard and Owen chat some about the features of the house, and Howard seems to be interested. The next day, Howard calls Owen and tells him that he'd like to make an offer on the house. At this point, what kind of relationship do Howard and Owen have?**
   A. Owen is Howard's fiduciary.
   B. Owen is Howard's principal.
   C. Howard is Owen's client.
   D. Howard is Owen's customer.

4. **When a broker manages real property for the owner, they have a**
   A. special agency relationship.
   B. major agency relationship.
   C. limited agency relationship.
   D. general agency relationship.

5. **During a 90-day listing agreement, the seller dies. What statement is true?**
   A. The agent can continue to show the property to any interested buyer.
   B. The agent's death is the only thing that would terminate the listing.
   C. The listing agreement can be enforced against the seller's heirs.
   D. The listing agreement is terminated.

6. **Ryan, a licensee working for a seller, hires another cooperating broker to hold an open house each Sunday for his sellers. Which of the following is true of this arrangement?**
   A. The arrangement is unethical as brokers are not permitted to enlist other brokers to show property on the seller's behalf.
   B. The cooperating broker has a duty to disclose any material information to the seller.
   C. The cooperating broker has no fiduciary duties; only Ryan himself has those responsibilities to the seller.
   D. The situation described is that of an in-house transaction.

7. **After listing a property that the agent believes is overpriced, the agent returns to the office and vents his frustration to a fellow licensee at the brokerage. The agent has breached his duty of**
   A. loyalty.
   B. disclosure.
   C. reasonable skill and care.
   D. accountability.

8. **When a brokerage practicing designated agency has different agents representing both buyer and seller, the agency relationship the broker assumes is**
   A. buyer's agent.
   B. dual agent.
   C. seller's agent.
   D. subagent.

9. **A salesperson is told by his client NOT to disclose the fact that, during heavy rains, the basement takes on water. The agent must**
   A. not disclose the defect, due to the duty of obedience.
   B. show the property only on sunny days.
   C. disclose the defect to any interested buyers.
   D. give up the listing.

10. **A seller tells the listing agent he wants to put a price of $280,000 on his house. The agent knows its value is only $200,000, and so she lists the home for $225,000. The agent has breached her duty of**
    A. obedience.
    B. disclosure.
    C. loyalty.
    D. accountability.

Law of Agency 2
Agency and Brokerage

Key Terms

Agency Relationship of trust created when one person (principal) gives another person (agent) the right to represent the principal in dealings with third parties.

Agency Disclosure Form Form that states whether an agent is representing the seller, buyer, or both in a transaction.

Antitrust A business activity that attempts to monopolize, contract, or conspire (or any of these things together) in a way that impact's negatively on another's ability to do business.

Brokerage The business of bringing together buyers and sellers of real property and assisting in negotiating such transactions.

Broker Protection Clause Provides the broker is still entitled to commission if the property is sold during a certain time period under certain circumstances.

Broker's Agent Engaged and works directly for the broker—a broker's agent is not a subagent of the seller or buyer. Still owes the same fiduciary duty to the broker's seller or buyer as the broker does.

Consensual Dual Agency Occurs when 1. the broker and all licensees are dual agents for both parties in the transaction, or 2. the buyer and seller each appoint a designated agent, who fully represents them. The broker, however, would (with consent) act as a dual agent in the transaction.

Cooperating Broker An outside broker from another company who brings the "other" party in a transaction.

Exclusive Agency Listing agreement between a broker and seller that provides the broker the exclusive right to represent the seller in the sale of the seller's property and the broker will be compensated if he or any other person or entity (excluding the seller) produces a purchaser in accordance with the listing agreement.

Exclusive Right to Sell Listing agreement that entitles the broker to a commission if anyone, including the seller, finds a buyer for the property during the listing term.

First Substantive Contact An event triggering agency disclosure (e.g., prior to entering into a listing agreement, prior to showing a property, at an open house when a buyer displays serious interest, etc.).

Group Boycott A boycott is a concerted refusal to deal with a particular party.

(continued on next page)

Agency Relationships

- **Agency** – relationship between a principal and a party representing her interests
- **Brokerage** – a business concept premised primarily on bringing parties together for the purpose of a transaction
- **Broker** – one who is licensed to represent one of the parties in a real estate transaction
- **Salesperson** – in most cases, it is a salesperson who brings sellers or buyers together with brokers
- **Subagent** – an agent of an agent; a person that an agent has delegated authority, so the subagent can assist in carrying out the principal's orders

Compensation

- Commission rate negotiated between the client and the broker
- May be based on percentage of sales price, flat fee, fee for specific services
- Generally earned when a ready, willing, and able buyer is found and a meeting of the minds occurs
- Should be included in a written agreement
- To earn commission, an agent generally must be the **procuring cause** of a sale
- Agents may accept compensation **only from their employing broker**
- An offer of compensation is be stated in MLS, for example:

  Subagency compensation 3% Buyer-agency compensation 3%
- Brokers representing buyers often earn commission through the listing broker's offer of cooperation
- RESPA prohibits licensees (brokers and salespersons) from accepting any compensation from a service company involved in a transaction without the prior written consent of the client

Key Terms - continued

Informed Consent Written evidence that a client is aware of and has given permission to an agent to perform a specific action or take on a specific role in the client-agent relationship.

Listing Agreement A written agency contract between a seller and a real estate broker, stating the broker will be paid a commission for finding (or attempting to find) a buyer for the seller's real property.

Market Allocation An antitrust violation where two or more brokers conspire to divide their customers in any way.

Net Listing A listing agreement in which the seller sets a net amount acceptable for a property; if the actual selling price exceeds that amount, the broker is entitled to keep the excess as commission; illegal in New York.

Offer of Compensation The commission that will be paid on the sale of property.

Offer of Cooperation An open invitation to other brokers to sell property listed by another broker.

Open Listing A nonexclusive listing given by a seller to as many brokers as he chooses. If the property is sold, the broker who was the procuring cause of the sale is entitled to the commission.

Price Fixing An antitrust violation in which competitors set a standard commission rate.

Procuring Cause The real estate agent who is primarily responsible for bringing about a sale, such as by introducing the buyer to the property or by negotiating the agreement between the buyer and seller. Sometimes more than one agent contributes to a sale.

Subagent An agent of an agent; a person that an agent has delegated authority to, so that the subagent can assist in carrying out the principal's orders.

Tie-in Arrangements Requiring the consumer, as a condition of a transaction, to use, or not use a particular service or product.

- **New York Commission Escrow Act** – protects broker commissions that are contractually earned but that sellers refused to pay at closing

Agency Contracts

- Sellers and buyers secure the services of a real estate professional using either listing agreements or buyer brokerage agreements
- Agreements establish the agency relationship between the seller or buyer and the broker and other licensees affiliated with the broker
- An agreement is binding between only the seller or buyer and the broker

Seller Agency Agreements

Exclusive Right to Sell Listing

- Grants the broker the exclusive right to represent the seller in the sale of the seller's property
- Requires the listing agency to actively promote the sale of the property
- Compensates the broker if the broker, the seller, or any other person or entity produces a purchaser in accordance with the terms specified in the listing agreement, or if the property is sold during the term of the listing agreement to anyone other than specifically exempted persons or entities
- Provides the greatest opportunity for the listing agent to earn commission
- Must have an expiration date

Exclusive Agency Listing

- Grants an agency the exclusive right to represent the seller in the marketing and sale of the seller's property
- Requires the listing agency to actively promote the sale of the property
- Compensates the broker only if someone other than the seller finds the buyer in accordance with the terms specified in the listing agreement
- Must have an expiration date
- Requires good record-keeping to provide evidence of who was the procuring cause of the sale in the event of any disputes

> **Note:** Most exclusive listing agreements contain a **broker protection clause** that covers a certain period after the listing expires; this clause provides that the broker is still entitled to a commission if the property is sold during a specified time period, and the buyer is someone the broker negotiated with during the listing term

Open Listing

- Grants an agency the non-exclusive right to represent the seller in the marketing and sale of the seller's property
- **Unilateral** contract – only one party makes a binding promise
- Allows seller to list with as many brokers as he or she chooses
- If property sells, broker entitled to a commission only if the procuring cause of the sale

Net Listing

- Not really a "listing" but an agreement in which the seller sets a net amount he is willing to accept for the property, with the broker being entitled to keep the excess as commission if the actual selling price exceeds that amount
- Illegal in New York and rarely used in other states

Buyer Agency Agreements

- **Exclusive buyer agency agreement** - broker is paid even if the buyer purchases property through another agent; usually icludes a protection clause similar to an exclusive listing agreement.
- **Nonexclusive / open buyer agency agreement** - like open listing agreement, broker earns a commission only for introducing the buyer to the property that is purchased.

COMMON OBLIGATIONS OF THE BUYER BROKER:

- Exercise diligence in locating a property, as specified, at the price and terms acceptable to the client
- Employ knowledge and skill in negotiating the purchase transaction on behalf of the client
- Assist the client throughout a transaction and act in the client's best interest

COMMON OBLIGATIONS OF THE BUYER CLIENT:

- During the effective period of the exclusive buyer broker agreement, work exclusively with the broker in all issues related to the purchase of the property
- Provide the broker with all requested financial and personal information needed to complete a transaction
- Observe the compensation agreement specified in the exclusive buyer brokerage agreement

---

Determining the Licensee's Role in the Transaction

Single Agency

- The most basic form of agency where one agent represents just one client.
- Seller's agent engaged by seller to represent his best interests in securing a buyer for his home.
- Buyer's agent engaged by buyer to represent his best interests in negotiating the purchase of a home.

Single Seller Agency

Seller (or Buyer) *Client/Principal*

Buyer (or Seller)
Customer

↑

Broker *Agent of Seller (or Buyer) Client* *Principal of Affiliated Licensees*

↑

All Affiliated Salespeople *Agents of Broker* *Subagents of Seller (or Buyer) Client*

In-House Transactions

It is more profitable for brokers to keep transactions in-company. When the seller is a client and the buyer is a customer with no representation, for example, there is no dual agency. When both the seller and buyer are clients, a dual agency situation exists and **informed written consent** of both parties is required. Options:

- **Dual agency:** All licensees owe fiduciary duties to both seller client and buyer client (though no duty of undivided loyalty)

- **Dual agency with designated agents:** Broker appoints specific agents to **advocate** for each client in negotiations (though no duty of undivided loyalty); broker assumes role of dual agent

Dual Agency with Designated Agents

Cooperative Transactions

Listing brokers commonly extend offers to outside brokerages to sell listings to outside buyers. When a broker submits a property listing to the multiple listing service (MLS), the act constitutes an unilateral blanket **offer of cooperation,** *an open invitation to other brokers to sell property listed by another broker.* Options:

- **Subagent:** Represents listing broker's seller and owes the same duties to the seller as does the listing broker. The client may direct the activities of a subagent and, therefore, has vicarious liability for that subagent.

- **Broker's agent:** Represents the listing broker's seller and owes the same duties to the seller as does the listing broker. The client may **not** direct the activities of a broker's agent and, therefore, does not have vicarious liability for a broker's agent.

Cooperative Transaction

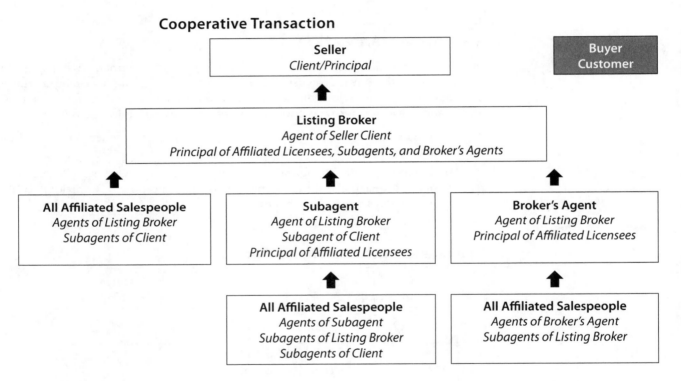

The Agency Disclosure Process

- Section 443 of Article 12-A of the New York Real Property Law requires disclosure of an agency relationship in the sale and rental of one- to four-unit residential properties
- Section 443 mandates the use of a specifically worded written agency disclosure form that details consumer choices in agency relationships and representation
- An agency disclosure form must be presented and consented to the prospective seller or buyer at the **earliest substantive contact**
- If someone refuses to sign, the agent must sign a simple affidavit recounting the situation
- New disclosures must be presented and signed if the agency relationship changes

- Copy of signed disclosure must be given to consumer; broker must maintain signed copies, along with all other contracts and records related to a real estate transaction, for **at least three years**

Explaining the Agency Disclosure Form

- Signing the disclosure form does not create an agency relationship or obligate the consumer as it is not a contract
- The disclosure form details the right of the consumer and the obligations of an agent in various roles
- The agent is required by New York Law to disclose who they are working for in a relationship and transaction
- The disclosure form affirms that an individual acting as a real estate agent is not qualified in fields other than real estate and that outside professionals should be consulted

Agency Relationship Disclosure

- Seller's agent – engaged by a seller to represent seller's best interests
- Buyer's agent – engaged by a buyer to represent buyer's best interests
- Broker's agents – buyers and sellers may authorize their respective agents to engage other agents in the transaction
- Dual agent – a real estate broker may represent both the buyer and the seller if both parties give their informed consent in writing
- Dual agency with designated sales agents – if the buyer and the seller provide informed consent in writing, the principals or the real estate broker who represents both parties as a dual agent may designate separate licensees to represent each party to negotiate the purchase and sale of real estate

Regulation 175.7

NYCRR Title 19 Part 175.7:

- Requires agents to make clear for which party they are acting.
- Limits compensation from more than one party in a transaction except when full disclosure and consent is granted by all parties

Antitrust Issues in Brokerage

- A business activity that attempts to monopolize, contract, or conspire (or any of these things together) in a way that negatively impacts another's ability to do business
- Result in restraint of trade

Antitrust Violations

- **Group boycotting** – when two or more real estate firms make a concerted refusal to deal with a particular party
- **Price-fixing** – when two or more real estate firms agree on the commission rate that each will charge
- **Market allocation agreements** – when two or more real estate firms conspire to divide up customers in any way
- **Tie-in agreements** – when a real estate broker requires the consumer, as a condition of a transaction, to use, or not use, a particular service or product

QUIZ

1. *The New York 443 Disclosure Form*
   A. creates a fiduciary relationship.
   B. defines the agency's commission structure.
   C. describes the nature of the agency relationship.
   D. documents the condition of the seller's property.

2. *Which situation does NOT represent a conflict of interest?*
   A. Alex is a disclosed dual agent, representing both buyer and seller.
   B. Kaye is a buyer's agent whose commission is based on the sale price of the home.
   C. Paul is showing his buyer client a house on which he had a prior listing.
   D. Susan is negotiating the purchase of a home for her client, who is also her sister.

3. *Which broker's action would NOT be a violation of New York license law?*
   A. accepting a referral fee from a title company without permission of the client
   B. commingling the money of a principal
   C. depositing earnest money in an escrow account two days after he receives it
   D. entering into a net listing agreement

4. *A seller who lives in a small town has posters made up advertising his house for sale. He posts them on many telephone poles around the neighborhood. As part of the poster, he advertises that he will pay 3% to any broker who brings him a buyer. What type of listing is this?*
   A. exclusive agency
   B. exclusive right to sell
   C. open listing
   D. net listing

5. *A broker takes a listing and one of his agents represents a buyer who makes an offer acceptable to the seller. Who is NOT a dual agent in this scenario?*
   A. buyer's agent
   B. listing agent
   C. other agents in the brokerage not involved in the transaction
   D. all of these are dual agents

6. *You met Tom to discuss listing his house. You went over the New York 443 Disclosure Form and he signed it that day. You did not, however, get a listing agreement with Tom. You may discard Tom's signed Disclosure Form*
   A. immediately, since he did not become a client.
   B. after one year.
   C. after three years.
   D. never.

7. *Which listing arrangement is illegal in New York?*
   A. exclusive agency
   B. exclusive right to sell
   C. open
   D. net

8. *The seller lists her house with New Age Realty. The next day, the seller goes to work and mentions listing her house. A co-worker expresses interest in the listing. What kind of listing would make the broker entitled to a commission if the co-worker makes a direct offer acceptable to the seller?*
   A. exclusive agency
   B. exclusive right to sell
   C. open listing
   D. net listing

9. *At a local convention of real estate licensees, broker Dan mentioned that he was going to have to raise his commission rates or close his office. Dan could be found guilty of*
   A. allocation.
   B. price-fixing.
   C. securities violations.
   D. nothing; he did not violate any rules or laws.

10. *Greg lists his home with PDQ Realty, allowing them to put a sign in the yard, list it in MLS, and advertise it in the local newspaper. During the listing period, Greg sells the home to his brother and is not obligated to pay PDQ any commission. What type of listing did Greg have with PDQ?*
    A. exclusive agency
    B. exclusive right to sell
    C. open listing
    D. net listing

Being an Independent Contractor

4

Key Terms

Employee Someone who works under the direction and control of another.

Independent Contractor Individual who is self-employed.

Statutory Employee Independent contractors specifically classified as employees by statute for Social Security and Medicare taxes.

Statutory Non-employee Direct sellers and licensed real estate agents; treated as independent contractors for all tax purposes if certain conditions are met.

Employee Classifications

A person's employment status may be classified by the Internal Revenue Service Code Section 3508 in one of four ways. The two major differences among these four classifications are:

- Who directs the licensee's activities
- Who pays payroll taxes

Independent Contractor

Controls the means and methods of accomplishing an assigned task; the paying entity has the right only to demand an end result

Employee

A person whose results are mandated by the employer and the employer controls how the results are accomplished

Statutory Employee

Independent contractors specifically classified as employees by statute for Social Security and Medicare taxes. Social Security and Medicare are withheld from the wages of statutory employees if all three of the following conditions apply:

- The service contract states or implies that substantially all services are to be performed personally by the individual
- The employee does not have a substantial investment in the equipment and property used to perform the services (other than an investment in transportation facilities)
- The services are performed on a continuing basis for the same payer

Statutory Non-employee

Direct sellers and licensed real estate agents are treated as independent contractors for all tax purposes if these conditions are met:

- The individual is a licensed real estate agent
- All payments for services as direct sellers or real estate agents are directly related to sales or other output, rather than to number of hours worked
- Services are performed under a written contract providing they will not be treated as employees for federal tax purposes

Common Law Rules

- Behavioral control
- Financial control
- Type of relationship of the parties

Elements of the Broker-Independent Contractor Relationship

Common characteristics of the broker-independent contractor relationship include:

- Compensation is paid only for output without regard for the number of hours worked.
- Compensation is paid without any deductions for taxes, and the independent contractor is solely responsible for the payment of the taxes to the appropriate agencies.
- Salespersons determine their own work hours, depending on the needs of their clients.

- Brokers can provide an office and supplies, but salespersons are responsible for expenses incurred (this may be in the form of a deduction from commissions when compensation is paid; however, this deduction does not fall into the disqualifying category of taxes withheld).
- The broker may direct and supervise, but does not fully control the actions of the salesperson.
- The agreement may be terminated by either the salesperson or broker at any time.
- Salespersons are free to engage in outside employment.
- Federal law also requires a written agreement, executed by both parties without duress or undue influence by either party (in New York State, the written contract must have been executed within the past 15 months).
- At the end of the tax year, an independent contractor receives a 1099 MISC form detailing any commission-based income instead of a W-2. A salesperson would receive a W-2, however, for any non-production income.

Consequences for Not Meeting Requirements

If the qualifications of the independent contractor relationship are not met, either party may be liable for additional consequences. The employer may be liable to pay the following:

- Unemployment insurance premiums (state and federal)
- Workers' Compensation premiums
- Social Security taxes
- Medicare taxes
- State and federal withholdings
- Interest and penalties on the amounts not paid

Independent Contractors and New York Law

There are two specific regulations found in Title 19 of the New York Codes, Rules, and Regulations directing a broker's relationship with licensees:

Section 175.21

Enforces the requirement for brokers to supervise affiliated salespersons – whether independent contractor or employee – and enumerates the specific controls granted to the broker, which are: Regular, frequent, and consistent personal guidance, instruction, and oversight.

Section 175.23

Requires the broker to maintain records of all sales of one- to four-family dwellings for three years. The records must contain the following information:

- Name and address of seller
- Name of buyer
- Mortgage, if applicable
- Purchase price
- Resale price, if applicable
- Amount of deposit paid on contract
- Amount of commission paid to broker
- Expenses regarding procuring a mortgage loan
- Net commission or net profit realized by the broker

Brokers engaged in soliciting and granting mortgage loans must also keep the following information for a period of three years:

- Name of applicant
- Amount of mortgage loan
- Closing statement with disposition of proceeds
- Verification of employment
- Financial status of applicant
- Inspection and compliance report as required by the FHA

QUIZ

1. *Of these options, which is not required by New York law to be included in the records a broker maintains about a sales transaction?*
   - A. amount of deposit paid
   - B. amount of commission paid
   - C. number of hours worked by the agent
   - D. purchase price

2. *What is a REALTOR®?*
   - A. a member of the New York Chamber of Commerce
   - B. a member of The National Association of REALTORS®, a private trade association
   - C. an active real estate licensee
   - D. the local real estate board

3. *Real estate salespeople, who are employed by a real estate broker, will be categorized by the IRS in two ways. They are:*
   - A. salesperson or broker.
   - B. employees or independent contractors.
   - C. staff or agents.
   - D. employees or agents.

4. *Walter works for XYZ Brokerage. He sets his own hours, but broker Bob requires Walter to use specific forms and follow certain procedures. Walter is most likely classified by the IRS as*
   - A. a common law employee.
   - B. a common law independent contractor.
   - C. a statutory employee.
   - D. a statutory non-employee.

5. *A common law independent contractor*
   - A. has no responsibility to the firm that employs her.
   - B. has taxes withheld from her paycheck.
   - C. is not subject to withholding requirements.
   - D. never pays taxes on her earnings.

6. *Which IRS classification would NOT be applicable to a real estate agent?*
   - A. employee
   - B. independent contractor
   - C. statutory employee
   - D. statutory non-employee

7. *Which is NOT one of the factors used by the IRS to determine that a real estate agent qualifies as a statutory non-employee?*
   - A. has a fiduciary relationship with clients
   - B. paid for output, not hours worked
   - C. properly licensed
   - D. written and signed contract with broker

8. *Sue decides to discontinue her brokerage and work as a salesperson. She then affiliates with another broker and orders business cards that read: Sue Smith, Broker. If she is acting as a salesperson, can she put "Broker" on her cards?*
   - A. Yes, Sue worked hard to achieve that status.
   - B. Yes, if she also includes the words "on deposit."
   - C. No, Sue can list herself only as an associate broker.
   - D. Only if she gets her broker's permission.

9. *At the end of the year, what form will a real estate salesperson who files as an independent contractor receive that details his or her compensation for the year?*
   - A. 1040 IND
   - B. 1099 MISC
   - C. W-2
   - D. W-4

10. *An important part of the relationship between a broker and an independent contractor salesperson is that the salesperson*
   - A. cannot be charged for office space or supplies provided by the broker.
   - B. earns commission based on the results of his work efforts.
   - C. is not subject to any direction or control by the broker.
   - D. is paid for the number of hours worked.

Estates, Interests, Liens, and Easements

5

Key Terms

Adverse Possession Acquiring title to someone else's real property by possession of it. Possession must be open and notorious, hostile and adverse, exclusive, and continuous for a prescribed number of years (e.g., in New York, 10).

Air Rights The right to undisturbed use and control of airspace over a parcel of land (within reasonable limits for air travel); may be transferred separately from the land.

Appropriative Rights Water rights allocated by government permit, according to an appropriation system. It is not necessary to own property beside the body of water in order to apply for an appropriation permit. *Also called*: **Prior Appropriation**.

Appurtenance A right that goes with real property ownership; usually transferred with the property, but may be sold separately.

Beneficiary Person designated to receive benefits from a certain act.

Bundle of Legal Rights All real property rights conferred with ownership, including right of use, right of enjoyment, and right of disposal.

Chattel Personal property.

Common Areas Land and improvements in a condominium, planned unit development, or cooperative that all residents use and own as tenants in common, such as the parking lot, hallways, and recreational facilities; individual apartment units or homes are not included. *Also called*: **Common Elements.**

Curtesy A husband's common law interest in his wife's property; not recognized in New York.

Dominant Tenement Property that receives the benefit of an appurtenant easement.

Dower A wife's common law interest in her husband's property; not recognized in New York.

Easement A right to use some part of another person's real property. An easement is irrevocable and creates an interest in the property.

Easement Appurtenant An easement that grants access.

Easement by Condemnation 1. Taking private property for public use through the government's power of eminent domain. 2. A declaration that a structure is unfit for occupancy and must be closed or demolished.

Easement by Express Grant An easement granted to another in a deed or other document.

(continued on next page)

Key Terms - continued

Easement by Implication An easement created by operation of law (not express grant or reservation) when land is divided, if there is a longstanding, apparent use that is reasonably necessary for enjoyment of the dominant tenement.

Easement by Necessity A special kind of easement by implication that occurs when the dominant tenement would be useless without an easement, even without a longstanding, apparent use.

Easement by Prescription An easement acquired by prescription.

Easement for Light and Air A view easement; considered a negative easement. In the case of negative easement, the dominant tenement can prevent the subservient tenement from doing something on the land because it could affect the dominant land.

Easement in Gross An easement that benefits a person instead of land; there is a dominant tenant, but no dominant tenement.

Emblements Another term for *fructus industriales*, meaning fruits of industry.

Encroachment Physical object intruding onto neighboring property often due to a mistake regarding boundary lines.

Encumbrance Non-possessory interest in property; a lien, easement, or restrictive covenant burdening the property owner's title.

Estate at Sufferance Possession of property by a tenant who came into possession of the property under a valid lease, but stays on after the lease expires without the landlord's permission.

Estate at Will A leasehold estate with no specified termination date and with no regular rental period.

Estate for Years Leasehold estate set to last for a definite period (e.g., one week, three years), after which it automatically terminates. *Also called*: **Term Tenancy**.

Fee on Condition Defeasible fee that may be assigned and terminated by the grantor upon the occurrence of an event.

Fee Simple Estate The greatest estate one can have in real property; freely transferable and inheritable, and of indefinite duration, with no conditions on title. *Also called*: **Fee Simple, Fee Title,** or **Fee Simple Absolute**.

Fixture A man-made attachment; an item of personal property attached to or closely associated with real property in such a way that it has legally become part of the real property.

General Lien A lien against all property of a debtor, instead of a particular piece of property.

Homestead Laws Laws that protect property owners from lien foreclosure by exempting some of their equity in real estate. In New York, homestead protection is limited to $10,000 individually and $20,000 for land co-owned by a married couple.

Involuntary Lien A lien that arises by operation of law, without the consent of the property owner. *Also called*: **Statutory Lien**.

Joint Tenancy A form of co-ownership in which the co-owners have equal undivided interests and the right of survivorship.

Joint Venture Two or more individuals or companies joining together for one project or a series of related projects, but not as an ongoing business.

Land The surface of the earth, the area above and below the surface, and anything attached to the surface.

Leasehold Estate An estate that gives the holder (tenant) a temporary right to possession, without title. *Also called*: **Less-than-Freehold Estate**.

License Revocable, non-assignable permission to enter another person's land for a particular purpose.

Life Estate A freehold estate that lasts only as long as a specified person lives. That person is referred to as the **measuring life**.

Life Estate Pur Autre Vie A life estate "for the life of another," where the measuring life is someone other than the life tenant.

Liquid When an investment can be easily converted to cash.

Lis Pendens Recorded notice stating a lawsuit is pending that may affect title to the defendant's real estate.

Littoral Rights Water rights of a landowner whose property is adjacent to a lake or contains a lake.

Mechanic's Lien A specific lien claimed by someone who performed work on the property (construction, repairs, or improvements) and has not been paid. This term is often used in a general sense, referring to materialmen's liens as well as actual mechanics' liens.

Mortgage An instrument that creates a voluntary lien on real property to secure repayment of a debt. The parties to a mortgage are the mortgagor (borrower) and mortgagee (lender).

Non-Possessory Interest An interest in property that does not include the right to possess and occupy the property; an encumbrance, such as a lien or easement.

Parcel A lot or piece of real estate, particularly a specified part of a larger tract.

Partition Allows any co-owner to end a joint tenancy.

Party Wall Easement A wall shared by two separate properties; the owners on each side share the right of use.

Periodic Estate A leasehold estate that continues for successive equal periods of time (i.e., week-to-week or month-to-month) until terminated by proper notice from either the lessor or the lessee. *Also called*: **Periodic lease** and **Periodic Tenancy**.

Personal Property Tangible items that (usually) are not permanently attached to, or part of, the real estate. *Also called*: **Personalty** or **Chattel**.

Possessory Interest An interest in property that entitles the holder to possess and occupy the property, now or in the future; an estate, which may be either a freehold or leasehold.

Qualified Fee When a grantor puts a condition or requirement in the deed and limits the title to real property. *Also called*: **Conditional**, **Determinable**, **Fee Simple Defeasible**, or **Defeasible Fee**.

Real Property The physical land and everything attached to it, and the rights of ownership (**bundle of rights**).

Restrictive Covenant 1. A limitation on real property use, imposed by the owner. 2. A promise to do, or not to do, an act relating to real property.

Right of Survivorship A characteristic of statutory survivorship tenancy, joint tenancy, and tenancy by the entireties; surviving co-tenants automatically acquire a deceased co-tenant's interest in the property.

Right of Way An easement giving the holder the right to cross another person's land.

Riparian Rights The water rights of a landowner whose property is adjacent to or crossed by a river (or any body of water).

Severalty When one part or provision in a contract can be held unenforceable without making the entire contract unenforceable.

Servient Tenement Property burdened by an easement. In other words, the owner of the servient tenement (the servient tenant) is required to allow someone who has an easement (the dominant tenant) to use his or her property.

Special Purpose Property Properties that are considered to have a limited use, such as a church or tennis club.

Specific Lien A lien that attaches only to a particular property.

Subordination Agreement a contract that gives a mortgage recorded at a later date the right to take priority over an earlier recorded mortgage.

Subsurface Rights The implication that an owner of land has rights to the land below the surface to the center of the earth, even though this part is not documented.

Tax Lien A lien on real property to secure the payment of taxes.

Tenancy by the Entirety A form of property co-ownership by husband and wife, in which each spouse has an undivided one-half interest and the right of survivorship, with neither spouse able to convey or encumber his or her interest without the other's consent.

Tenancy in Common A form of co-ownership in which two or more persons each have an undivided interest in the entire property (unity of possession), but no right of survivorship.

Trade Fixture Equipment a tenant installs for use in his or her trade or business, and which can be removed by the tenant before the lease expires.

Trust Allows the owner of property, known as the trustor, to transfer ownership to someone else, the trustee, in order for them to manage the property for a third party, the beneficiary.

Undivided Interest A co-tenant's interest, giving him or her the right to possession of the whole property, rather than a particular section of it.

Unities of Interest, Possession, Time, and Title Four unities required to form a joint tenancy whereby all owners share equally and simultaneously in these conditions.

Voluntary Lien A lien placed against property with the consent of the owner; a mortgage (or, in other states, a deed of trust).

The Nature of Property

Bundle of Legal Property Rights

- **Right of possession** – gives the owner the right physically occupy the land and to use the land in any way and make it productive as long as it is legal and does not interfere with other people's rights
- **Right of quiet enjoyment** – gives the owner the freedom to possess and use the land without interference from other people or society, including a responsibility to make sure that their neighbors' enjoyment is not hindered or adversely affected.
- **Right of disposition** – allows the owner to transfer all or some of the rights to other people, for example, landowners normally have the right to sell, lease, give away, divide, and retain part of the land or to dispose of it completely.
- **Right of exclusion** – (or the right of restriction) allows the owner to stop others from using the property or even from entering the property
- **Right of control** – allows the owner to physically alter or change the property (for example, build a garage or put in a pool)

Interference

- **Trespassing** – a physical invasion of land by another person who has no lawful right to enter it
- **Encroachment** – a legal synonym for trespass, but the term refers to objects, such as buildings whereas trespass refers to people
- **Nuisance** – interferes with the quiet enjoyment of land from outside causes like loud noises, unsightliness, and obnoxious odors; does not involve possessory rights

Real Property and Personal Property

- **Real property** – land and its attachments, as well as all of the rights associated with it
- **Personal property** – (also called **chattel**) any property that is not real property and not fixed to land
- **Land** – legally considered to include the surface of the earth, the subsurface to the center of the earth, and the air above the land within reasonable limits to permit commercial air travel
- **Attachments** – things attached to the land, whether natural or man-made
  - **Fixtures** – personal property items that have been permanently attached to the land or its improvements (become fixtures through annexation, close association, or adoption). Can be detached from the land and revert back to personal property through the process of **severance**
  - **Trade fixtures** – any equipment or personal property a commercial tenant installs for business purposes
  - **Natural attachments** – the plants growing on the land; can be personal property (fructus industrials or emblements) or real property (fructus nuturales)

Appurtenances

Rights that go with real property:

- **Subsurface rights** – the implication that a land owner has rights to use the land below the surface to the center of the earth, even through this part is not documented, such use might be for power lines, sewers, etc.
- **Air rights** – include the right to undisturbed use and control of airspace over a parcel of land (within reasonable limits for air travel)
  - **Easement for light and air** – a negative easement in which the dominant tenement can prevent the subservient tenement from doing something on the land because it could impact the dominant land
- **Water rights** – categorized as:
  - **Riparian** – water rights of a landowner whose land adjoins a river
  - **Littoral** – water rights of a landowner whose land adjoins a lake
  - **Appropriative** – water rights granted by government permit independent of land ownership
  - **Percolating** – water rights that involve the use of underground water (for example, the right to install wells)
- **Mineral rights** – a landowner owns all the solid minerals in or under the land

A lender must know if the entire bundle of rights is being transferred (fee simple) or if there are restrictions or past transactions that may limit the current transfer of ownership in any way as this can affect the value of real property.

Estates

A **possessory interest** in real property that entitles the holder to possession of the property now or in the future.

Freehold Estates

- **Fee simple estate** – the fullest freehold estate interest that exists in real property (also called fee title or fee simple absolute)
- **Qualified fee** – also called conditional, determinable, fee simple defeasible, or defeasible fee, means a grantor puts a condition or requirement in the deed that terminates the estate automatically if the condition or requirement is not met and reverts the title back to the grantor or the grantor's heirs
- **Fee on condition** – a grantor puts a condition or requirement in the deed that gives the grantor the "right of reentry" if the condition or requirement is not met.
- **Life estate** – a freehold estate that lasts only as long as a specified person, the "measuring life," lives; holder of a life estate is called a life tenant
  - Conventional life estate measuring life and life tenant are same person
  - Life estate pur autre vie, the measuring life is someone other than the life tenant
  - Future interest may be reversionary (property reverts to grantor) or remainder (property goes to someone other than grantor) upon the death of the measuring life
  - Life tenant may not commit an **act of waste** to the property (use the property in a way that damages it or reduces its market value)

- **Dower** and **curtesy** – special real property interest the law gives as statutory life estates to spouses when married couples own real property (not recognized in New York)

Leasehold Estates

- **Leasehold estate** – an interest that gives the holder a temporary right of possession of the estate without title
- **Estate for years** – any leasehold estate for a fixed time period
- **Periodic estate** – a leasehold estate for a time period not limited to a specific term
- **Estate at will** – a leasehold estate with no specified termination date and with no regular rental period
- **Estate at sufferance** – describes possession of property by a tenant who came into possession of the property under a valid lease, but stays on after the lease expires without the landlord's permission (a holdover tenant)

Encumbrances

Non-possessory interests that someone may have in someone else's property, or burdens on the property

Easements

An easement is a right to use another person's real property for a particular purpose.

- Restricts how a parcel of land may be used because a structure usually cannot be put on an easement
- Creates limited rights for the easement holder related to the land surface, its airspace, or subsurface
- Should be recorded in the public records
- Categorized as:
  - **Appurtenant easements**, burden a piece of land (the servient tenement) for the benefit of another piece of land (the dominant tenement); also called **right of way**
  - **Easements in gross** benefit a person, not a piece of land; the person can be an individual or a corporation, such as a utility company

Easement Creation

- **Easement by express grant** – a landowner divides land and includes deed language so the seller retains an easement across his former land
- **Easement by implication** – created by operation of law (not express grant or reservation) when land is divided if there is a longstanding, apparent use that is reasonably necessary for enjoyment of the dominant tenement
- **Easement by necessity** – a special kind of easement by implication that occurs when the dominant tenement would be completely useless without an easement, even if it is not a longstanding, apparent use
- **Easement by prescription** – created by open and notorious, hostile and adverse use of another person's land for a specific period of time determined by state law, 10 years in New York
- **Easement by condemnation** – the government's exercise of the right of eminent domain, condemning for an easement instead of full ownership

- **Party wall easement** – when a party wall is shared between two connected properties

Easement Termination

- **Release** – document in which a legal right is given up, releasing an easement holder's interest in the property if they are willing to give up or be paid for the easement; should always be recorded
- **Merger** – unites two or more separate properties by transferring ownership of all the property to one person
- **Abandonment** – the failure to occupy and use property, which may result in a loss of rights
- **Prescription** – just as an easement can be created by prescription, an easement can be lost by prescription after a specified number of years of non-use
- **Destruction**– the involuntary destruction of the building (e.g., by fire)
- **Failure of purpose** – the purpose for which it was created no longer exists

Easements vs. Licenses

- **License** – a temporary revocable, non-assignable permission to enter another's land for a particular purpose
- Differences include:
  - Easements are usually for an indefinite period of time
  - Easements are created by written agreement or action of law, but licenses may be created by oral contract
  - Easements run with the land, but licenses do not have to
  - Easements cannot be revoked, whereas licenses may be revoked at any time
  - A license cannot be assigned and becomes invalid if the licensee dies

Easements vs. Encroachments

- Encroachment – a physical object intruding onto a neighbor's property
- Encroachments are **not** easements since there is no legal claim or right to another person's property
- Encroachments may, over time, turn into adverse possession

Liens

Not only a financial interest in property, but also a financial encumbrance

- **General** – attached to all property, personal or real, owned in the country by the debtor
- **Specific** – attached only to specific property
- **Voluntary** – placed against property with consent of the owner
  - **Mortgages** – written instruments that use real property to secure payment of a debt
- **Involuntary** – arise by operation of law without consent of the property owner
  - **Mechanic's** – liens claimed by someone who performed work on real property and was not paid
  - **Tax** – liens on real property to secure the payment of property taxes
  - **Estate tax** – estate tax is administered to the estate of the deceased. An estate tax is an involuntary, general lien

- ◆ **Corporation franchise tax** – corporations operating in New York are required to pay an annual state tax based on net profit; a corporation franchise tax lien is an involuntary, general lien
  - ◆ **Judgment** – liens against a person's property through court action; involuntary, general liens
  - ◆ **Attachment** – liens intended to prevent transfer of property pending the outcome of litigation; notice of pending suit, called a **lis pendens**, may also be recorded
- **Lien priority** – property tax liens usually take precedence over other liens, then, liens are generally paid in the order they were attached to the land
- **Subordination agreement** – a lender voluntarily puts its lien in a lower order of priority

Forms of Ownership

Ownership or title to property is created and conveyed in one of three ways:

- By **deed**, which is *a document that transfers ownership of real property*, as when someone sells a house to someone else
- By **devise**, which is *when real property is transferred because of a will*
- By **descent**, which is *an operation of law when real property is transferred to an heir after the death of the owner who leaves no will*

Ownership in Severalty

A **sole** form of ownership, meaning that only **one person** or legal entity holds the title to that property

Co-Ownership

Co-ownership – also known as concurrent ownership, is any form of ownership where two or more legal persons share title to real property, with each person having an undivided interest in the property. **Undivided interest** gives each co-owner the right to possession of the whole property, not just part of it.

Unities of Co-Ownership
- Unity of **possession** – all co-owners hold the same undivided right to possess the whole property
- Unity of **interest** – all co-owners hold equal ownership interests
- Unity of **time** – all co-owners acquired their interests at the same time
- Unity of **title** – all co-owners acquired their interests by the same deed or will
- Unity of **person** – husband and wife are legally considered one person

Survivorship is a characteristic of statutory survivorship tenancy, joint tenancy, and tenancy by the entireties where surviving co-tenants automatically acquire a deceased co-tenant's interest in the property.

Co-Ownership Options
- **Tenancy in common** – a form of co-ownership with two or more persons having an undivided interest in the entire property, but no right of survivorship

- **Joint tenancy** – exists when each joint tenant has an equal undivided interest in the property and right of survivorship; when a joint tenant conveys an interest, only the survivorship right in that interest ends; requires unities of possession, interest, time, and title; all owners share equally and simultaneously
- **Tenancy by the entirety** – a form of co-ownership, available only to husband and wife owners, that involves each having an equal and undivided share of the property with the right of survivorship; requires all five unities

Community Property

- Says that two people in a marriage are equal but separate partners, and so marital property is automatically equally divided between spouses when they divorce
- These states observe community property laws: Arizona, California, Idaho, Louisiana, Nevada, New Mexico, Texas, Washington, and Wisconsin

Ownership by Associations

Corporation

- A legal entity created and operated according to the laws of each state
- Regarded by the law as a legal person separate from the individual stockholders
- Property is owned **in severalty** as the legal person
- Shareholders are not personally liable for the corporation's debts
- Can be public (cities, counties, school districts, etc.), private for profit, or private non-profit

Partnerships

- An association of two or more individuals as co-owners of a business, as specified in the partnership agreement
- May take title to property in the name of the partnership as tenants in partnership
- May also take title to property in the name of individual partners as tenants in common or as joint tenants
- May be general partnerships or limited partnerships

General Partnership

- An association of two or more individuals as co-owners of a business
- All partners share in the financial liability both individually and as a member of the partnership

Limited Partnership

- An association of two or more persons as co-owners of a business with one or more general partners and one or more limited partners
- Rights and duties of general partners in a limited partnership are the same as in a general partnership, but limited partners have no say in partnership matters
- The partner's liability is limited to their original investment

Syndicate

- Type of joint participation of individuals, partnerships, and / or corporations in a real estate investment
- Generally used for large-scale ongoing projects or multiple projects

Joint Venture

- Arrangement where two or more individuals or companies pool resources to engage in one or a series of projects but not as an ongoing business

Condominiums and Cooperatives

- **Condominiums** – property developed for co-ownership, where each co-owner has a separate fee simple interest in the interior of an individual unit and an undivided interest in the common areas of the property; in the event of default on the mortgage, individual owner's lender can place lien against specific unit and undivided interest in common areas
- **Cooperatives** – buildings owned by corporations, with the residents as shareholders who each receive a proprietary lease on an individual unit and the right to use common areas
- **Townhomes** – properties developed for co-ownership where each co-owner has a separate fee simple interest in an individual unit, including its roof and basement, as well as the land directly beneath the unit, and an undivided interest in the common areas of the property

QUIZ

1. **Which is NOT an example of real property?**
   A. minerals lying just under the surface of the land
   B. peach trees growing in the orchard
   C. a shed that was built in the yard on a bed of gravel
   D. wheat growing in the field that is sold with the farm

2. **Which item is NOT a fixture?**
   A. barn built five years ago
   B. brick patio used only in the summer
   C. built-in kitchen cabinets
   D. new kitchen water faucet still in its box

3. **Paul agrees to rent an apartment for six months for $700 a month. At the end of the six months, Paul agrees to rent for another six months. What does this situation describe?**
   A. appurtenant easement
   B. estate for years
   C. estate from year to year
   D. tenancy at will

4. **Which is NOT an example of an encumbrance?**
   A. a gas company's right to enter your property to fix a gas leak
   B. a mortgage lender placing a lien for non-payment
   C. a neighbor driving across your property to get to the road
   D. a neighbor's shrubs hanging over your property line

5. **Darrell has a written agreement to drive across Lin's property to get to his own. This is an example of a(n)**
   A. appurtenant easement, where Darrell's property is the dominant tenement and Lin's property is the servient tenement.
   B. defeasible easement, which puts a condition on Darrell to follow the rules established by Lin.
   C. easement in gross, where the easement is attached to Darrell and he can't transfer the easement if he sells the land.
   D. encroachment, since Darrell is allowed to encroach on the rights of Lin.

6. **A windstorm rips down power lines on farmer John's property. Big City Telecommunications enters John's property without his permission to fix the lines. What is this an example of?**
   A. easement in gross
   B. lien
   C. nuisance
   D. trespass

7. **Mark and Paula are married. They co-own a property with Tom as joint tenants with right of survivorship. Tom dies. What is Paula's interest in the property?**
   A. 33%
   B. 50%
   C. 100%
   D. It depends on who is named in Tom's will.

8. **The co-owner of an undivided interest in land with no rights of survivorship owns it by**
   A. absolute ownership.
   B. joint tenancy.
   C. severalty.
   D. tenancy in common.

9. **Ownership of property by one person or legal entity is called**
   A. exclusive tenancy.
   B. severalty.
   C. tenancy by the entirety.
   D. tenancy in common.

10. **The unities of person, possession, interest, time, and title are required for which type of ownership?**
    A. joint tenancy
    B. tenancy by the entirety
    C. tenancy in common
    D. tenancy in severalty

Contracts and Contract Preparation

6

Key Terms

Acceptance Agreeing to the terms of an offer to enter into a contract, thereby creating a binding contract; taking delivery of a deed.

Actual Eviction Physically forcing someone off property, preventing someone from re-entering property, or using the legal process to make someone leave.

"As Is" Clause Provision in a purchase agreement stating the buyer accepts the property in its present condition.

Assignment One party (assignor) transferring rights or interests under a contract to another person (assignee). In New York, all contracts are assignable unless the contract states otherwise.

Bilateral A contract in which each party promises to do something.

Consideration Anything of value such as money, goods, services, or promises, given to induce another person to enter into a contract. *Also called*: **Valuable Consideration**.

Constructive Eviction When a landlord's act (or failure to act) interferes with the tenant's quiet enjoyment of the property, or makes the property unfit for its intended use, to such an extent that the tenant is forced to move out.

Contingency Provision in a contract or deed that makes the parties' rights and obligations depend on the occurrence (or nonoccurrence) of a particular event. *Also called*: **Condition**.

Contract Agreement between two or more parties to do, or not do, a certain thing. The requirements for an enforceable contract are **capacity**, **mutual consent**, **lawful objective**, and **consideration**.

Counteroffer A response to an offer to enter into a contract, changing some of the terms of the original offer; a rejection of the original offer (not a form of acceptance).

Covenant 1. A contract. 2. A promise. 3. A guarantee (express or implied) in a document such as a deed or lease. 4. A restrictive covenant.

Earnest Money Deposit 1. Money offered as an indication of good faith regarding the future performance of a purchase agreement. 2. A tenant's security deposit.

Eviction Dispossessing or expelling someone from real property.

Executed Contract Contract under which both parties have completely performed their contractual obligations.

Executory Contract A contract under which one or more parties have not yet completed performance of their obligations.

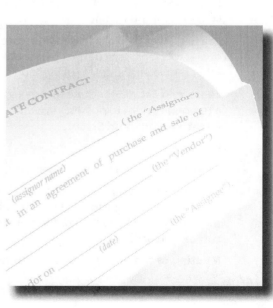

(continued on next page)

Key Terms - continued

Express Contract Contract that has been put into words, either spoken or written.

Forbearance A legally binding promise to refrain from doing a particular act.

Graduated Lease A lease in which the rent changes throughout the lease term. The contract specifies how much as well as when the rent will change.

Gross Lease A lease in which the lessor pays all operating and maintenance costs associated with the property.

Ground Lease A lease in which a tenant leases unimproved land on a long-term basis. Ground leases typically include a provision that provides the tenant will construct a building on the property, which he will own upon completion. However, the lessor retains the rights to the land. Essentially, ownership of the land and improvements (building) are separated. Also known as a **Land Lease**.

Holdover Tenant A lessee who remains in possession of property after the lease has expired; a tenant who refuses to surrender possession of property at the tenancy's end.

Implied Contract A contract that has not been put into words, but is implied by the actions of the parties.

Index Lease Method used to determine rent for long-term leases.

Land Contract A real estate installment agreement where a buyer makes payment to a seller in exchange for the right to occupy and use property, but no deed or title transfers until all, or a specified portion of, payments have been made. *Also called*: **Installment Land Contract**, **Installment Sales Contract**, and **Land Sales Contract.**

Land Lease Lease in which a tenant leases unimproved land on a long-term basis.

Lease Conveyance of a leasehold estate from the fee owner to a tenant; a contract where one party pays the other rent in exchange for possession of real estate.

Leasehold Estate An estate that gives the holder (tenant) a temporary right to possession, without title. *Also called*: **Less-than-Freehold Estate**.

Lessee Person who leases property; a tenant.

Lessor Person who leases property to another; a landlord.

Liquidated Damages A sum of money the parties to a contract agree in advance (at the time of entering into the contract) will serve as compensation in the event of a contract breach.

Meeting of the Minds Also known as mutual agreement.

Net Lease Lease for which a tenant pays all taxes, insurance, etc., plus utilities and rent.

Novation 1. When one party to a contract withdraws and a new party is substituted, with the consent of all parties, relieving the withdrawing party of liability. 2. The substitution of a new obligation for an old one.

Offer When one person proposes a contract to another and that offer is accepted, a binding contract is formed.

Option A contract giving one party the right to do something within a designated time period, without obligation to do it.

Option to Renew Renewal methods and the terms by which a renewed lease will exist.

Percentage Lease Lease under which a tenant pays a percentage of gross sales in addition to rent.

Periodic Lease A leasehold estate that continues for successive equal periods of time (i.e., week-to-week or month-to-month) until terminated by proper notice from either the lessor or the lessee. *Also called*: **Periodic Estate** and **Periodic Tenancy**.

Power of Attorney An instrument authorizing one person (called an attorney in fact) to act as another's agent, to the extent stated in the instrument.

Proprietary Lease Exclusive, longer term lease given to a person who lives in a cooperative and owns stock in the cooperative.

Quiet Enjoyment Use and possession of real property without interference from the previous owner, the lessor, or anyone else claiming title.

Reformation A legal action to correct a mistake, such as a typographical error, in a deed or other document.

Rescission When a contract is terminated and each party gives anything acquired under the contract back to the other party (verb form is **rescind**).

Rider An amendment to a contract.

Right of First Refusal A right to have the first chance to buy or lease property if the owner decides to sell or lease it. *Also called*: **Right of Pre-emption**.

Sales Contract Contract in which a seller promises to convey title to real property to a buyer in exchange for the purchase price. *Also called*: **Purchase Agreement**, **Sale Agreement**, **Purchase and Sale Agreement**, **Offer to Purchase**, and **Earnest Money Agreement**.

Security Deposit Money a tenant gives a landlord at the beginning of tenancy to ensure the tenant will comply with the terms of the lease. The landlord may retain all or

Contract Law

A **contract** is an agreement between two or more competent parties to do, or not do, something. It is a legally enforceable promise, with the law providing remedies for breach.

Contract Classifications

- **Bilateral** – each party makes a binding promise to the other, a promise for a promise
  - Example: A listing agreement where the seller agrees to pay commission to the broker if she carries out her responsibilities
- **Unilateral** – only one party makes a binding promise to another party as a way to induce the second party to act in some way
  - Example: An option where one party has the right to do something within a designated amount of time, without obligation to do it
- **Express** – an agreement that's been expressed in words, either oral or written
  - Example: Signing a work order at the garage to fix your car is an express contract
- **Implied** – an agreement that has not been put into words but is implied by actions of the parties
  - Example: Eating at a restaurant; it's understood that you agree to pay the bill, even if you don't actually discuss it before you sit down or finish eating
- **Executory** – one or both parties have not yet completed performance of their contractual obligations, though they may be in the process of carrying out their duties
  - Example: Party A and Party B sign a listing agreement; the broker is actively seeking a buyer but has not yet fulfilled his side of the contract

---

Key Terms - continued

part of the deposit to cover unpaid rent, repair costs, or other damages, if necessary.

Sit Down Contract When all negotiating is conducted in one place at one time with all parties to the contract and their attorneys present.

Specific Performance A legal remedy in which a court orders someone who has breached a contract to perform as agreed, rather than simply paying monetary damages.

Statute of Frauds A law that requires certain types of contracts to be in writing and signed to be enforceable; codified in New York General Obligations Law.

Statute of Limitations A law requiring a particular type of lawsuit to be filed within a specified time after the event giving rise to the suit occurred; in New York, it is six years for real estate transactions.

Sublease When a tenant transfers only part of his right of possession or other interest in leased property to another person for part of the remaining lease term.

Time is of the Essence A contract clause that means performance on the exact dates specified is an essential element of the contract; failure to perform on time is a material breach.

Triple Net Lease A lease in which the tenant pays *all* the expenses associated with the property, including rent.

Uniform Commercial Code (UCC) Sets out certain requirements for negotiable instruments.

Unilateral When only one party makes a legally binding promise and the other has not. The promise will become legally binding if the other party chooses to accept it (similar to an offer).

Void Having no legal force or effect.

Voidable A contract that one of the parties can disaffirm, without liability, because of a lack of legal capacity or a negative factor such as fraud or duress.

- **Executed** – both parties have fully performed their contractual obligations
  - Example: Party A and Party B sign a listing agreement; after a buyer is found, the seller pays the broker's commission at closing

Essential Elements of a Contract

For a contract to be valid, it must have these **six** essential elements:

1. **Competent parties** – in New York, a person must be at least 18 years old, mentally competent, and have proper authorization
2. **Lawful objective** – the purpose or objective of a contract must be lawful at the time the contract is made; when one person promises to pay someone for committing an illegal act, the contract is void
3. **Consideration** – (also called valuable consideration) anything of value such as money, services, goods, or promises given to induce another to enter into a contract
   - **Forbearance** – a promise to refrain from doing something
   - **Promisor** – one making a promise
   - **Promisee** – one who gets the benefit of a promise
   - **Adequacy** – the value of the consideration one party gives does *not* have to be equal to the value of what the other gives
4. **Description** – any contract must include a description of what is being contracted
5. **Mutual agreement** – generally involves an offer and acceptance; indicates a **meeting of the minds**
6. **Written format and signatures** – every state has a version of the **statute of frauds**, a law requiring certain types of contracts to be in writing and signed to be enforceable
   - In New York, the statute of frauds requires real estate contracts be written and contain all the essential elements for a valid contract
   - Applies to any power of attorney authorizing someone to sell another's real estate; a **power of attorney** is an instrument authorizing one person (called an attorney-in-fact) to act as another's agent to the extent stated in the instrument
   - The *Doctrine of Part Performance* allows a New York State court to enforce an oral agreement that should have been in writing if the promisee has taken irrevocable steps to perform his side of the bargain, and failure to enforce the contract would result in an unjust benefit for the promisor
   - *Parole evidence* provides that the written agreement overrides any oral agreements

Contract Validity

In addition to be express or implied, unilateral or bilateral, executory or executed, a contract is valid, void, voidable, or unenforceable:

- **Valid** – a binding, legally enforceable agreement if it meets all of the legal requirements for contract formation; if one party doesn't fulfill his side of the bargain, the other party can sue to have the contract enforced
- **Void** – not enforceable because it lacks one or more of the requirements for contract formation, or is otherwise defective

- **Voidable** – can be terminated or nullified by one party *without* liability because of a lack of legal capacity or other factor such as fraud or duress
- **Unenforceable** – a contract that may have been valid between the parties but a court would refuse to enforce; for example, an oral contract for the sale of real estate or a vaguely worded contract

Offer and Acceptance

Contracts are required to show mutual agreement or meeting of the minds.

Offer

One party proposing a contract to another party—only if the other party accepts the offer is a contract formed.

- **Intent to contract** (objective intent vs. subjective intent) – explicit words and actions of the offeror must reasonably indicate the intention of forming a contract
- **Definite terms** – offer must be complete in its terms and details; an offer isn't binding if it's vague or does not include the essential elements of a contract
- **Earnest money deposit** – made with an offer to purchase is not consideration. Earnest money is an inducement to have the buyer's offer accepted and a means of showing the seller the buyer is serious and able to follow through with the financing necessary to buy the property
- **Termination of an offer** – an offer can be terminated by:
  - Lapse of time
  - Death or incapacity of one of the parties
  - Revocation

Acceptance

Acceptance (also called a meeting of the minds) occurs when a party agrees on price, down payment, financing method, and other essential terms. **When an offer is accepted, a contract is formed** and the parties are legally bound. Four basic requirements for acceptance:

- When an offer does not specify how it is to be accepted, any reasonable method of acceptance effectively binds the offeror and prevents revocation
- Must be communicated to the offeror
- Must be made in the manner specified
- Must not vary the terms of the offer; changed terms indicate a **counteroffer**

Genuine Assent

Consent must be freely given to create a binding contract. Offer and acceptance are not freely given when either the result of one of four negative factors is:

- **Fraud** – intentional or negligent misrepresentation of material facts; occurs when a person relies on another to be truthful
- **Undue influence** – excessive pressure on someone, preventing him from making a rational or prudent decision
- **Duress** – threatening violence against or unlawfully confining a person, or any member of that person's family, to force him to sign a document
- **Mistake** – when one or more parties to a contract are mistaken about a fact or law

Performance and Breach of Contract

A **breach of contract** occurs when a party to a contract fails to perform with no legal cause. A party who fails to perform and the failure is not excused has breached the contract. When one party breaches, the other party may not be required to perform, depending on whether there has been substantial performance or material breach.

- **Substantial performance** – the promisor doesn't perform all contractual obligations, but does enough so that the promisee is required to fulfill that part of the deal

- **Material breach** – a breach of contract that is significant enough to excuse the non-breaching party from performing the contractual obligations

Clauses

- **Time is of the essence clause** is a specific clause that emphasizes timely performance as an essential part of the contract; failure to perform on time is a material breach. The contract can be saved by an agreement to extend. If this clause is not included and the buyer was late in performing, the seller could give the buyer a reasonable time to perform even though the deadline in the contract has passed.

- **Conditions**, also called contingency clauses, are contract provisions that make the parties' rights or obligations dependent on the occurrence (or non-occurrence) of certain events. When a contract is conditional, the promisor must make a good faith effort to fulfill the condition.

Remedies for Breach of Contract

If one party to a contract does not perform the contractual obligations, or breaches the contract, the non-defaulting party may take legal action by filing suit against the defaulting party in a court of law. Remedies include:

- **Cancellation** – termination of a contract without undoing acts that have been performed under it

- **Compensatory damages** – an award, usually money, intended to compensate the plaintiff for harm caused by the other's act or failure to act; award is usually the amount that will put the non-breaching party in the same position as if the other party had fulfilled the contract

- **Injunction** – a court order that orders a party to do or refrain from doing a certain act (or acts) as opposed to a monetary award

- **Liquidated damages** – the amount specified in a clause of the contract that states how much money a party collects if the contract is breached; usually included as a way to avoid expensive litigation

- **Reformation** – a contract is modified by the court to reflect the true intention of the parties

- **Rescission** – the destruction, annulment, or termination of a contract and all parties to a the contract must give back anything acquired under it to the other party

- **Specific performance** – a legal remedy in which a court orders someone who has breached a contract to perform as agreed, rather than simply paying damages

Discharge of Contracts

- **Agreement of the parties** – when all parties to a contract agree, any executory contract can be discharged, or terminated; also known as release of contract
- **Partial performance** – when both parties agree to accept something different, usually less, than the terms of the original contract, and the original obligation is extinguished
- **Full performance** – all terms and contractual obligations have been carried out by all parties and the contract is thus released
- **Impossibility of performance** – the performance of a contractual obligation becomes illegal because of a change in the law after the contract was created, terminating the contract
- **Operation of law** – the rights and liabilities of the contracting parties are changed by application of the law, for example:
  - Alteration of contract
  - Bankruptcy
  - Death of a party to the contract
  - Statute of limitations (6 years in New York)

Assignment and Novation

- **Assignment** – one of the parties (assignor) transfers rights or interests under a contract to another person (assignee); assignor is not relieved of liability but remains secondarily liable to the other party and can be sued if the assignee doesn't perform; consent required for personal services contracts
  - In NY, most contracts assignable by either party without consent unless contract specifically states otherwise
- **Novation** – when a new contract is substituted, relieving the withdrawing party of liability; requires consent of both parties

Sales Contracts

Sales contracts are contracts in which a seller promises to convey title to real property to a buyer in exchange for the purchase price; also called purchase agreements, sale agreements, purchase and sale agreements, installment sales contracts, and earnest money agreements. A sales contract is the:

- Buyer's offer
- Receipt for the earnest money deposit
- The contract between the buyer and seller

Contract Preparation

New York does not dictate the use of a standard form; actual process usually determined by local customs and practices.

Standardized Sales Contracts

New York allows brokers to use a standardized sales contract form that has been approved by a recognized Bar Association in conjunction with a local Board of REALTORS® as long as it meets certain criteria, including:

- Broker may fill in only nonlegal provisions
- Clearly and prominent indication that it is a legally binding document and it is recommended all parties seek an attorney's advice before signing
- Brokers cannot add any provisions to the standard preprinted contract form unless they make the entire contract subject to the review and approval of the attorneys representing all parties.

Binders

A **binder** is an agreement that may accompany an earnest money deposit for the purchase of real property as evidence of the purchaser's good faith and intent to complete the transaction. A binder is *not* a sales contract or purchase contract but contain the essential elements that will go into a contract that an attorney prepares. Binders are most often used in New York City and Long Island.

Essential Elements of a Sales Contract

All of the essentials of a valid contract must be present in a sales contract and it must identify:

- **Parties** to the contract, including the names and addresses of the buyer(s) and seller(s).
- Specific **property** to be sold.
- **Interest** in the property to be sold
- **Terms** of the sale as clearly as possible
- Total purchase **price** and **method of payment**

Data Needed for Contract Preparation

Some specific information or documents that may be needed include:

- **Survey** of the property's boundaries.
- Evidence of any **encumbrances** such as easements or liens.
- Prior **deed**, which is used to draft a new deed.
- Property **tax bills**, the most recent available, as well as special assessments and water and fuel bills needed to adjust expenses at closing.
- **Certificate of occupancy** to indicate that the property is habitable after local authorities perform required inspections.

Other Contract Provisions

- **"As is" clauses** – a provision in a purchase agreement stating the buyer accepts the property in its present conditon
- **Contingencies** – conditions or provisions that must occur in order for the contract to be performed
- **Escape clauses** – when a buyer has to sell their home in order to purchase the property in the present contract, the seller can request an escape clause be included in the contract, to allow them to pursue other buyers, while giving the offeror the right to perform or cancel, should another contract be considered
- **Lead-based paint disclosures** – buyers who write a contract on almost any residential property built prior to 1978 must be given a booklet discussing lead-based paint hazards. Buyers of pre-1978 residential property must be allowed

ten days to investigate potential lead-based hazards before the contract becomes binding. New York law also requires sellers to provide buyers with a Property Condition Disclosure statement

- **Riders** – amendments to contracts

Leases

Leases are conveyances that temporarily transfer the right of possession of property from the owner (the landlord or lessor) to another (the tenant or lessee), creating a **leasehold estate**. Lessees, or tenants, are entitled to **quiet enjoyment** of the property, which is the right to the use and possession of real property without interference from the previous owner, the lessor, or anyone else claiming title. A lease, or rental agreement, is also a contract:

- Stating the terms of the relationship between lessor and lessee, for example, the rent the tenant pays in exchange for possession of the real estate.
- That reverts possession to the lessor at the conclusion of the lease.

Types of Leases

- **Gross lease** – property owner pays all expenses associated with the property, including property taxes, insurance, and maintenance
- **Net lease** – tenant pays some or all of the expenses associated with the property – taxes, insurance, and maintenance – in addition to rent and utilities
  - Single net – tenant pays one of these expenses
  - Double net (or net-net) – tenant pays any two of these expenses
  - Triple net (or net-net-net) – tenant pays all three of these expenses
- **Percentage lease** – the tenant pays a percentage of his or her gross sales to the landlord, often in addition to a fixed monthly rental payment
- **Land lease/ground lease** – tenant leases unimproved land on a long-term basis; typically includes a provision that provides the tenant will construct a building on the property, which the tenant will own upon completion
- **Index lease** – amount of the rent is tied to some common index indicator such as the Consumer Price Index or the Wholesale Price Index. As the agreed upon index increases, the rent goes up by the same percent of change
- **Graduated lease** – spells out step-by-step rent increases (or decreases), generally paid in installments or set at fixed intervals

Standard Lease Provisions

- **Legal capacity to contract**, in which both parties must be competent and over the age of 18
  - **Demising clause** that grants possession of the property to lessee
  - **Terms** of the lease must be clearly stated, including the duration of the tenancy, its expiration date, and an adequate description of the property
  - An adequate **description** of the property
  - **Consideration**, which usually is a sum of money paid as rent in exchange for possession of property
  - **Security deposit** – money the tenant pays to the landlord that provides monetary security in case of damage to the residence or failure by the lessee

to comply with the lease agreement; must be held in escrow and must be in interest-bearing account if 6 or more units (interest belongs to the lessee)

- **Lease renewal** – New York does not provide for statutory rights to be renewed; many leases include an **option to renew**, which sets forth the renewal methods and terms by which the renewed lease will exist

- **Specification of rent and payment** – lease agreements usually stipulate rent is paid in advance on a month-to-month basis

- **Use provisions** – residential leases typically assert the premises cannot be used for anything other than its intended purpose—a place to reside

  - **The terms listed in writing** if it will last for more than one year to comply with the statute of frauds. In New York, an oral lease for less than one year is generally enforceable
  - **Signatures** of both parties

Other Lease Considerations

- **Apartment sharing** – in New York, a lease may not restrict the immediate family of the named lessee from occupancy

- **Improvement** – New York's Multiple Dwelling Law states an owner renting a multiple-family dwelling must keep it in good repair

- **Habitability** – New York's Warranty of Habitability Law requires property owners to lease property that is habitable and livable at the beginning of the lease term and to maintain the premises in habitable and livable conditions throughout the lease term

- **Sublease** – occurs when a tenant transfers only part of his right of possession or other interest in leased property to another person for part of the remaining lease term; original tenant remains responsible to owner for all lease provisions

Rent Regulations

- **Rent control** – a series of state and local regulations that restrict the amount of rent charged by property owners

  - In New York City, rent control operates under the maximum base rent (MBR) system
  - A maximum base rent is established for each apartment and is adjusted every two years to reflect changes in operating costs

- **Rent stabilization** – limits the amount that rents may be raised

  - In New York City, apartments in buildings of six or more units, built between February 1, 1947 and January 1, 1974, are subject to rent stabilization. Tenants who moved in after June 30, 1971 are also covered
  - The Rent Regulation Reform Act of 1997 and New York City Local Law Number 4 provide for the deregulation of apartments with legal monthly rents of $2,000 or more and that are occupied by tenants with an income in excess of $175,000 in each of the two successive years prior to the owner's application for deregulation

Lease Termination

Leases are terminated in a number of ways. The most common is when a lease term expires. Another method is when the property owner and the tenant mutually agree to cancel a lease agreement prior to its expiration.

- **Abandonment** – If a tenant abandons the premises and the owner re-enters to repossess it, a lease can be terminated.

- **Eviction**

  - **Actual eviction** – The forced removal, by **legal means**, of a tenant and the tenant's belongings from a leased premise.

  - **Constructive eviction** – A landlord forces a tenant to leave the property by making it uninhabitable or prevents the tenant from the quiet enjoyment of the property.

  - **Self-help eviction** – A landlord uses physical force, threats, or other means to get rid of a tenant instead of going through the legal process; **illegal** in New York

Death of Property Owner or Sale of Property

When one party to the lease dies or the property is sold, it does not terminate the lease. The heirs or new owner must honor the existing lease contracts.

Other Real Estate Contracts

Cooperative Apartment Purchase and Contract

Cooperatives are buildings owned by corporations with the residents as shareholders who each receive a proprietary lease on an individual unit and the right to use common areas.

- Purchaser buys shares in the corporation (personal property)

- Proprietary leases have longer terms than ordinary leases and offer more rights than an ordinary tenant lease

- Shares, and thus the apartment, transferred to purchaser along with assignment of the long-term proprietary lease to the apartment

- Financing governed by the Uniform Commercial Code, which provides for the lender to retain a security interest in the personal property or chattel until the lender is paid in full

Options

- Contracts that give one party the right to do something, without obligating him to do so; a unilateral contract

- Allows the optionee to exercise the option within the defined timeframe, but does not obligate the optionee to exercise the option

- Is supported by consideration; the optionee pays the optionor for the option right

- Includes consideration that is usually separate and independent of the purchase price

- Must be in writing and signed by the optionee and the optionor

- Can be recorded (to protect the optionee) only if it states a definite expiration date (recorded option is no longer a cloud on the title as of the expiration date).
- Is still binding on the optionor's heirs if optionor dies before option expires
- Generally serves as the purchase contract when an option is exercised
- **Right of first refusal** – the right to have the first opportunity to buy or lease property if the owner decides to put it up for sale or lease

Land Contracts

Installment sales contracts, also referred to as land contracts, are real estate installment agreements where the buyer, or vendee, makes regular payments to the seller, or vendor, in exchange for the right to occupy and use the property.

- A buyer can typically qualify more easily than for a conventional loan
- The seller actually holds the title to land as security, not just a mortgage lien
- Deed or legal title is not transferred until all, or a specified substantial portion of, the payments have been made

QUIZ

1. *Adam and Jenny enter into an agreement wherein Adam will buy Jenny's house at the asking price if Jenny will install a new roof and if Adam can qualify for a loan sufficient to cover the purchase. Until the roof is installed and the financing obtained, the contract is said to be*
   A. executed.
   B. executory.
   C. rescinded.
   D. voidable.

2. *Walton decides to sell his cabin on the lake and offers it in a letter to his regular postman, Bill, at a price of $5,000. The next day, Walton receives a note from a neighbor, a close friend of the postman, who says, "I accept your offer." Is Walton obligated to sell to the neighbor?*
   A. no, because no licensed agent was involved
   B. no, because only the offeree can accept an offer
   C. yes, because both the offer and the acceptance were in writing
   D. yes, because the acceptance was within three days

3. *Who is authorized to rescind a voidable contract?*
   A. either party
   B. neither; only a void contract may be rescinded
   C. only a minor
   D. the agent and the seller only

4. *Larry has entered into a lease option to purchase Susie's home. The option binds*
   A. Larry only.
   B. Susie only.
   C. neither Larry or Susie.
   D. both Larry and Susie.

5. *The Statute of Frauds is a statutory law that requires contracts regarding real estate to*
   A. be in writing to be enforceable.
   B. have a definite expiration date.
   C. have adequate consideration.
   D. include a non-discrimination clause.

6. *Once a contract is terminated, it is considered*
   A. discharged.
   B. executory.
   C. mitigated.
   D. unilateral.

7. *Identify which of the following is NOT a requirement for a valid contract.*
   A. acceptance
   B. consideration
   C. lawful and possible objective
   D. substantial performance

8. *What is a novation?*
   A. an amendment to a contract
   B. an assignment of a contract
   C. an assumption of a contract
   D. a new contract

9. *Dr. Gitwell pays his landlord rent for his office and also pays all of the utility bills for the office. His landlord pays the property taxes, mortgage, and insurance. What type of lease is this?*
   A. gross lease
   B. land lease
   C. net lease
   D. percentage lease

10. *Top Cuts Lawn Service has an agreement to mow all of Lots-O-Wealth Realty Co. properties for sale. Top Cuts is now concentrating their efforts on the east side of town, and so they have assigned the properties on the west side of town to another lawn service, Under Cuts. Who is liable under an assignment?*
    A. Top Cuts remains primarily liable.
    B. Top Cuts remains secondarily liable.
    C. Top Cuts and Under Cuts share the liability equally.
    D. Top Cuts is relieved of liability.

The Valuation Process and Pricing Properties

Key Terms

Appraisal An estimate or opinion of property value (parcel of land) as of a certain date, supported by objective data.

Arm's Length Transaction One that occurs under typical conditions in the marketplace, with each party acting in his or her own best interest.

Assemblage Combining two or more parcels of land into one larger parcel.

Assessed Value Value placed on property to which a local tax rate is applied to calculate the amount of real property tax.

Comparative (Competitive) Market Analysis (CMA) A method of determining the approximate market value of a home by comparing the subject property to other homes that have sold, are presently for sale, or did not sell in a given area. *Also called:* **Competitive Market Analysis** and **Comparable Market Analysis.**

Conformity "Rule" that says a particular home (or neighborhood) achieves maximum value when it is surrounded by homes similar in style and function.

Contribution "Rule" that says a particular item or feature of a home is worth only what it actually contributes in value to that property.

Cost Money needed to develop, produce, buy, or build something.

Cost Approach Appraisal method that estimates the value of real estate by figuring the cost of building the house or other improvement on the land, minus depreciation, plus the value of the vacant land.

Depreciation A loss in value for any reason.

Direct Cost The cost in labor and materials.

Evaluation Determining the usefulness or utility of property without specifying an estimate of value.

External Obsolescence Any influence that falls outside the actual property site and negatively affects a property's value. *Compare:* **Functional Obsolescence**.

Functional Obsolescence Loss in property value resulting from changes in tastes, preferences, or market standards.

Highest and Best Use The most profitable, legally permitted, feasible, and physically possible use of a property.

Income Approach Appraisal method that estimates the value of real estate by analyzing the amount of revenue, or income, the property currently generates or could generate, often comparing the subject property to other similar properties.

(continued on next page)

Real Estate Agents and Appraisals

An **appraisal** is a professional estimate or opinion of value of a piece of property as of a certain date. It must be defendable and supported by objective evidence and data.

- Generally, only licensed real estate appraisers may perform actual appraisals on property. Real estate licensees in New York State may perform some less formal appraisals

- Real estate licensees typically perform a type of informal appraisal or valuation called a competitive market analysis (CMA)

- Appraisers are primarily hired by lenders to determine property values for mortgages or investments

- Appraisers may also be hired by buyers or sellers before they buy, sell, or exchange property

Key Terms - continued

Indirect Cost Costs associated with a construction project, other than labor and materials.

Insurable Value The amount that property can be insured for, usually only representing the replacement costs of the structure and disregarding any value for land.

Investment Value The highest price an investor would pay for a property based on how well it will serve her investment goals.

Market Position The position an agent's listing is in compared to similar homes in the same neighborhood at a similar price.

Market Price The actual open market price paid in an arm's length transaction.

Market Value The theoretical price a property is most likely to bring in a typical transaction.

Mortgage Value The value of an asset for purposes of securing a mortgage loan.

Personal Property Tangible items that (usually) are not permanently attached to, or part of, the real estate. *Also called*: **Personalty** or **Chattel**.

Physical Deterioration The actual wear and tear due to age, the elements, unrepaired damage, or other forces.

Plottage An increase in value (to cover the cost of acquiring the parcels) by successful assemblage, usually due to use.

Price The amount a ready, willing, and able buyer agrees to pay for a property and a seller agrees to accept.

Progression Is when the value of the worst home in a particular area is positively affected by other homes in the area.

Property Valuation The process of gathering and analyzing information to determine the value of a piece of property.

Real Property The physical land and everything attached to it, and the rights of ownership (bundle of rights).

Regression Is when the value of the best home in a given area is negatively affected by other homes in the area.

Residential Market Analysis In-depth study of a listing as it stands on its own, as well as in light of current market conditions.

Sales Comparison Approach An appraisal method that estimates the value of real property by performing a market analysis of the area where the subject property is located. Data are collected and adjustments made for differences.

Site A plot of land with enhancements that make it ready for a building or structure.

Situs Place where something exists; an area of preference thus giving it economic attributes (value).

Substitution Theory that an informed buyer will not pay more for a home than a comparable substitute.

Supply and Demand The law of supply and demand says that for all products, goods, and services, when supply exceeds demand, prices will fall and when demand exceeds supply, prices will rise.

Value in Use The present worth of the future benefits of ownership.

- Appraisers are used any time that a client needs to have a supportable value estimate for a piece of property, e.g., civil lawsuits and dispute resolution, divorces, bankruptcies, estates and trusts, zoning changes, impact or feasibility studies, eminent domain valuations, insurance coverage or claims, tax matters (donations or property exchanges), or determining construction or remodeling costs

Value Characteristics

Value is the amount of goods or services offered in the marketplace in exchange for something else. Before anything can have value, certain value characteristics must be present and perceived by the user and other potential users of the property. All four characteristics must be present and in harmony for the item to achieve maximum value. The four value characteristics are (remember D U S T):

- **Demand** – the need or desire for a specific good or service by others
- **Utility** – the ability of a good or service to satisfy human wants, needs, or desires
- **Scarcity** – the perceived low supply of a good or service relative to the high demand for it
- **Transferability** – the ability to freely buy, sell, encumber, or dispose of property in any way the owner sees fit

Physical Characteristics

Real estate has three physical characteristics that serve to give land inherent value. The three physical characteristics are:

- **Uniqueness** – (also called non-homogeneity) refers to the fact that every piece of land, every building, and every home is different—no two are the same
- **Immobility** – the physical characteristic that refers to the fact that real estate itself cannot move from one place to another
- **Indestructibility** – refers to the fact that real estate cannot be destroyed

Broad Forces That Affect Value

There are essentially four broad forces that affect all aspects of life and the economy. These forces also have a significant impact on value in the real estate market (remember **P E G S**):

- **Physical** – influences on property caused by the elements, such as water or environmental issues, which may be natural or man-made
  - Topography
  - Water
  - Location
  - Popularity
  - Environment
- **Economic**
  - **Business cycles** – general swings in business activity
  - **Economic base** – the main business or industry that a community uses to support and sustain itself

- ◆ **Supply and demand** – for all products, goods, and services when supply exceeds demand, prices will fall and when demand exceeds supply, prices will rise
- ◆ **Inflation** – an increase in the cost of goods or services
- ◆ **Cost of money** – the interest rate paid to borrow money
- **Governmental** – some of these laws impact all businesses, and, others specifically impact real estate
  - ◆ **Revenue generating laws** – consist of taxation and specific tax policies
    - ▲ **Taxation** – the process of government levying a charge upon people or things
    - ▲ **Specific tax policies** – enacted to encourage or discourage certain behavior or activity
  - ◆ **Fiscal policy** – the government's plan for spending, taxation, and the debt management
  - ◆ **Monetary policy** – is the means by which the government can exert control over the supply and cost of money
    - ▲ **Secondary mortgage** – secondary mortgage markets are the private investors and government entities that buy and sell real estate mortgages
  - ◆ **Government programs** – assistance mechanisms enacted by legislation and administered by the executive branch of the government.
    - ▲ The **FHA (Federal Housing Administration)** and the **VA (Veterans Administration)** both offer loan guarantees to banks, allowing them to loan money to people who might otherwise have trouble qualifying
- **Social**
  - ◆ **Demographic changes** – changes within the general population, including population growth, age, and family size
  - ◆ **Migration** – involves general trends to move toward one city or area of town versus another
  - ◆ **Social trends** – similar to previous two categories, but also includes such things as single parent households, people buying houses later in life, and the growing number of empty nest households
  - ◆ **Buyer tastes and standards** – includes everything from specific features of a property to overall trends in the real estate market

Market Factors

Change is constantly occurring, such that none of the great forces or property-specific factors affecting value remains constant. This is why an appraisal is only valid as of its effective date. Change affects specific factors for every property differently.

- **Supply and demand** – in real estate, when prices are high due to a temporary housing shortage, the housing supply increases. And when the market has an oversupply of homes for sale, prices decrease
- **Scarcity** – perceived low supply of a good or service relative to the high demand for it

Property-Specific Factors

- **Highest and best use** – the most profitable, legally permitted, economically feasible, and physically possible use of a property. This is the most important property-specific factor an appraiser considers before making a determination of value. Involves a three step process:

1. The land is valued as if it were vacant

2. The property is valued as it is improved

3. The appraiser's determination of highest and best use

- **Location** – sometimes called **situs**, describes the place where something exists, recognizing certain preferences can impact the value of that property

   - An individual home's location *within* a neighborhood affects its value

- **Progression** – when the value of the worst home in a particular area is positively affected by other homes in the area

- **Regression** – when the value of the best home in a given area is negatively affected by other homes in the area

- **Substitution** – an informed buyer will not pay more for a home than a comparable substitute

- **Conformity** – a particular home achieves its maximum value when surrounded by homes similar in style and function

- **Contribution** – a particular item or feature of a home is worth what it actually contributes in value to that property

- **Assemblage** – combining two or more parcels of land into one larger parcel. This is typically done to increase the usefulness of the land by allowing one larger building to be constructed on the larger parcel

   - **Plottage** – when assemblage results in an actual increase in land value (over simply the combined value of the individual parcels)

- **Anticipation** – when a future benefit or event may affect a particular parcel of land, its value may increase or decrease based simply on the anticipation of that benefit or event

Defining Value

Although at times the term "value" seems to be synonymous with "price" and "cost," it really is not:

- **Market value** – the theoretical price real estate will likely bring in a typical transaction; the expected price

   - **Arm's length transaction** – a typical transaction; the transaction occurred under typical conditions in the marketplace, and each of the parties is a relative stranger to one another and was acting in their own best interests

- **Market price** – the actual price a ready, willing, and able buyer offers and the seller accepts

- **Cost** – the total money needed to develop, produce, or build something, which includes both direct costs, such as labor and materials, and indirect costs, such as fees or marketing costs

More Types of Value

- **Mortgage value** – the amount of money a lender is willing to let someone borrow to finance, or re-finance, property

- **Investment value** – the highest price investors would pay for a property based on how well they believe it will serve their financial goals

- **Insurable value** – the amount a property can be insured for, usually representing only the replacement cost of the structure and disregarding any value for the land
- **Assessed value** – the amount used to calculate taxes due, and sometimes representing a percentage of market value
- **Value in use** – also known as **utility value**; the present value to an owner of a property that is not currently being put to its highest and best use

Three Approaches to Value

The appraisal process requires extensive collection of data, determination of highest and best use, and consideration of these three methods:

- **Sales comparison approach** – the most relied upon when there is recent sales data in the subject property's area, assuming that appropriate data is available
- **Cost approach** – the most relied upon for properties with new or almost new improvements or for unique properties
- **Income approach** – the most relied upon in appraising investment properties,when income data for comparable properties is available

Estimates of value derived from these three approaches are reconciled in the end to come up with the final conclusions.

Sales Comparison Approach

- The **sales comparison approach** is an accepted appraisal method that develops an opinion of value of real property by comparing the property being appraised with other properties that reflect a typical buyer's action in a sales transaction
- The sales comparison approach is considered the most useful and accurate of the three appraisal methods for typical residential properties because it is rooted in actual market activity
- The main disadvantage to the sales comparison approach is that it requires properties in the area to have been sold recently
- The sales comparison approach may not be suitable for special purpose properties, such as schools, churches, etc., and other unusual or unique properties for which there are no recent sales data to analyze
- A minimum of three comparables is required by most secondary market lenders. Most appraisers use three to five comps
- The subject property is the base; it never changes. If the comp is superior, subtract from the comp's value; if the comp is inferior, add to comp's value
- Some features are objective—the number of bedrooms, while other features are subjective—the overall condition. Significant features can change from area to area
- Matched pair analysis looks at sales data in the area where (ideally) only one feature is different to determine the amount that feature added to the price

Sample Property Adjustment

	Subject Property	Comparable 1	Comparable 2	Comparable 3
Feature	1-car garage	No garage	1-car garage	2-car garage
Adjustment Needed	Never adjust!	Missing something, so add more to make it equal to subject property	Equal to subject property, so no need to adjust	Has more, so subtract something to make it equal to subject property
Pre-adjustment Value	????	$190,000	$197,000	$206,000
Adjustment	Never adjust!	+ $5,000	+/- $0	- $5,000
Final Value	????	$195,000	$197,000	$201,000

Cost Approach

The **cost approach** is a valuation method that develops an opinion of value for a property by calculating the cost of the land, site improvements, and the cost to build the structure on the land.

Depreciation

Depreciation is the loss in value to property for any reason. It is a component of valuation that allows an appraiser to consider a property's effective age in comparison to its actual age. Depreciation can be "curable," that is, remedied at a reasonable cost; or "incurable," only remedied with a cost that cannot be returned in the market. Types of depreciation include:

- **Physical deterioration** – often called deferred maintenance, it is actual wear and tear due to age, the elements, unrepaired damage or other forces; the most common and most curable

- **Functional obsolescence** – when a building is less desirable because of something inherent in the design of the structure

- **External** or **economic obsolescence** – when something outside the control of a property makes it less desirable; the most serious and most likely to be incurable

Replacement vs. Reproduction

- **Replacement** – of a structure is building the *functional equivalent* of the original building. Usually cost estimates are done for replacing a building with one that's similar in size, layout, quality, and utility

- **Reproduction** – of a structure is building an *exact replica* of the original building

Cost of Building and Improvement

- **Cost manuals** – give the appraiser an estimated cost per square foot to build a particular type of structure with particular features in a specific part of the country. The appraiser then makes any necessary adjustments for variations in materials used or other features not reflected in the cost manual

- **Quantity survey** – has the appraiser count the number of each type of part and material used to construct the building. The total cost for all of these components is added together with an appropriate charge for the labor, builder's profit, cost of permits, etc.

Other Data Needed for the Cost Approach Method

- The site value used in the cost approach always represents the value of the site at its highest and best use
- Most often, the contributory value of other site improvements will be considered "as is," or in their depreciated state

Income Approach

The **income approach** is relevant for appraisal assignments in which the subject property is leased, or could reasonably be leased, producing an income stream for the owner. It is considered an objective appraisal method because it relies on the analysis of historical data for income, expenses, and other figures from the subject and comparable properties. Future income and expenses are estimated based on that historical data. While the income approach works well for income producing properties, it can be difficult to use when dealing with single-family homes because it is not always possible to find other income-producing residential homes in the same area.

Capitalization Rate

The capitalization rate is a percentage rate used by investors to calculate the present value of future income as a means for estimating the value of real estate. We can estimate the value of a real estate investment using three variables:

Income. The amount of money a property earns from rent and other sources. The capitalization rate method needs the annual net income or net operating income (NOI), which is the income after expenses (does not include depreciation or debt service). To find NOI:

Annual Gross Income – Vacancy Loss – Expenses = NOI

Rate. Represents the return on the purchase price of the property. An appraiser evaluates comparable properties in the marketplace to determine the appropriate rate to use for estimating value.

Value. The *worth of the investment*, what someone is willing to pay for a property at a given moment in time.

If we know any two variables, we can use the IRV formula to solve for the third variable:

Net Operating Income (NOI) ÷ Rate = Value

Gross Rent Multiplier

The **gross rent multiplier** (GRM) is a number used to estimate *the value of one- to four-unit residential properties*. The GRM is the relationship between a property's value and the total gross monthly rent. An appraiser analyzes comparable rental properties to find the GRM:

Rental Home Sale Price ÷ Gross Monthly Rent = GRM

Then determines an appropriate GRM to apply to the subject property to arrive at an estimate of value:

Gross Monthly Rent (or Expected Monthly Rent) x GRM = Estimated Value

Analyzing the Three Appraisal Approaches

Sales Comparison Approach

- **Advantages**
  - The most accurate of the three appraisal methods (if you have good data)
  - Relies on information rooted in marketplace activity
  - Works for most types of residential and commercial property
- **Disadvantages**
  - Requires properties to have been sold recently in the area
  - Not suitable for special-purpose properties, such as schools, churches, etc., and other unusual or unique properties
  - Fails to take into account properties currently for sale

Cost Approach

- **Advantages**
  - A very useful and accurate estimate of value for special-purpose properties
  - Uses extensive data
  - Excellent for new properties and for insurance purposes
- **Disadvantages**
  - The cost of a building does not necessarily equal its value
  - Consideration of several market factors is necessary to make an accurate estimate of value

Income Approach

- **Advantages**
  - Most useful when analyzing income-producing properties, such as commercial or investment real estate
  - Ability to solve for any variable: Income, value, rate of return
  - Gives a method to analyze the value of a future income stream
- **Disadvantages**
  - Seldom useful for residential property due to lack of data
  - Income figures and expenses represent past income performance of property
  - Attempts to introduce vacancy, collections, and other losses into the equation are merely a guess
  - Does not account for depreciation, building condition, and other factors

The Appraisal Process

The steps that must be performed for all appraisals are:

1. Define the appraisal, state the problem
2. Define the data and sources necessary to do the appraisal
3. Collect and analyze the relevant data
4. Determine the highest and best use for the subject property
5. Determine the value of the land separate from the structures
6. Estimate the value of subject property using applicable approaches
7. Reconcile estimates of value from the three approaches
8. Report conclusions of valuation process, including all data used

The Appraisal Report

The fundamental elements of every appraisal report are:

- Be clear, accurate, and not misleading
- Contain sufficient information to be understood properly by the intended users
- Disclose any extraordinary assumptions, hypothetical conditions, or other assignment conditions that directly affect the appraisal

The **Uniform Residential Appraisal Report** (**URAR**) is the predominant appraisal report used for single family residential appraisals.

Competitive Market Analysis

A **competitive market analysis (CMA)** is a method of determining the approximate market value of a home by comparing the subject property (your buyer's or seller's property) to other homes in the same neighborhood or vicinity that have sold, are presently for sale, or did not sell (either the listing expired or was withdrawn). Sometimes called a residential market analysis or a comparable market analysis. A CMA:

- May be performed by a real estate licensee
- Could be considered an "informal" valuation similar to an appraisal using the sales comparison approach
- Is **never** equal to an appraisal
- Is generally quicker and easier to perform than an appraisal
- Does not require the mass collection and analysis of data that an appraisal does
- Considers all comparable listings: Active, sold, expired, and withdrawn
- Puts most emphasis on observable differences
- Should produce results that will provide a meaningful basis of comparison for clients

Elements to Consider

- **Recently sold properties** – when researching recently sold properties, choose several located in the same area

- **Currently listed competing properties** – when analyzing competing listings, pay close attention to:
  - The number of competing properties on the market
  - Length of time the properties have been listed
  - Whether the list price has been reduced
  - How many times the list price has been reduced
- **Recently expired listings** – when listings expire because the price was more than market conditions justified, researching these properties can give you valuable insight on what is an acceptable list price
- **Curb appeal** – items like landscaping, color, building materials, and the distance from the house to the road
- **Market position** – compared to your listing, how many similar properties are for sale in the same neighborhood and for a similar price?
- **Assets and drawbacks** – your residential market analysis should include a comparison of the assets and drawbacks of your listing relative to competing properties
- **Area market conditions** – the stability and health of the real estate market as a whole directly impacts your business and what your clients can expect
- **Recommended terms of sale** – these terms may directly affect how long a home is on the market
- **Market value range** – after conducting your research, you will want to assign a price range to the listing

Agent's Role and Responsibilities

Even though a competitive market analysis is not an official appraisal report, real estate salespeople do have a specific role and certain responsibilities when preparing them:

- Competence
- Diligence
- Documentation
- Communication

QUIZ

1. *Market value can best be defined as a property's*
   A. appraised value for property tax purposes.
   B. listing price.
   C. most probable selling price.
   D. most recent selling price.

2. *An appraisal*
   A. establishes the selling price of a property.
   B. guarantees the value of a piece of real estate.
   C. is an opinion of value based on a typical buyer.
   D. is a prediction of future value.

3. *Which homes should an appraiser consider when finding comps?*
   A. homes currently listed for sale in the market
   B. homes where the listing agreements have expired
   C. homes that have sold recently in the subject's area
   D. homes that were taken off the market

4. *Vincent is tasked with deriving the value for a large, custom home that was constructed nine months ago on a secluded 10-acre lot. Which approach could be considered the most reliable for valuation?*
   A. cost approach
   B. income approach
   C. sales comparison approach
   D. All are equally reliable.

5. *Steve and Jana bought an empty lot on a quiet street of small, 40-year-old ranch homes. On the lot, they built a luxurious two-story, 3,500 square foot home. A year later when they put their home on the market, its value will likely be held down by the other homes in the neighborhood. This is an example of the principle of*
   A. anticipation.
   B. balance.
   C. progression.
   D. regression.

6. *After freeway construction, a home experiences noise from traffic. This can be considered*
   A. functional obsolescence.
   B. poor urban planning.
   C. poor smog control.
   D. external obsolescence.

7. *If an industrial building needs a sprinkler system at a cost of $30,000, and if this will result in an increase in value $40,000, the depreciation is referred to as*
   A. incurable external obsolescence.
   B. incurable physical deterioration.
   C. incurable functional obsolescence.
   D. curable functional obsolescence.

8. *Comp #3 has five bedrooms; the subject property has four bedrooms. Through matched pair analysis, the appraiser has determined that a bedroom in that neighborhood is worth $7,500. What is the appropriate way to apply this information when performing the sales comparison approach to valuation?*
   A. add $7,500 to Comp #3 value.
   B. subtract $7,500 from Comp #3 value.
   C. add $7,500 to the subject base.
   D. subtract $7,500 from the subject base.

9. *A property has been renting for $750 per month. Based on comparables, the GRM is 110. What is the estimated value of the property?*
   A. $68,182
   B. $82,500
   C. $99,000
   D. $990,000

10. *Complete the following statement. A competitive market analysis is _____ the equivalent of an appraisal.*
    A. never
    B. sometimes
    C. usually
    D. always

Deeds and Real Estate Closings

8

Key Terms

Abstract of Title A brief summary of the history of title to a property, listing all recorded documents that affect the title.

Accession Gives property owners the right to everything produced by their land. Also, the acquisition of title to land by its addition to real estate already owned, through human actions or natural processes.

Accretion The gradual addition of land by the forces of nature.

Acknowledgment The act of a party signing a document before a notary public, stating it was signed voluntarily.

Actual Notice Actual knowledge; that which is known.

Adverse Possession Acquiring title to someone else's real property by possession of it. Possession must be open and notorious, hostile and adverse, exclusive, and continuous for a prescribed number of years (10 years in New York).

Alluvion Solid material deposited along a shore by accretion.

Assessments A percentage of a property's market value.

Avulsion When real property is lost due to sudden acts of nature like tornadoes or earthquakes.

Bargain and Sale Deed Deed without any warranties against liens or other encumbrances but does imply grantor has the right to convey title.

Chain of Title Chain of deeds and other documents transferring title to land from one owner to the next, as disclosed in public records.

Closing Statement Document prepared by the closing agent itemizing all expenses and costs paid by the buyer and seller to close the real estate transaction. *Also called*: **Settlement Statement** or **HUD-1.**

Clouds on a Title Claim, encumbrance, or defect that makes title to real property unmarketable.

Consideration Anything of value such as money, goods, services, or promises, given to induce another person to enter into a contract. *Also called*: **Valuable Consideration**.

Constructive Notice Provides protection to a landowner against all unrecorded titles.

Conveyance Instrument that conveys a grantor's interest, if any, in real property. *Also called*: **Deed**.

Credits Money received for an obligation given,

(continued on next page)

Debits An expense or money applied against a credit.

Dedication Gift from a landowner to the government. *Also called*: **Dedication by Deed.**

Deed An instrument that conveys a grantor's interest, if any, in real property. *Also called*: **Conveyance.**

Delivery and Acceptance Delivery of the deed by the grantor with the intention of transferring title and acceptance by the grantee receiving the land. When a deed has been properly executed, both have occurred.

Devise To transfer land through a will is to devise it (thus heirs who are left the land are devisees).

Executor Person named in a will to carry out its provisions, including disbursement of land.

Foreclosure When real property is involuntarily transferred because the owner defaulted on debts secured by the property.

Full Covenant and Warranty Deed Contains the strongest and broadest form of guarantee of title of any type of deed, and provides the greatest protection of any deed to the grantee. In this type of deed, the grantor makes various covenants, or warranties.

Grant To transfer or convey an interest in real property by means of a written instrument.

Grantee The person who receives a conveyance of real property in a real estate transaction.

Grantor The person who transfers title to real property in a real estate transaction.

Habendum Clause Clause within a deed that describes the type of estate granted and that must always agree with the granting clause.

HUD-1 Settlement Statement An accurate accounting of all expenses buyers and sellers pay in a real estate transaction; required by RESPA.

Involuntary Alienation When title to property is transferred during the owner's lifetime without his consent.

Lot and block A type of legal description used for platted property. The description states only the property's lot number and block number in a particular subdivision.

Marketable Title Title free and clear of objectionable encumbrances or defects, so that a reasonably prudent person with full knowledge of the facts would not hesitate to purchase the property.

Metes and Bounds A land survey process whereby a licensed land surveyor starts at an easily identifiable point of beginning (POB) and describes a property's boundaries in terms of courses, (compass directions), and distances, ultimately returning to the point of beginning.

Plat Also called a plat map, plat is a detailed survey map of a subdivision recorded in the county where the land is located. Subdivided property is often called platted property.

Proration The division of expenses between buyer and seller in proportion to the actual usage of the item represented by a particular expense. *Also called*: **Adjustments**.

Quitclaim Deed Conveys any interest in a parcel of land the grantor has at the time the deed is executed. It conveys whatever right, title, or interest the grantor holds in the property without representation that there is any interest at all.

Real Estate Settlement Procedures Act (RESPA) Requires lenders, mortgage brokers, or servicers of home loans to provide borrowers with pertinent and timely disclosures of the nature and costs of the real estate settlement process.

Reconciliation Verifying debits and credits have been added and subtracted correctly on a real estate settlement statement.

Referee's Deed Deeds that contain no covenants or warranties although ownership is implied.

Reference to a Plat A description on a deed that includes the property's location on a plat map.

Settlement Statement A document prepared by the buyer's and seller's attorney or bank representatives that itemizes all expenses and costs paid by the buyer and seller to close the real estate transaction.

Sheriff's Deed A deed issued by the court to a property purchaser from a foreclosure sale.

Survey The process of locating and measuring the boundaries of a property, and indentifying improvements, encroachments, and easements associated with the land.

Title The actual lawful ownership of real property and refers to holding the bundle of rights conveyed. Title is not a document, but rather a theory pertaining to ownership.

Title Closing The final stage in a real estate transaction; transfer of real property ownership from seller to buyer occurs, according to the terms and conditions in a sales contract or escrow agreement.

Title Insurance An insurance policy that protects the lender (and sometimes the property owner) against loss due to disputes over the ownership of a property and defects in the title that were not found in the search of the public record.

Title Search An inspection of the public record to determine all rights and encumbrances affecting title to a piece of property.

Voluntary Alienation When title to property is transferred voluntarily through a sale, gift, dedication, or grant.

Deeds and Title

Deeds are the means by which property ownership is transferred. However, a deed to property does not necessarily prove ownership. A **deed** is:

- An instrument (written document) that conveys a grantor's interest in real property to someone else, the grantee
- Evidence that the transfer of title took place
- Also known as a *conveyance*

Title is:

- The actual lawful ownership of real property
- A reference to holding the bundle of rights conveyed
- **Not** a document but rather a theory dealing with ownership

The seller is the **grantor**, and the buyer is the **grantee**.

Essential Elements for a Valid Deed

For a deed to be valid in New York, it must be in writing and contain necessary information on its face. The essential elements for a valid deed include:

- **Competent grantor** – a person who wishes to grant or convey land, is of sound mind for the purposes of entering a contract, and has reached the age of majority, which in New York is 18
- **Identifiable grantee** – the person to whom the interest in real property is to be conveyed and identified in such a way to reasonably separate this person from all others in the world
- **Act of Conveyance** – a clause in the deed that states the grantor intends to convey title to the land (also called the granting clause, these words identify the document as one that involves the transfer of interest from one person to another)
- **Consideration** – anything of value such as money, goods, services, or promises, given to induce another person to enter into a contract
- **Legal description** – the legal description of the property being conveyed should be thorough and complete
- **Habendum clause** – is typically included after the granting clause in many deeds (describes the type of estate granted, which must be consistent with any estate indicated in the granting clause); usually indicated by words "to have and to hold"
- **Limitations** – must be noted; describes how property may or may not be used, such as a deed restriction
- **Exceptions and reservations** – anything that affects the property, such as an easement; must be expressly noted on the deed
- **Signatures** – a deed must include the signatures of all grantors
- **Acknowledgement** – is the signature of a notary public or other authorized party declaring that the signing of the deed took place in their presence and was a free and voluntary act
- **Delivery** – a deed has no legal effect until there has been delivery of the deed by the grantor with the intention of transferring title

- **Acceptance** – a deed has no legal effect until delivery and acceptance by the grantee receiving the land. At this point:
  - The title transfers from the grantor to the grantee
  - The deed's job is done; it is simply evidence that the transfer of title took place
  - Title cannot be re-conveyed by destroying the deed or returning it to the grantor
  - A deed cannot be reassigned or transferred to the next owner; each transaction requires a **new** deed

Recording Deeds

Deeds are **not** required to be recorded to be valid, but recording a deed ensures that its existence is clear to third parties as part of the public record. It also ensures against lost documents. In addition to the elements required to create a valid deed, these elements must be present in order to record the deed:

- A **certificate of the address of grantee** ensures that tax authorities are informed as to where to send tax bills
- To record a deed, New York requires both the grantor and grantee be identified by address
- Evidence of **real estate transfer tax** (in most states and some local governments), often in the form of a stamp

Types of Deeds

Full Covenant and Warranty Deed

Full covenant and warranty deeds contain the strongest and broadest form of guarantee of title of any type of deed and provide the greatest protection of any deed to the grantee. Basic warranties include:

- **Covenant of seizen** – grantor guarantees that he or she truly holds title to the property and has the right to convey it
- **Covenant of right to convey** – grantor promises that he owns the land and has the right to convey it
- **Covenant against encumbrances** – grantor promises that the property will not have any encumbrances except for those specifically listed on the deed
- **Covenant of quiet enjoyment** – grantor promises that the grantee will not be bothered by others claiming the title
- **Covenant of further assurances** – requires the grantor to remedy any defects in the title being conveyed and any errors or deficiencies in the deed itself
- **Covenant of warranty forever** – provides the grantor will defend the grantee's interest against all lawful claims of title

Deeds without Warranties

Deeds without warranties also transfer title to real property, but with them, the grantor makes no warranties regarding title, nor does the grantor guarantee he has the right to convey title. Examples include:

- **Bargain and sale deed** – implies that the grantor owns the property and has a right to convey it, but there are no warranties with it.

- **Bargain and sale deed with covenants** – (sometimes called a special warranty deed) is a guarantee that the grantor has not encumbered the property in any way except what is stated in the deed.

- **Executor's deed** – a type of judicial deed used to convey property of the deceased.

- **Quitclaim deed** – conveys any interest in a parcel of land the grantor has at the time the deed is executed without any guarantees. Also known as a deed of release, quitclaim deeds are often used to remedy **clouds on a title**, which is when someone may have a claim on the title.

- **Referee's deed** – a type of judicial deed used in bankruptcy or foreclosure proceedings.

Legal Property Descriptions

The legal description of property provides the ability to identify and distinguish that property from any and all other parcels of land. A legal description of a specific parcel of land is usually required on three documents:

- **Deed** – an instrument that conveys ownership of real property from the grantor to the grantee. The legal description provides an exact explanation of what the grantee is receiving from the grantor.

- **Mortgage** – an instrument that creates a voluntary lien on real property to secure repayment of a debt. The parties to a mortgage are the mortgagor (borrower) and mortgagee (lender). The mortgagee needs the legal description of the property because the property is the collateral for the loan that they have made.

- **Title insurance** – indemnifies the property owner against losses resulting from undiscovered title defects and encumbrances on the property. The legal description defines exactly what is insured.

> **Note:** If there is a discrepancy with the legal description among these documents, the title company should do the research to resolve it.

Systems of Legal Description

Metes and Bounds System

A metes and bounds description generally starts from an identifiable permanent reference point, and from there, finds the first corner of the property, the point of beginning. A licensed surveyor describes a property's boundaries in terms of distance (metes) and compass direction (bounds). The description continues by indicating a compass direction and distance to define the boundaries of the lot, moving clockwise, until returning to point of beginning and enclosing the lot. **Commonly used by land surveyors in New York**.

Monument System

The monument system may be used in place of the metes and bounds system. It is often used to describe multi-acre tracts of land. The description is drawn from permanent objects on the land, such as wells, large trees, stone walls, and boulders.

Block and Lot System

Descriptions, indicating the lot and block numbers of a parcel in a subdivision, are contained in a plat map (also called a plot plan or a recorded plat) recorded in the public records of the county in which the land is located.

Methods of Transferring Title

In New York, title to real property must be transferred during an owner's lifetime by voluntary alienation and involuntary alienation. After a landowner dies, title to property is transferred by will or descent.

Voluntary Alienation

Voluntary alienation is the most common way to transfer ownership of land. Voluntary alienation is an action, which the property owner undertakes of his own free will and is accomplished through:

- **Sale** of property, in which the owner agrees to hand over title in exchange for consideration; usually completed with a **deed**
- **Gift** of a deed, in which the owner may transfer title without receiving something of value from the recipient
- **Dedication** of private property for public use, (e.g., a developer who dedicates land for streets within a new subdivision or someone who dedicates land for a park to a municipality)
- **Grant,** as when the government transfers title to land to an individual

Involuntary Alienation

Involuntary transfer, or alienation, is the transfer of title in an interest in real property **against the will** of the owner, or **without action by the owner**, occurring through operation of law:

- **Eminent domain** is *the government's constitutional power to take private property for public use, as long as the owner is paid just compensation.* The actual act of taking private property for public use through eminent domain is known as **appropriation** or **condemnation.**
- If a landowner *defaults on debts secured by real property, the property can be transferred without consent* through **foreclosure**.
- Possession and use of property can mature into title. Acquiring title to land by **adverse possession** requires *open and notorious, hostile and adverse, exclusive, and continuous use* of another's land for a designated period of time, which is **ten years** as defined by the laws of the State of New York.

Devise and Descent

Transfer of property upon the death of the owner:

- **Devise** – when someone dies with a will (testate), the property is transferred to heirs (the devisees) as indicated in the will.
- **Descent** – when person dies **without a will** (intestate), his property automatically descends to his heirs or next of kin as provided for by state law. Also called **intestate succession** or **intestate descent.**

Real Estate Closings

The final stage in a real estate transaction is the closing, or settlement. Here, transfer of real property ownership from seller to buyer occurs, according to the terms and conditions in the sales contract or escrow agreement. This is also when funds required for the sale are disbursed. Closings are normally conducted by a closing agent (also called escrow agent or settlement agent), who may be an employee of the title company, an attorney, or a broker.

Participants at the Closing

- **Buyers** attend to pay for and receive title to property
- **Sellers** attend to grant their property to the buyers and to receive payment
- The **buyer's** and **seller's attorneys** may be present to review all closing documents
- **Real estate agents** represent their clients, confirm the necessary documents are there, ensure all elements of the sales contract are satisfied, and collect their commission
- A **mortgage company representative** examines all loan documents and makes sure the property for which a mortgage is being issued has a clear title
- **Title company representatives** review the documents and, once satisfied, deliver evidence that the title is insured

Documents and Procedures for Closing

Among the documents you are most likely to see at a closing are:

- Deed or other title document, such as a land contract; supplied by the seller
- Evidence of title, such as a title report or title insurance; supplied by the title company
- Discharge of mortgage; supplied by the seller's lender
- Loan documentation, such as promissory notes and mortgages; supplied by the buyer's lender
- Checks; usually supplied by the buyer, the buyer's lender, and perhaps an escrow officer
- Settlement statement; generally supplied by a settlement officer or escrow officer
- Property inspection reports for insects, lead, occupancy permits, etc.; supplied by the seller
- Bill of sale for personal property; supplied by the seller
- Surveys; supplied by a surveyor on behalf of the buyer or the seller
- Homeowner's insurance; supplied by the buyer
- IRS Form 1099; supplied by the settlement officer or escrow officer
- New York Transfer Tax return; all transfers of real property in New York require the use of Form TP 584
- Real Property Transfer Report; the New York State Office of Real Property Services (ORPS) requires that Form RP-5217 accompany the deed when it is recorded
- **Photo identification**; necessary to prove that the person signing the documents is indeed who he says he is

Titles and Title Insurance

Chain of Title

The **chain of title** is a clear and unbroken chronological record of the ownership of a specific piece of property.

- Each owner is linked to the previous owner and the subsequent owner through deeds, forming a chain of title as disclosed in the public records.

- A gap in the chain of title creates uncertainty, which is called a **cloud on the title**.

- A deed outside the chain of title is a **wild deed**.

- A **suit to quiet title** may be required to close any missing links and remove the cloud on the title. The purpose of this suit is to clear a particular, known claim, title defect, or perceived defect; in New York, this is accomplished through an **Article 15 proceeding**

Title Search and Title Abstract

When conveying real property, the seller is generally expected to deliver clear title, also known as marketable title. A title search is necessary to determine ownership and the quality of the title prior to conveyance. A title search, usually performed by an abstractor or a title company, starts with the chain of title and results in the creation of an **abstract of title**:

- Complete chronological and **historical summary** of title to a piece of property

- Lists **all documents in the public record** that have affected title to the property

- Shows all grants and conveyances from the chain of title

- Should show every lien, easement, restriction, lawsuit, mortgage, and other encumbrances that have ever affected the property, even if the encumbrance has been removed or satisfied

- Lists the public records that were searched, as well as the public records that were **not** searched

- Does **not** reveal encroachments on the property, which would need to be documented through a survey of the property, not through public records

- Does **not** ensure the validity of the title

Title Insurance

- Protects lenders (and sometimes property owners) against loss due to disputes over ownership of a property and defects in the title not found in the search of the public record

- Protects property owners from claimants not listed in the insurance policy, including defects in the public record such as forged documents, improper deeds, undisclosed heirs, errors in a property's legal description, and other mistakes

- Does not cure defects, but insures against losses due to title defects other than those specifically excluded

- Requires the title company to go to court if necessary and defend its policyholder against any claim against the ownership of the land

- Is generally paid for with a one-time premium at closing

Real Estate Settlement Procedures Act

The **Real Estate Settlement Procedures Act** (RESPA) requires lenders, mortgage brokers, or servicers of home loans to provide borrowers with pertinent and timely disclosures of the nature and costs of the real estate settlement process. As a real estate professional, you must be aware that RESPA:

- Prohibits kickbacks and fees for services not performed during closing.

- Requires a HUD information booklet be given to buyers explaining settlement costs.

- Requires a Good Faith Estimate of closing costs be given to the buyer within three business days of applying for a mortgage.

- Requires the use of the HUD Settlement Statement (HUD-1) for all federal-related residential loans (one-to four-family units).

- Gives the buyer the right to inspect the HUD-1 one business day prior to closing.

- Requires brokers and lenders to disclose multiple relationships without obligating parties to use suggested referrals.

- Sets limits on the amount of escrow reserves a lender can hold or require a buyer to deposit in advance to cover real estate taxes, real estate insurance premiums, and other similar costs.

Typical Seller Costs

Though negotiable, the following are among the costs sellers can generally expect to pay:

- Attorney fees
- Broker's commission
- Condo or co-op fees; cooperative flip tax
- Existing lien payments
- Recording fees
- New York State transfer taxes (real property transfer tax); $4 per $1,000 of purchase price

Typical Buyer Costs

Though negotiable, the following are among the costs that buyers can generally expect to pay:

- Appraisal, credit report, and survey fees
- Attorney's fees
- Bank fees
- Origination fee
- Points
- Escrow
- Tax service fees
- Private mortgage insurance
- Condo or co-op fees
- Home inspection fees
- Mortgage insurance

- Mortgage recording tax
- Recording fees
- Title search/title insurance
- Flood certification fee

Debits vs. Credits

- **Debits** (like debts) are sums of money **owed**
  - ♦ A debit is charged to a particular party on a balance sheet to represent money that *must be paid to the other party.*
- **Credits** are sums of money **received**
  - ♦ A credit is given to a particular party on a balance sheet to represent money that *should be paid by the other party.*

Proration

- Proration, also known as **adjustment**, is the allocation of an expense between buyer and seller in proportion to the actual usage of the item represented by that expense.
- **Accrued** expenses, or retrospective expenses, are items on a settlement statement for which the cost has been incurred, but the expense has not yet been paid.
- **Prepaid** expenses, or prospective expenses, are items on a settlement statement the seller has *paid in advance,* usually at the beginning of the year for the rest of the year or longer.
- Items often prorated include property tax and homeowner's insurance.
- When determining expense per day, it is customary to calculate to three or four places past the decimal point, then adjust the final answer for exact dollars and cents.

 Note: In New York, buyers become the owners of a property on the closing date. In practice, the buyer or seller may be charged with that day's fees and expenses. Since actual possession may take longer, in these instances, the sales contract should note who is responsible for what expenses until the new owner takes possession.

Calculating Prorations

Expenses may be prorated using:

- A statutory year (360 days), 12 months of 30 days each.
- A calendar year (365 days), counting the exact number of days in each month (taking leap years into account).

The steps to calculate the adjustment are to:

1. Determine if the expense is accrued or prepaid.
2. Divide the expense by the appropriate period to find a monthly/daily rate.
3. Determine how many months/days are affected by the expense.
4. Multiply the monthly/daily rate by the number of affected months/days.
5. Determine which party is credited and which is debited.

QUIZ

1. **Which type of deed provides the greatest protection to the grantee?**
   A. bargain and sale deed
   B. general warranty deed
   C. quitclaim deed
   D. special warranty deed

2. **A valid deed requires the signature of the**
   A. grantee.
   B. grantor.
   C. grantor and grantee.
   D. notary of public.

3. **During a person's lifetime, title to real estate may be transferred by which method?**
   A. deed
   B. descent
   C. devise
   D. escheat

4. **Which statement is NOT true regarding quitclaim deeds?**
   A. They are often used to clear clouds on a title.
   B. They offer the grantee the most warranty protection.
   C. They convey whatever interest the grantor holds in the property, if any.
   D. They may be used by a spouse to release dower interest not conveyed.

5. **An abstract of title is a**
   A. chronological summary of the essential provisions of every recorded document pertaining to a particular parcel of land.
   B. contract whereby a title insurance company indemnifies the owner that title is free of defects and hidden risk.
   C. sworn statement from an attorney that title is good.
   D. written declaration by a person executing an instrument before an officer authorized to give a note.

6. **In New York, how many years must one possess the land in an open, continuous, notorious, and hostile way before claiming adverse possession?**
   A. 5
   B. 10
   C. 15
   D. 20

7. **Title insurance protects policyholders from all of the following defects EXCEPT**
   A. a forged deed.
   B. an unrecorded lien that the buyer knew about.
   C. improper deeds.
   D. mistakes in the public records.

8. **In the metes and bounds system of legal description, metes indicates _____ and bounds indicates _____.**
   A. direction / distance
   B. distance / direction
   C. distance / reference point
   D. reference point / direction

9. **The habendum clause**
   A. follows the granting clause in a deed and includes a "to have and to hold" statement.
   B. holds the property for designated period of time.
   C. states that consideration given is love and affection.
   D. states that a deed must be in writing.

10. **In New York, who pays the transfer tax at a closing?**
    A. the buyer who receives the transfer
    B. the seller
    C. the mortgage lender
    D. both A and B

Overview of Real Estate Finance

Key Terms

Acceleration Clause Contract clause giving the lender the right to declare the entire loan balance due immediately because of default, or other reasons stated in the contract.

Alienation Clause Contract clause giving the lender certain stated rights when there is a transfer of ownership in the property; prohibits loan assumption.

Amortizing Loans When monthly payments retire the debt over the life of the loan instead of leaving the borrower with a large balloon payment at the end of the loan term.

Buydown Additional funds in the form of points paid to a lender at the beginning of a loan to lower the loan's interest rate and monthly payments.

Conforming Loan A loan that meets Fannie Mae and Freddie Mac standards, and thus can be sold on the secondary market.

Conventional Loan Mortgage loan not insured or guaranteed by a government entity.

Default Failure to fulfill an obligation, duty, or promise, as when a borrower fails to make payments, a tenant fails to pay rent, or a party to a contract fails to perform.

Defeasance Clause 1. Clause used to defeat or cancel a certain right upon the occurrence of a specific event (e.g., on final payment, words of grant in a mortgage are void and the mortgage is thereby cancelled and title is revested to the mortgagor). 2. Clause used to give a borrower the right to redeem real estate after default on a note by paying the full amount due plus fees and court costs.

Discount Points Amount paid to a lender when a loan is made to lower the interest rate; one point equals one percent of the loan amount.

Fannie Mae (Federal National Mortgage Association) Nation's largest investor in residential mortgages.

Finance Instruments Legal documents that establish the rights and duties of all parties involved in transaction.

Freddie Mac (Federal Home Loan Mortgage Corporation) Non-profit federally chartered institution that functions as a buyer and seller of savings and loan residential mortgages.

Ginnie Mae (Government National Mortgage Association) Government-owned corporation that guarantees payment of principal and interest to investors who buy its mortgage-backed securities on the secondary market.

(continued on next page)

Key Terms - continued

Grace Period The time a borrower is allowed after a payment is due to make that payment without incurring penalties.

Graduated Payment A buydown plan for which payment subsidies in the early years keep payments low, but payments increase each year until they are sufficient to fully amortize the loan.

Hypothecate To make property the security for a loan without giving up possession of it (as with a mortgage).

Loan-to-Value Ratio (LTV) The amount of money borrowed, compared to the value (or price) of the property.

Mortgage An instrument that creates a voluntary lien on real property to secure repayment of a debt. The parties to a mortgage are the mortgagor (borrower) and mortgagee (lender).

Mortgage Banker One who originates, sells, and services mortgage loans, and usually acts as the originator and servicer of loans on behalf of large investors, such as insurance companies, pension plans, and the secondary market.

Mortgage Broker One who, for a fee, places loans with investors, but typically does not service such loans.

Mortgage Insurance Premium (MIP) Insurance offered through FHA to insure a lender against default on a loan by a borrower.

Mortgagee A lender who accepts a mortgage as security for repayment of the loan.

Mortgagor A person who borrows money and gives a mortgage to the lender as security.

Points One percent of a loan amount. Points can be charged for any reason, but are often used for buydowns. *Also called*: **Discount Points**.

Prepayment Penalty Clause Additional money charged by a lender for paying off a loan early.

Primary Mortgage Markets Lenders who make mortgage loans directly to borrowers. *Also called*: **Primary Markets**.

Private Mortgage Insurance (PMI) Insurance offered by private companies to insure a lender against borrower default.

Promissory Note A written, legally binding promise to repay a debt.

Purchase Money Mortgage A mortgage used to finance the purchase of a home; may be used specifically when the seller finances all or part of the sale price of property for a buyer. Here the seller retains a mortgage and title passes to the buyer.

Real Estate Settlement Procedures Act (RESPA) Requires lenders, mortgage brokers, or servicers of home loans to provide borrowers with pertinent and timely disclosures of the nature and costs of the real estate settlement process.

Secondary Mortgage Markets Private investors and government agencies that buy and sell mortgages. *Also called*: **Secondary Markets**.

Securitization Act of pooling mortgages and then selling them as mortgage-backed securities.

State of New York Mortgage Agency (SONYMA) Offers programs funded by the sale of tax-exempt bonds and designed to make housing affordable to low- and moderate-income households.

Subordination Clause A contract that gives a mortgage recorded at a later date priority over an earlier recorded mortgage. *Also called*: **Subordination Agreement**.

Usury Laws limiting the maximum interest rate that can be charged.

Wraparound Mortgage When a seller keeps the existing loan and continues to pay on it, while giving the buyer another mortgage. *Also called*: **Wraparound Financing**.

Overview of Mortgage Lending

Finance instruments are legal documents that establish the rights and duties of all parties involved in a transaction. There are two types of real estate finance documents: The **financing instrument**, which is typically a promissory note, and the **security instrument**, which is usually a mortgage or deed of trust.

- A **promissory note** is a written promise to pay. On the note, the person promising to pay is called the maker of the note and is usually the homebuyer or mortgagor. The person who is promised payment is called the payee, usually the lender but may also be the seller.

- In most real estate transactions, a promissory note is accompanied by a security instrument that allows a debtor to **hypothecate** property, meaning a debtor can pledge property as security for debt without giving up possession of it. A **mortgage** is a type of security instrument where the borrower (called the **mortgagor**) pledges property to the lender (called the **mortgagee**) as collateral for the debt, creating a lien against the real property.

Types of Primary Lenders

The primary mortgage market consists of lenders (and individuals) who make loans directly to borrowers. Examples of primary lenders include:

- Commercial banks
- Savings and loans
- Mortgage companies
- Credit unions
- Finance companies
- Mutual savings banks

Secondary Mortgage Markets

Secondary mortgage markets are private investors and government sponsored enterprises that buy and sell real estate mortgage loans. Major secondary market buyers include:

- The Federal National Mortgage Association, **Fannie Mae**
- The Federal Home Loan Mortgage Corporation, **Freddie Mac**
- The Government National Mortgage Association, **Ginnie Mae**

Conventional Financing

- "Conventional" mortgages are those not insured or guaranteed by a government entity (generally meaning the FHA or the VA).

- Conventional loans are available to anyone who meets the lender's requirements; they are considered the most secure type of loan available.

- Borrowers generally take out a 30-year loan to finance the purchase of a home; 15-year loans are available and loan terms of even longer than 30-years are possible.

Conforming vs. Nonconforming Loans

Conforming loans:

- Follow the criteria set by secondary markets, primarily Fannie Mae and Freddie Mac
- May be sold to the secondary market
- Are generally preferred by lenders

Nonconforming loans:

- Do not follow Fannie Mae/Freddie Mac criteria and therefore cannot be sold to these agencies
- May be classified as such due to the size of the loan (jumbo loans) or the credit quality of the borrower (subprime loans)

Loan-To-Value Ratio (LTV)

- Used by lenders to determine how much they will loan a potential borrower based on the value of the property
- Refers to the amount of money borrowed compared to the value of the property
- Defines value as the appraised value or the sale price, whichever is less
- Generally, lower LTV means a bigger down payment

Private Mortgage Insurance (PMI)

- Purpose is to compensate the lender in case of borrower default
- Makes loans somewhat easier for borrowers to obtain and relatively safer for lenders to offer
- Insures only the upper portion of the loan—the amount that exceeds the standard 80% loan-to-value ratio (LTV)
- New York State law requires lenders to stop charging PMI once the borrower has 25% equity in his home (federal law is even stricter at 78% LTV)
- Once the increased risk of borrower default is eliminated, the mortgage insurance has fulfilled its purpose and can be cancelled

Homebuyer Assistance Programs

- Can be down payment assistance programs (DPA programs), subsidized mortgage interest rates, help with closing costs, or a combination
- Offered by government or nonprofit organizations to promote home ownership or by lenders as part of their obligation under the Community Reinvestment Act
- Money is limited and administered on a first-come, first-serve basis

Types of Financing Alternatives

Seller Financing

- Seller extends credit to a buyer to finance the purchase of the property, retaining a mortgage as security
- Title passes to the buyer
- May be called a **purchase money mortgage** (PMM) when a seller finances all or part of the sale price of a property for a buyer
- Simplest when the property sold is unencumbered, meaning it is commonly considered to be free and clear of mortgages or other liens

Loan Assumption

- Buyer agrees to take over payments of a seller's debt on an existing mortgage with terms of the note staying unchanged
- Seller remains secondarily liable unless he or she gets a release from the lender
- Lenders may charge an assumption fee and/or increase the loan's interest rate
- Lenders may not allow the assumption and call the note or demand full payment of the loan now (as stated in the note or mortgage)
- When reassigned to the buyer through novation, original borrower is released from liability

Wraparound Financing

- Seller keeps the existing loan and continues to pay on it while extending credit to buyer through another mortgage
- Could be used for seller financing or could be a second, larger mortgage a borrower gets from a second lender that encompasses the original loan
- Not an option when the mortgage contains an alienation clause
- **Not allowed in New York State**

Discount Points

- Allow a borrower to get a discount on a loan's interest rate
- Cover the difference between the current market interest rate and the rate a lender gives a borrower on a note
- Paid by buyer or seller, as negotiated
- One point equals 1% of the loan amount
- Called a **buydown** if additional points paid to the lender at the beginning of the loan to reduce the buyer's interest rate and thus the monthly payment

Be careful when using the word "points." This can refer to loan origination fees charged by a lender or the optional "discount points" a buyer may pay to lower interest rates in a buydown.

Government Agency Financing

Federal Housing Administration (FHA)

- Part of the Department of Housing and Urban Development (HUD)
- Primary function is to insure loans for lenders
- Does not make loans or build homes
- Loans made by FHA-approved lenders
- Regulations, procedures, and practices shape real estate finance
- Sets maximum loan amounts that vary with the location of the property based on the average price in the area

FHA-Insured Loans

- Must be for one- to four-family owner-occupied property
- Requires minimum investment of 3.5% (with no secondary financing)
- Requires upfront mortgage insurance premium (MIP); may require annual MIP paid on monthly basis
- Assumable (with credit checks if loan was made after December 1, 1986)
- Prohibits prepayment penalties
- Limits loan origination fees to no higher than one point or one percent of the loan amount

Veterans Administration (VA) Guaranteed Loans

- Guarantees repayment of top portion of certain residential loans made to eligible veterans in the event of borrower default
- Must be for one- to four-family owner-occupied property
- Made by an approved lender; the VA rarely makes loans
- Require a Certificate of Eligibility (COE) to establish the veteran's entitlement
- May be obtained with no down payment
- No maximum loan amounts
- Secondary financing is permitted
- Assumable (with credit checks if the loan was made after March 1988)
- Prepayment penalties prohibited
- No MIP or PMI, but there is a funding fee that may be financed
- Limits loan origination fee to no higher than one point or one percent of the loan amount

USDA Rural Development Housing Programs

- Provides loans in rural areas for households at or below 80 percent of the adjusted median income level
- Will make loans in rural areas or small towns with no available lender
- No down payment requirements
- No mortgage insurance premiums

State of New York Mortgage Agency (SONYMA)

- Created in 1970 to reduce shortages of funds from private banks for mortgage lending in New York
- Serves as a direct lender
- Designed to make housing affordable to low- and moderate-income households
- Offers below-market interest rates, low or no down payment requirements, no prepayment penalties, and some closing cost assistance
- Requires recapture tax if the house is sold for profit within nine years

Mortgage Bankers and Brokers

Mortgage Bankers

- Originators of loans, lending mortgage money in the primary market
- Typically charge the borrower a loan origination fee and annual interest for the use of the money during the term of the loan
- Originate mortgage loans with the intention of selling mortgages to third-party investors in the secondary market
- May continue to service loans for investors who have purchased the loans in the secondary market and charge these investors servicing fees

New York Mortgage Banker License

A New York Mortgage Banker License is required for an individual or entity that:

- Originates at least five mortgage loans per year.
- Has at least $250,000 in adjusted net worth, which shall be maintained at all times.
- Can show written documentation of a line of credit provided by a banking institution or an insurance company outside the applicant's corporate structure, in an amount not less than $1,000,000.
- Has a corporate surety bond in a principal amount of not less than $50,000 or more than $500,000 based on its volume of business.
- Has five years of verifiable experience in the making of mortgage loans on either a retail or wholesale level.

Mortgage Brokers

- Earn a fee to act as an intermediary to bring together borrowers and lenders who originate the actual loans
- May solicit, process, place, and/or negotiate residential loans
- Enter into an agency relationship with a buyer through a fee agreement
- Can also be compensated by the lender

Role of Mortgage Broker

- Pre-qualifying, which involves a high-level examination of the borrower's financial situation to determine the type and amount for which he may qualify
- Helping the borrower gather the necessary documentation to assist the lender with pre-approval

- Submitting loan applications to lenders
- Explaining the terms of various loan options, such as interest rates, discount points, origination fees, etc.
- Negotiating a rate lock, which is when the agreed-upon interest rate and points are frozen until the loan closes
- Securing a mortgage commitment from a lender, which is a written letter that confirms that lender's willingness to loan the money

New York Mortgage Broker Registration Requirements

Brokers are supervised and regulated by the State of New York Banking Department. Requirements include:

- A minimum of two years verifiable experience in the mortgage field
- A corporate surety bond or pledged deposit with a principal amount not less than $10,000 or more than $100,000, based on the number of applications
- Fingerprint cards
- References attesting to their character, fitness, and reputation
- A recent original credit report
- The application/investigation fee
- A list of the three mortgage lenders the broker uses or intends to use the most

Dual Agency

A real estate agent who is acting as a mortgage broker must explain the concept of **dual agency** to both the buyer and the seller and **obtain consent from both parties** before taking on that role. She must also complete the dual agency **disclosure form** and as with other documentation of a transaction, maintain a hard or electronic copy of the disclosure form and signed acknowledgment for at least **three years.**

QUIZ

1. *The document that uses real property to secure debt is called a*
   A. chattel mortgage.
   B. mortgage.
   C. promissory note.
   D. trustee's deed.

2. *The mortgagor is*
   A. the borrower.
   B. the broker.
   C. the lender.
   D. the seller.

3. *When a lender originates a mortgage for a buyer by providing loan money, this is known as*
   A. primary mortgage market.
   B. secondary financing.
   C. secondary mortgage market.
   D. seller financing.

4. *What is the required down payment if the purchase price is $85,000 and the lender will approve a loan-to-value ratio of 80%?*
   A. $5,000
   B. $6,800
   C. $8,500
   D. $17,000

5. *What is the legal clause that gives the lender certain stated rights when there is a transfer of ownership in the property?*
   A. acceleration clause
   B. alienation clause
   C. power of sale clause
   D. subordination clause

6. *The defeasance clause ensures that*
   A. a mortgage recorded at a later date takes priority over an earlier recorded mortgage.
   B. at default, the borrower must assign any rental income over to the lender.
   C. upon final payment, the mortgage is satisfied, cancelled, or void, and the title is re-vested from mortgagee to mortgagor.
   D. upon sale of the property, the lender may accelerate the debt, change the interest rate, or charge an assumption fee.

7. *A borrower is buying a house for $100,000. He provides a down payment of $5,000. If he pays two discount points, what is the total cost of the points?*
   A. $1,500
   B. $1,900
   C. $2,000
   D. $2,100

8. *The clause that allows the lender to declare the entire balance remaining immediately due and payable if the borrower is in default is the*
   A. acceleration clause.
   B. alienation clause.
   C. defeasance clause.
   D. prepayment clause.

9. *A type of buydown plan that has lower monthly payments in the early years with increases at specified intervals until the payment amount is sufficient to amortize the loan over the remaining term is known as a(n)*
   A. adjustable rate loan.
   B. graduated payment.
   C. participation plan.
   D. seller financing.

10. *If the LTV is 80%, and the property was appraised at $86,500.00 and is selling for $88,000.00, how much would the purchaser be permitted to borrow?*
    A. $73,500
    B. $70,400
    C. $65,200
    D. $69,200

Mortgage Basics

Key Terms

Adjustable Rate Mortgage (ARM) Mortgage that permits the lender to periodically adjust the interest rate so it reflects fluctuations in the cost of money.

Annual Percentage Rate (APR) Total cost of financing a loan in percentage terms, as a relationship of total finance charges to total amount financed.

Blanket Mortgage 1. Mortgage that covers more than one parcel of real estate. 2. Mortgage that covers an entire building or development, rather than an individual unit or lot.

Bridge Mortgage Short-term mortgage loan that covers the gap between selling one property and buying another.

Construction Mortgage Temporary loan used to finance a construction project.

Equitable Right of Redemption The right of a debtor to save (redeem) property from foreclosure proceedings prior to confirmation of sale.

Graduated Payment Mortgage Allows the borrower to make smaller payments early in the mortgage, with payments increasing yearly until they are sufficient to fully amortize the loan.

Home Equity Line of Credit A credit line secured by a second mortgage on the homeowner's principle residence. Home equity lines of credit are available to the homeowner as expenses arise and payments are made according to the credit terms. Interest is usually tax deductible.

Home Equity Loan A loan secured by a second mortgage on the homeowner's principle residence. Home equity loans are usually one-time loans for a specific amount of money obtained for a specific, and often non-housing-related, expenditure. Payments are made according to the loan terms and interest is usually tax deductible.

Home Ownership and Equity Protection Act (HOEPA) Amended the Truth-in-Lending Act in 1994; prohibits equity stripping, whereby a homeowner loses equity in a home due to excessive fees, and other abusive lending practices.

Housing Expense Ratio The relationship of total monthly housing expense to income, expressed as a percentage: Total Housing Expense ÷ Income = Ratio %.

Interest Rate Cap A limit on the amount of interest rate increase that can occur with an adjustable rate mortgage.

(continued on next page)

Types of Mortgage Loans

A **mortgage** is a written financial instrument that uses real property to secure the payment of a debt. There are various mortgage loans available:

- **Fixed rate mortgage** – has an annual percentage rate (APR) that remains constant for the duration of the loan

- **Graduated payment mortgage (GPM)** – a payment structure that lets the mortgagor make smaller monthly payments in the early years, with payments increasing yearly until they are sufficient to fully amortize the loan; lower monthly payments made at the beginning that do not cover the amount of interest due result in **negative amortization**

- **Pledged account mortgage** – an escrow account is established for the borrower with part of the down payment; lender withdraws money from the account each month and applies it to the borrower's monthly payments

- **Reverse equity mortgage** – a qualified homeowner age 62 or older with only a few or no outstanding liens mortgages his home, and, in return, may receive a monthly check or a lump sum from the lender

- **Home equity line of credit** – money available to the homeowner to access on an as-needed basis up to a pre-determined limit; a type of **open-end mortgage**

- **Home equity loan** – a one-time loan against the borrower's residence for a specific amount of money (and often for a specific purpose)

- **Bridge mortgage** - covers the gap between selling one property and buying another; designed to be temporary and is used most commonly for construction financing (also referred to as a *swing loan*)

Key Terms - continued

Judicial Foreclosure A lawsuit filed by a lender or other creditor to foreclose on a mortgage or other lien; a court-ordered sheriff's sale of property to repay the debt.

Margin Difference between the index value and interest rate charged to the borrower with an ARM loan.

Mortgage An instrument that creates a voluntary lien on real property to secure repayment of a debt. The parties to a mortgage are the mortgagor (borrower) and mortgagee (lender).

Negative Amortization The principal balance of a loan grows when the amount paid does not cover the interest that is due.

Open-End Mortgage Mortgage loan that allows borrowers to request additional funds from the lender, up to a certain pre-determined limit, even re-borrowing part of the debt that has been repaid (at the lender's discretion) without having to re-negotiate the loan.

Package Mortgage Personal property, such as an appliance, is included in a property sale and financed together with one contract.

Payment Cap Protects borrowers from large payment increases in their mortgages.

Pledged Account Mortgage An escrow account established with part of a buyer's down payment. The borrower/buyer's lender then withdraws money from the account each month and applies it to the monthly payment.

Pre-Approval Process by which a lender determines that potential borrowers can be financed through the lender for a certain amount of money.

Predatory Lending Practice of making loans with excessively high fees and misrepresented loan terms; predatory lenders often target borrowers who are financially unstable and who do not qualify for conventional loans.

Pre-Qualification Process by which an agent or lender reviews potential borrowers to determine if they are likely to get approved for a loan, and for approximately what amount.

Rate Cap Used with ARMs to protect borrowers from large interest rate increases.

- **Package mortgage** – includes both real estate property and personal property, such as appliances installed on the property; commonly used to finance furnished condominium units or resort properties
- **No doc mortgage** – also known as a **stated doc mortgage**, it can be available for those who cannot pass a credit review but have a large down payment, or who cannot prove income stability because they are self-employed
- **Blanket mortgage** – covers two or more parcels or lots, often to finance new subdivision developments; usually contains a release clause allowing certain parcels to be removed from the mortgage when the loan balance is reduced by a specified amount
- **Straight**, **interest-only**, or **term mortgage** – the borrower pays the principal at the end of a specified term, during which only interest was being paid
- **Construction mortgage** – a temporary loan used to finance the construction of buildings or developments on land; the collateral is the land, though the land itself is not worth the total amount of the loan until the construction occurs; replaced with a permanent loan when construction is complete
- **Sale-and-leaseback** – in a sale and leaseback transaction, the purchaser, usually a real estate investor, buys the property and leases it back to the seller
- **Variable balance mortgage** – has a variable interest rate, but not a variable payment
- **Bi-weekly mortgage** – Repayment plan with biweekly, rather than monthly, payments to achieve an earlier pay-off and lower interest paid throughout the life of the loan
- **Shared appreciation mortgage** – the lender originates a mortgage at a low interest rate (several points below the current rate) in exchange for a share of the gains the borrower realizes when the property is eventually sold; may be used for developers of large real estate properties

Release Clause A clause in a mortgage agreement for a subdivision that allows the borrower to pay a certain amount of money to release one or more lots with the mortgage continuing to cover the other lots.

Residual Income The amount of income a borrower has left after subtracting taxes, housing expense, and all recurring debts and obligations (used for VA loan qualifying).

Reverse Equity Mortgage When a homeowner age 62 or over with little or no outstanding liens, mortgages his or her home to a lender and, in return, receives a monthly check. *Also called*: **Reverse Mortgage.**

Sale and Leaseback Financing A method for financing commercial or industrial properties in which a company constructs the building then becomes a tenant by selling the building to an investor.

Straight Mortgage A loan that comes due on a specified date, often before the periodic payments would pay it off. *Also called*: **Term Mortgage.**

Total Debt Service Ratio Relationship of total monthly debt obligations to income, expressed as a percentage. *Also called*: **Debt-to-Income Ratio.**

Truth-in-Lending Act (TILA) Federal law that requires lenders to disclose consumer credit costs to promote informed use of consumer credit; implemented by **Regulation Z**.

Underwriter A person who evaluates a loan application to determine its risk level for a lender or investor.

Veterans Administration (VA) Government agency that guarantees mortgage loans for eligible veterans.

Voluntary Conveyance When a debtor returns property to the lender in lieu of foreclosure. Generally, the debtor does not receive any compensation for surrendering title to the property, but does avoid foreclosure.

Foreclosure

Judicial foreclosure allows the creditor to work through the courts to obtain ownership of the collateral property in the event of default. While the process differs from jurisdiction to jurisdiction, here are the steps in the typical judicial foreclosure process:

1. Borrower defaults on a loan

2. Lender accelerates the due date of the debt to the present and gives the debtor a notice of default, demanding that the debtor pay off the entire outstanding balance of the loan at once

3. If the debtor fails to do so, the lender starts a lawsuit, called a foreclosure action, in Common Pleas Court in the county in which the land is located

4. If the court determines that the lender is rightfully owed the money, a judge will issue an order of execution, allowing the lender to take ownership; if the lender decides to sell, it will direct an officer of the court to sell the property

5. The officer of the court, usually the county sheriff, notifies the public of the place and date of the sale, through advertising that runs for four consecutive weeks in a newspaper circulated in the county

6. On the sale date, a public auction is held, where anyone can bid on the property

7. Once the property is sold to the highest bidder at or in excess of the minimum bid, the proceeds are used to pay any back property taxes, then the cost of the foreclosure (sheriff, appraisers, transfer tax, auctioneer, etc.), and then the lien holders are paid in priority order (first lien, second lien, etc.); any surplus funds go to the debtor

8. After the sale, a document called a confirmation of sale is filed to finalize the sale

9. The officer then makes out a sheriff's deed to the purchaser of the property, which is executed, acknowledged, and recorded just like any other deed, although it does not include any warranties

Avoiding Foreclosure

- **Equitable right of redemption** – in New York, a debtor can save property from the time the foreclosure action is brought up until the confirmation of the foreclosure sale by paying the court what is due, which may include court costs and attorneys' fees; once redemption is made, the court will set aside the sale, pay the parties, and the debtor has title to the property again.

- Other states use the **statutory right of redemption**, which allows debtors to redeem themselves after the final sale.

- **Voluntary conveyance** – a debtor can make a voluntary conveyance (also called a **deed in lieu of foreclosure**) to transfer ownership to the lender without court proceedings; debtors still lose the property, but avoid having a judicial foreclosure on their credit report.

Lien Status

Lien status is especially important in the event of foreclosure because the proceeds from a foreclosure sale pay the liens in the order they were applied to the property.

- **First mortgage** – a security instrument with a first lien position; always has priority over all other mortgages; may only be preempted by a tax lien

- **Senior mortgage** – any mortgage with a higher lien position than another. Thus, a first mortgage is always in a senior mortgage position

- **Second mortgage** – a security instrument in a second lien position

- **Junior mortgage** – any mortgage with a lower lien position than another (subordinate); thus, a second mortgage is a junior mortgage to a first mortgage, but a second mortgage is a senior mortgage to a third mortgage

Adjustable Rate Mortgages

An **adjustable rate mortgage** (ARM) has an interest rate that may be periodically adjusted by the lender based on a standard index of economic conditions. ARMs usually have a lower initial interest rate than a fixed rate loan. ARMs may help borrowers qualify more easily for a home loan.

How ARMs Work

The borrower's interest rate is determined initially by the cost of money at the time the loan is made. The three main elements of an ARM are rate, index, and margin. To determine a current ARM interest rate, simply add the current index value to the margin:

Current Index Value + Margin = Interest Rate

Elements of ARM Loans

- **Index** – a statistical report that is a generally reliable indicator of the approximate cost of money; since rate adjustments for ARM loans are based on fluctuations in the index, most lenders try to use one that is responsive to economic fluctuations, e.g., the Cost of Funds Index (COFI)

- **Margin** – the lender's profit; the lender's margin generally remains fixed for the duration of the loan and is not affected by the movement of interest rates or other factors in the financial markets

- **Rate adjustment period** – the interval at which a borrower's interest rate changes and can range from a few months to many years

- **Mortgage adjustment period** – the interval at which a borrower's mortgage payment changes

- **Interest rate cap** – limits the number of percentage points an interest rate can be increased during the term of a loan; helps eliminate large and frequent mortgage payment increases

- **Mortgage payment cap** – protect borrowers from large payment increases

- **Negative amortization cap** – negative amortization occurs when a loan balance grows because payments do not cover the interest due on the loan; a cap on negative amortization results in loan re-amortization where payments are recalculated so the new payment will fully amortize the loan over the remaining loan term

- **Conversion option** – gives the borrower the right to convert from an adjustable rate loan to a fixed rate loan

Financial Disclosure Laws

Real estate professionals must be aware of the various disclosure requirements for real estate loans. The source of the duty to disclose varies according to which disclosures are involved.

Truth in Lending Act

The **Truth in Lending Act** was enacted to prevent abuses in consumer credit cost disclosures and requires lenders to disclose consumer credit costs in a uniform manner when lenders offer credit to borrowers and when credit terms are advertised to potential customers in order to promote informed use of consumer credit in residential loans. Specific provisions of the Act are implemented by **Regulation Z**.

- Requires that borrowers be shown exactly how much they are going to pay for credit in dollars and percentages in a **Truth in Lending Statement** provided by loan originator within three business days of applying for a loan; includes:
  - Annual percentage rate
  - Finance charge (cost of consumer credit as a dollar amount)
  - Amount financed
  - Total amount of money to be repaid (principal + interest
- **Annual percentage rate (APR)** is a combination of the interest rate and all other charges for obtaining the loan, such as a loan application fee, loan origination fees, interest, PMI premiums, discount points, etc.
- 2009 provisions require that a loan cannot close until the seventh business day after the required disclosures are given to the borrower
- Provides for the **right to rescind** for borrowers with loans on their primary residence (refinances and home equity loans and home equity lines of credit) for three business days after a loan contract is signed
- Requires an advertisement using a triggering term (words or phrases that describe loan terms such as down payment, interest rate, monthly payment), to disclose the annual percentage rate (spelled out in full)

The Home Ownership and Equity Protection Act

The Home Ownership and Equity Protection Act (HOEPA), amending the Truth in Lending Act, prohibits equity stripping and other abusive lending practices on loans defined as high cost loans.

Consumer Protections
- **Balloon payments** – prohibited on most HOEPA loans having terms less than five years
- **Negative amortization** – prohibits loans having any kind of interest or payment adjustment that could result in negative amortization
- **Pressure tactics** – requires lenders to include text in the disclosure stating the consumer is not required to complete the credit transaction
- **Loan pricing** – must not include more than two advance payments from the loan proceeds
- **Acceleration clauses** – prohibits increasing interest rates if the customer is in default

- **Prepayment penalties** – limits prepayment penalties to avoid unfair practices that lock customers into loans that may not be, or are no longer, in their best interest
- **Loan flipping** – prohibits refinancing a HOEPA loan within a one-year period unless it is clearly in the borrower's best interest
- **Demand clauses** – prohibits any provision that would enable the creditor to call the loan before maturity
- **Income verification** – prohibits making a loan to a customer without verifying the customer can repay
- **Right of rescission** – allows three business-day right to rescind

Getting a Mortgage

Pre-Qualification

Pre-qualification is the process of determining the size of loan for which a potential home buyer might be eligible.

- No formal credit report is ordered
- Not binding on the lender
- Often done informally by the real estate licensee

Pre-Approval

Pre-approval is the process by which a lender determines that a potential borrower will be financed through the lender for a specific amount of money.

- Includes a lender analysis of a formal credit report
- Lender gives the buyer the pre-approval information in writing, which is sometimes referred to as a certificate of pre-approval or letter of pre-approval

The Loan Approval Process

The real estate loan approval process consists of four steps:

Consulting with the Lender

It is important for borrowers to select the right lender. After the buyer selects a lender, initial discussions usually involve the various mortgages available. Buyers can expect to incur expenses to process a real estate loan, including for:

- Pulling a credit bureau report
- A property appraisal report
- A preliminary title report
- Required inspections
- Loan origination fee

Completing the Loan Application

Buyers typically complete a loan application during the initial consultation with the lender. The sections on a loan application include:

- Type of mortgage and terms of loan
- Property information and purpose of loan

- Borrower information
- Employment information
- Monthly income and combined housing expense information
- Assets and liabilities
- Details of the transaction
- Declarations
- Acknowledgement and agreement
- Information for government monitoring purposes

Processing the Loan Application

Once the application is complete, the lender gathers other pertinent information about the buyer, including the required verifications of income, assets, liabilities, etc., that are necessary for the lender when considering the five C's:

- **Capacity** – the borrower's financial ability to make mortgage payments along with other debts and obligations
- **Collateral** – the value of the borrower's down payment and property being sufficient for the lender to recoup the loan money if foreclosure is necessary
- **Credit** – the borrower's history of making payments on past debts and obligations
- **Character** – the borrower's employment stability and history of responsibility in meeting financial obligations
- **Conditions** – external factors, such as the economic health of the borrower's field of employment, as well as general economic conditions

Analyzing the Borrower and Subject Property

When the lender receives the credit report, verification forms, the preliminary title report, and appraisal, a loan package is put together and given to an **underwriter**, who evaluates a loan application to determine its risk level for a lender or investor. The lender's underwriter is usually the final decision maker on loan approval.

Underwriting Standards

Income

Stable monthly income is *the monthly income amount that can reasonably be expected to continue in the future.* Before deciding if there is sufficient income, the underwriter must decide what portion of the borrower's total verified earnings are acceptable as a part of stable monthly income. This is accomplished by studying the *quality* (dependability) and the *durability* (probability of continuance) of the income sources. The maximum mortgage payment must include principal, interest, taxes, and insurance (known as PITI), plus monthly homeowner's association fees, if applicable.

Qualifying Standards

Lenders primarily look at two ratios to evaluate the borrower's income. Borrowers must qualify under both ratios, with the lesser amount being what is acceptable.

Payment-to-Income Ratio

The payment-to-income ratio examines whether a borrower's stable monthly income is considered adequate to cover the proposed monthly PITI mortgage payment. For a conventional mortgage loan, income is considered adequate if the proposed monthly mortgage payment of PITI does not exceed 28% of stable monthly income. You may also hear this referred to as the housing expense ratio or the front-end ratio.

Gross Monthly Income x Payment-to-Income Ratio % = Maximum PITI

Debt-to-Income Ratio

For the purposes of this calculation, housing expenses (PITI) are considered as part of the total debt, as well as any recurring monetary obligation that will not be cancelled. For example:

- Installment loans for cars, furniture, etc., usually with 10 or more payments remaining
- Credit card payments
- Retail account payments
- Child support payments
- Alimony payments
- Stock pledges
- Other mortgage loans

(Gross Monthly Income x Debt-to-Income Ratio %) - Recurring Debts = Maximum PITI

You may also hear this referred to as the debt service ratio or the back-end ratio.

Loan Standards

Conventional payment-to-income ratio:	28%
Conventional debt-to-income ratio:	36%
FHA payment-to-income ratio:	31%
FHA debt-to-income ratio:	43%
VA – no payment-to-income ratio but may look at residual income	
VA debt-to-income ratio:	41%

Credit History

Credit history is a record of debt repayment, detailing how a person paid credit accounts in the past and is a guide to whether she is likely to pay them on time and as agreed in the future. Borrowers must inform a lender of all debts—even things that may not show up on a credit report.

Evaluating Credit History

When evaluating a borrower's credit history, lenders use a number of methods. Lenders are moving toward more objective evaluation methods to ensure compliance with the Equal Credit Opportunity Act (ECOA). The Act prohibits discrimination in lending based on age, sex, race, marital status, color, religion, national origin, or receipt of public assistance. Credit scoring is an objective means of determining the creditworthiness of potential borrowers based on a number system.

Fico/Beacon Scores

FICO is a credit score developed by Fair, Isaac, & Co. and used by Experian; **BEACON** is a credit score used by Equifax. FICO and BEACON scores are the result of very complex calculations carried out by a computer that takes into account every aspect of a borrower's credit file. The FHA and VA use the scores to calculate interest rates offered (and perhaps the required down payment).

Net Worth

Net worth is determined by subtracting liabilities from total assets. It is the value of all property (real and personal) accumulated, after subtracting all debts or obligations owed. Lenders and underwriters are interested in:

1. Confirming the borrower has sufficient personal assets and funds to make the down payment, pay closing costs, and cover prepaid items such as taxes, homeowner's insurance, and interest on the property without borrowing.

2. Determining the borrower has adequate reserves (cash on deposit or other highly liquid assets a borrower has available) to cover two months of PITI mortgage payments, after making a down payment and paying closing costs.

3. Identifying other assets, demonstrating an ability to manage money, and identifying what could be sold to handle emergencies and make mortgage payments. Equity (the difference between the market value of the property and the sum of the mortgages and other liens against it) should also be included on the loan application.

Verifying Assets

When verifying a borrower has sufficient cash to cover the down payment and required reserves, underwriters will typically send a Request for Verification of Deposit directly to the borrower's bank. The bank then returns it directly to the underwriter without passing through the borrower's hands.

Gift Letter

If an applicant lacks the necessary funds for a down payment or closing costs, a gift of the required amount from relatives or employers is usually acceptable to the underwriter. The gift should be confirmed by a gift letter signed by the donor and should clearly state the money represents a gift and does not have to be repaid. Even if the gift letter requirements are satisfied, borrowers typically have to make some cash payment from personal cash resources.

Loan Decision

Loan underwriters carefully examine a loan package and decide to approve, reject, or approve the loan with conditions. The Equal Credit Opportunity Act requires a lender to make a credit decision within 30 days after receiving a loan application. After the loan is approved and all conditions are met, the necessary documents are prepared for closing (sometimes called settlement or escrow). Closing is the transfer of ownership of real property from seller to buyer according to the terms and conditions in the sales contract or escrow agreement. In order to comply with provisions of the Truth in Lending Act, the soonest a loan could close is the seventh business day after application.

Hot Mortgage Topics

Subprime Loans

- Loans made by lenders and investors to borrowers with questionable credit or limited documentation
- Typically these loans have higher-than-normal fees and interest rates based on the risk the lender associates with the loan
- Not all subprime lenders are predatory lenders
- Subprime lenders may be mainstream lenders also offering conventional loans to borrowers or brokers specializing in working with the "credit impaired"

Predatory Lending

Predatory lending is when a lender willfully deceives a consumer by targeting uninformed borrowers or borrowers with lower incomes, weak credit, and bankruptcy issues. The motive for predatory lending is profit. The law specifically prohibits certain practices, including:

- Packing a loan with credit insurance and other extra fees, such as exorbitant prepayment penalties
- Extending credit to people with little or no income or with high debt (extreme lending)
- Refinancing the lender's own high-cost loan with another fee-rich loan in less than a year's time (skimming equity)

Addressing Predatory Lending

- HUD task force on predatory lending
- Government agencies have filed lawsuits, criminal and civil, against lenders, requiring them to stop predatory practices and return money to consumers they defraud
- In New York City, the PACE program is designed to educate homeowners in targeted segments of the community; members work with other organizations to provide assistance to homeowners who may have been victimized by scams
- New York State Anti-Predatory Lending Law, enacted in 2003, applies restrictions to high-cost loans that are first or junior lien mortgages
- The New York State Banking Department created the Halt Abusive Lending Transactions (HALT) and Mortgage Fraud task force in 2007 to fight against rising foreclosures stemming from predatory lending
- The Home Ownership and Equity Protection Act (HOEPA), amending the Truth in Lending Act, established disclosure requirements and prohibits equity stripping and other abusive practices in connection with high-cost mortgages, and the most recent amendment to TILA which defines requirements for "higher-priced" loans

Rising Foreclosure Rate

Foreclosure is a risk when the interest rate on adjustable rate mortgages increases, or when the principal payments on an interest-only loan kick in and many homeowners find they can no longer afford the payments.

Common Foreclosure Scams

Unfortunately, when foreclosure rates rise, so do the number of scams targeting those in default. Scam artists, known as "rescuers," use a variety of tactics on distressed homeowners:

- **Phantom help** – the rescuer charges high fees for minimal help to the borrower
- **Bailout** – homeowners surrender title to their home, believing they will be able to rent it back, and eventually buy it back
- **Bait and switch** – homeowners believe they are signing new loan documents, when in reality, they are actually selling or giving up the home

Avoiding Foreclosure Scams

Advise customers and clients about the various scams and educate them on how to avoid becoming a victim; for example:

- Avoid doing business with anyone calling himself a foreclosure consultant
- Do not work with anyone who solicits business door-to-door or who advertises to those on pending foreclosure lists
- Avoid working with anyone who wants an upfront fee
- Avoid anyone claiming to pay closing costs on a new loan or who wants to buy a home "as is"
- Do not sign title over to anyone to avoid foreclosure

QUIZ

1. *Just one day prior to a foreclosure sale, the homeowner pays to the bank all the past-due payments, late charges, attorney fees, etc. The homeowner saves the property under the right called*

    A. anticipatory repudiation.
    B. defeasance clause.
    C. equitable right of redemption.
    D. statutory right of redemption.

2. *The federal statute that requires a lender to give a borrower a statement of total interest being paid over the life of a loan is the*

    A. Equal Credit Opportunity Act.
    B. Fair Credit Reporting Act.
    C. Federal Fair Housing Act.
    D. Truth in Lending Act.

3. *A bridge mortgage is described as*

    A. a mortgage that allows homeowners to finance expensive purchases, pay off credit card debt, or pay for medical, educational, or home improvements.
    B. a mortgage that a borrower gives to a lender in order for the borrower to redo or expand a loan on an existing property.
    C. a mortgage that occurs between the termination of one mortgage and the beginning of the next.
    D. a new mortgage plus an existing mortgage, treated as a single obligation by the buyer with one payment made on the entire debt.

4. *What is an important distinction between pre-qualification and pre-approval?*

    A. Pre-qualification of a buyer is more costly than pre-approval.
    B. Pre-qualification of a buyer is not binding on the lender.
    C. Pre-qualification of a buyer is not useful to the real estate agent.
    D. Pre-qualification takes longer to complete than pre-approval.

5. *Which is LEAST LIKLEY to be an indicator of predatory lending?*

    A. changing loan terms at the closing
    B. charging excessive prepayment penalties
    C. increasing interest charges on late loan payments
    D. requiring mortgage insurance

6. *Once the initial rate has been set for an adjustable rate mortgage (ARM), future interest rate adjustments are based on the upward and downward movements of*

    A. income tax rates.
    B. the price of houses.
    C. a standard index.
    D. the stock market.

7. *For a conforming loan, the lender wants to be sure a borrower's debt service ratio does NOT exceed*

    A. 29%.
    B. 36%.
    C. 41%.
    D. 43%.

8. *A quick computation of the buyer's income and debt ratio may serve as a*

    A. credit report.
    B. loan application.
    C. pre-approval.
    D. pre-qualification.

9. *A borrower's stable monthly income is $3,000. He has three monthly debts: $350 car payment, $50 personal loan payment, and $50 credit card payment. What is the maximum monthly mortgage payment he would qualify for using the total debt-to-income ratio of 36% for a conventional loan?*

    A. $390
    B. $630
    C. $840
    D. $1,080

10. *What is the maximum payment-to-income ratio allowed for an FHA loan?*

    A. 28%
    B. 29%
    C. 31%
    D. 36%

Land Use Regulations

11

Key Terms

Abutting Property Directly contiguous properties, sharing at least one common boundary.

Accessory Apartment An apartment within a single-family dwelling.

Accessory Use The use or occupancy incidental or subordinate to the principal use or occupancy of a property.

Area Variance Permission to use land in a way typically not allowed by current zoning laws.

As of Right Zoning Prohibits discrimination among landowners in a particular zone.

Building Codes The Uniform Fire Prevention and Building Code, as modified by local amendments. Governs the construction details of buildings and other structures in the interest of the safety of the occupants and public.

Building Permit Official documents from a local government or other authority that allow the beginning of a construction or remodeling project.

Census Tract Relatively small areas used by the U.S. Census Bureau to track the population of the United States.

Certificate of Occupancy Permit issued to the builder after all inspections have been made and the property is deemed fit for occupancy.

Cluster Zoning A varied selection of lot sizes and housing choices within a single area.

Comprehensive Plan Written document prepared by a city's planning board that identifies the goals, objectives, principles, guidelines, policies, standards, and strategies for growth and development of a community. *Also called*: **Master Plan.**

Condemnation The act of taking property for public use through the government's power of eminent domain.

Deed Restriction Limitations on real property use, imposed by an owner through language included in the deed.

Demography Study of the social and economic status of a given area or population.

Doctrine of Laches Loss of legal rights because of failure to assert those rights in a timely manner.

Eminent Domain Government's constitutional power to appropriate or condemn private property for public use, as long as the owner is paid just compensation.

Escheat When property reverts to the state after a person dies without leaving a valid will and without heirs, or when property is abandoned.

11

(continued on next page)

Key Terms - continued

Family An individual, or two or more people related by blood, marriage, or adoption living together in one dwelling; or a group of up to three people not related by blood, marriage, or adoption living together as a single housekeeping unit; or one or more people living together in a single housekeeping unit in a hotel or club.

Group Home A residential facility in a residential zone for three or more unrelated people (i.e., foster homes, rehabilitation centers, and halfway houses).

Home Occupation Small business or other occupation conducted in a residence.

Incentive Zoning A system by which developers receive zoning incentives on the condition that specific physical, social, or cultural benefits are provided to the community.

Infrastructure The support facilities and services for a community, such as roads, parks, sewers, water, schools, trash collection, etc.

Lead Agency The agency under the State Environmental Quality Review Act principally responsible for determining whether an environmental impact statement is required in connection with the action and for the preparation and filing of the statement if required.

Moratorium Suspends the right of property owners to obtain development approval while local legislatures consider, draft, and adopt land use regulations or rules to respond to new or changing circumstances not adequately dealt with by current laws.

New York State Office of Parks, Recreation, and Historic Preservation (OPRHP) Oversees public recreation areas and administers federal and state preservation projects.

New York State Uniform Fire Prevention and Building Code Sets forth the construction, materials, safety, and sanitary standards for buildings in New York as well as standards for the condition, occupancy, maintenance, rehabilitation, and renewal of existing buildings.

Nonconforming Use Land use that does not conform to current zoning laws but is legally allowed because the land use was established before the new laws were enacted. Most nonconforming uses are allowed to continue but may not be expanded or enlarged.

Official Map A final and conclusive map with respect to the location and width of a municipality's streets, highways, drainage systems, and parks.

Plat A detailed survey map of a subdivision, recorded in the county where the land is located. Subdivided property is often called platted property. *Also called*: **Plat Map.**

Police Power The constitutional power of state and local governments to enact and enforce laws that protect the public's health, safety, morals, and general welfare.

Restrictive Covenant 1. A limitation on real property use, imposed by the owner. 2. A promise to do, or not to do, an act relating to real property.

Setback Requirements Provisions that require residences be located a specified distance between the front property line to the building line, as well as from the interior property lines.

Special Use Permit Permit issued in certain zoning districts when conditions designed to protect surrounding properties are met.

Spot Zoning The illegal rezoning of a single parcel or a small area to benefit one or more property owners rather than carry out the objectives of the master plan.

Subdivision Regulations State and local laws with which developers must comply before the land can be subdivided.

Surveys The process of locating and measuring the boundaries of a property, and indentifying improvements, encroachments, and easements associated with the land.

Taking When the government acquires private property for public use by appropriation. The difference between a "taking" and eminent domain is that the property is regulated by a government authority to the economic detriment of the owner, without compensation.

Topography The physical characteristics of the contour of a parcel of land.

Transfer of Development Rights The exchange of zoning privileges from areas with low population needs to areas of high population needs.

Use Variance Allows landowners to use their land in a way that is not permitted under current zoning laws. This type of variance is granted only in cases of unnecessary hardship. To prove unnecessary hardship, owners must establish that the requested variance meets four statutorily prescribed conditions.

Vacant Land Unimproved land or land with no building on it.

Variance A form of administrative relief that allows property to be used in a way that does not comply with the literal requirements of the zoning ordinance. There are two basic types of variances: use variance and area variance.

Zoning Ordinance Sets forth the type of use permitted under each zoning classification and specific requirements for compliance.

Land Use Regulations

Even when land ownership is considered absolute, meaning the complete bundle of rights belongs to the owner, it does not necessarily mean landowners have the absolute right to use and enjoy the land. Restrictions can be placed on land by:

*   The government
*   Private companies
*   Individuals

Private Land Use Controls

Private land use controls are imposed by individual owners and community developers and can affect individual deeds, or an entire neighborhood.

Conditions and Covenants

*   **Conditions** – provisions in a deed or other document that make the landowners' rights and obligations dependent on the occurrence or non-occurrence of some event
*   **Covenants** – promises or guarantees in a deed or other document

Deed Restrictions

Deed restrictions, also known as **restrictive covenants**, are typically created to prevent objectionable land use by new owners. Restrictive covenants:

*   Are limitations placed in a deed by a grantor that restrict the way in which the land may be used, improved, or maintained
*   Run with the land, which means they move with the title in future conveyances and apply to all future landowners
*   Are often imposed by developers or sub-dividers of land on all lots in a subdivision to maintain uniformity of character and/or value of the properties in a development; recorded in a declaration of **covenants, conditions, and restrictions** (CC&Rs)
*   May appear in the deed itself or in a separate document that is referenced by the deed; either way, they should be recorded in the public records
*   May be enforced by the grantor or the other grantees by petitioning the court
*   May **not** be enforced if the court determines that the right to enforce was lost through undue delay or failure to assert (Doctrine of Laches)
*   May **not** violate the law in any way
*   Cannot be so restrictive as to prevent the free and reasonable transfer of the property

Terminating Deed Restrictions

A deed restriction can be removed only if it is in violation of a discriminatory act or impinges upon the owner's bundle of rights. Ways to terminate restrictive covenants include:

*   Setting a termination date
*   Releasing the owner from the covenant
*   Abandoning the property
*   Changing the circumstances of the property and/or the owner

Subdivision Regulations

Subdivision regulations can be both private and public. Private subdivision regulations enable property owners to maintain the quality and consistency of the residences in the subdivision. A typical subdivision regulation is that residences must meet certain **setback requirements**, which means they are located a specified distance between the front property line to the building line, as well as from the front, rear, and side property lines. If a resident does not adhere to the setback requirements, which are covenants, property owners within the subdivision may take legal action.

Public Land Use Controls

Public land use controls (or restrictions) are imposed by the government at the local, state, and federal level.

The government's right to restrict land use is much broader as an exercise of **police power**, which is the constitutional power of the state and local governments to enact and enforce laws that protect the public's health, safety, morals, and general welfare.

Police Power

- **Land use controls/zoning** – public or private restrictions on how land may be used
- **Building and fire codes** – set of rules that specify the minimum acceptable level of safety for buildings
- **Rent control** – limit the amount of rent a property owner can charge for residential housing
- **Environmental protection laws** – restrictions to protect wildlife, endangered species, wetlands, or to protect against pollution or hazardous waste

Local Powers

In New York State, property taxes are local taxes and the income from them is spent locally. Property taxes:

- Create a lien on real property
- Take priority over all other liens

State Powers

- New York Office of Parks, Recreation, and Historic Preservation
  - The OPRHP oversees public recreation areas and administers federal and state preservation projects
  - Oversees the Certified Local Program, which supports local preservation and is the link between local communities and state and federal programs
- New York State Article 9-A
  - Requires subdividers to file with the DOS before offering to sell or lease subdivided vacant land to NY residents on an installment plan
  - Applies only to vacant land sold on an installment plan
- Power of Escheat
  - Occurs when abandoned or unclaimed property reverts to the state, such as when a person dies without leaving a valid will and without heirs or creditors, or when a property is abandoned

- ◆ Applies to both real property and personal property
- ◆ Ensures that land is not ownerless and therefore, someone is paying taxes on it
- State Environmental Quality Review Act (SEQRA)
  - ◆ Requires a state environmental quality review to assess the environmental impact of any activity or action approved by a state agency or unit of local government
  - ◆ A state environmental quality review requires the government entity that sponsored or approved the activity to not only identify, but to mitigate its significant environmental impact
  - ◆ If a proposed action may significantly impact the environment, an environmental impact statement (EIS) is necessary
  - ◆ If multiple agencies are involved, a **lead agency** oversees the entire evaluation process and makes the final decision regarding whether an EIS is necessary
- Transportation
  - ◆ The New York State Department of Transportation (NYSDOT) builds and maintains state-owned roadways, bridges, and overpasses. State-owned roads in New York City are the exception, however, because it has its own department of transportation.

Federal Powers: Eminent Domain

Eminent domain is the government's constitutional power to appropriate private property for public use, as long as the owner is paid just compensation. Eminent domain is the power, whereas **condemnation** is the *actual act of taking* the property for public use through the government's power of eminent domain. Condemning authorities include:

- The state and its authorized agencies
- Municipalities
- School districts
- Railroads
- Public utilities
- The federal government

Before government can exercise eminent domain, two conditions must be met:

- The condemned property must be for the use and benefit of the public
- The property owner must be paid fair market value for the property lost

A **taking** occurs when the government acquires private property for public use by appropriation. In this case, the property is regulated by a government authority to the economic detriment of the owner, **without compensation** (unlike eminent domain, where the owner is paid fair market value).

Zoning Ordinances

Zoning ordinances set forth the type of use permitted under each zoning classification and specific requirements for compliance. Typically, zoning is the responsibility of local governments. Zoning ordinances have two parts:

- A zoning map that divides the community into designated districts
- A text of the zoning ordinance that sets forth the type of use permitted in each zone

According to New York State law, municipalities are required to refer certain planning and zoning actions to respective county planning boards for review. Sometimes, planning boards impose a **moratorium** that temporarily suspends the right of property owners to obtain development approvals while the local legislature takes time to consider, draft, and adopt land use regulations or rules to respond to new or changing circumstances not adequately dealt with by its current laws.

Zoning Classifications

- Residential
    - For residences; not commercial buildings
    - Consists of single-family and multi-family dwellings
    - Accessory **use** such as a **home occupation** is common in residential areas
    - Group **homes** are also found in residential areas
- Commercial
    - Hotels, retail shops, restaurants, malls, etc.
- Industrial
    - Includes manufacturing facilities
- Institutional
    - Schools, college campuses, hospitals, correctional facilities, etc.
    - May appear in residential or commercial zones as well, depending on local zoning ordinances
- Agricultural
    - Areas where animals may graze and crops may be grown
- Public Open Space
    - Forests, public parks, lakes, bays, shorelines, etc.
    - Land intentionally left undeveloped
    - Can be owned either publicly or privately
- Vacant Land
    - Unimproved land, or land with no building on it
    - Can still be considered vacant if the building/improvement does not serve a purpose
- Parklands
    - Specifically used for recreational activities
    - Maintained for their ecological, aesthetical, and educational value
    - Local, state, and federal authorities all can exercise their power over parklands
- Recreational
    - Greenways, trailways, public fishing areas, parks, shorelines, waterway access, etc.
    - Owned primarily by municipalities and private citizens

Types of Zoning

- **As of right zoning**
    - Prohibits discrimination among landowners in a particular zone
    - Ensures all landowners in a particular zone have the same rights to do as they wish to their land

- **Cluster zoning**
  - Allows developers to provide a varied selection of lot sizes and housing choices within a single area
  - Zones typically include open spaces or green spaces
  - May consist of **abutting properties**
  - May take the form of a **planned unit development (PUD)**
- **Incentive zoning**
  - System by which developers receive zoning incentives on the condition that specific physical, social, or cultural benefits are provided to the community
- **Spot zoning**
  - Illegal rezoning of a single parcel or small area to benefit one or more property owners rather than carry out the objectives of the community's master plan
  - When rezoning happens, the zoning law is changed; it is not a variance or exception

The Planning Board

Nearly every municipality in New York has a planning board that holds public hearings, investigates solutions for the planning issues at hand, and makes recommendations to the appropriate legislative authority. Responsibilities include:

- Creating a capital budget
- Creating and controlling the city's comprehensive plan
- Regulating plat, density, street, and traffic patterns
- Regulating subdivision development
- Reviewing site plans
- Taking specific zoning actions

The Zoning Board of Appeals

New York State statutes require a zoning board of appeals be formed when a local legislature adopts its zoning law. The essential functions of this board are to:

- Grant variances
- Interpret ordinances

Planning and Zoning in New York City

The planning board and the zoning board in New York City are one entity known as the Board of Standards and Appeals. A zoning board's determinations can be challenged in New York State Supreme Court through **Article 78 Proceeding**, which is an article of the New York Civil Practice Law and Rules.

Exceptions to Zoning Laws

A zoning law is constitutional only if it applies in the same manner to all similarly situated property owners. To prevent undue hardships, zoning laws usually provide for limited exceptions, such as:

- **Nonconforming uses** – established uses that violate new zoning laws, but must be allowed to continue since the use was established before the zoning was enacted (sometimes called being "grandfathered in")

- **Variances** – a variance is a form of administrative relief that allows property to be used in a way that does not comply with the literal requirements of the zoning ordinance
  - **Area variances** – entitle landowners to use land in a way that is typically not allowed by the dimensional or physical requirements of the zoning law
  - **Use variances** – allow landowners to use their land in a way that is not permitted under current zoning laws—such as commercial use in a residential zone
- **Conditional uses** – allowed in certain zoning districts, but only upon issuance of a **special use permit**, subject to conditions designed to protect surrounding properties and the community (from possible negative impact caused by the permit)

Local Enforcement

Zoning laws and regulations are enforced through codes, departments, and individuals within a community, municipality, city, and state. Enforcement mechanisms include:

- **Building codes**
  - Protect the public by setting minimum standards requiring builders to adhere to certain construction standards, including using particular methods and materials, sanitary equipment, electrical wiring, and fire prevention standards
  - **Building permit** – issued only if the plans comply with the codes
  - **Certificate of occupancy** – a permit issued to the builder after all inspections have been made and the property is deemed fit for occupancy
  - **Certificate of compliance** – issued for an altered building
- **The New York State Uniform Fire Prevention and Building Code**
  - Sets forth the construction, materials, safety, and sanitary standards for buildings in New York as well as standards for the condition, occupancy, maintenance, rehabilitation, and renewal of existing buildings
- Building departments
  - Protects residents by seeing that code restrictions are followed and construction and renovations are done by licensed professionals
  - Oversee code enforcement
- Professional service providers
  - Professionals that represent both public and private interests
  - Architects, urban designers, project managers, surveyors, engineers, planners etc.
- Local courts
  - Have the responsibility of controlling local land use decisions

QUIZ

1. *All of the homes in the Prairie Acres Subdivision appear to be built a uniform distance of 30 feet from the street. What is the probable reason?*
   A. a zoning variance
   B. coincidence
   C. homeowner's association rules and regulations
   D. setback requirements in the subdivision regulations

2. *The physical act of taking private land for public use is*
   A. appropriation.
   B. economic development.
   C. eminent domain.
   D. just compensation.

3. *Constitutionally, the government has the right to take private land under certain circumstances. This right is known as*
   A. adverse possession.
   B. appropriation.
   C. eminent domain.
   D. police power.

4. *The concept of escheat means that property*
   A. can be appropriated by the state when there's a public need.
   B. can be confiscated for non-payment of taxes.
   C. must meet specific zoning requirements before it can be developed.
   D. reverts to the state when a person dies with neither a will nor an heir.

5. *The illegal rezoning of a single parcel of land or a small area to benefit one or more property owners rather than carry out objectives of the master plan is known as*
   A. as of right zoning.
   B. cluster zoning.
   C. incentive zoning.
   D. spot zoning.

6. *A restriction may be removed from a deed if*
   A. it is found to violate a landowner's bundle of rights.
   B. no one comes forward to enforce the deed restriction.
   C. the current deed owner sells the property to another buyer.
   D. the statute of limitations on the deed restriction has expired.

7. *Government regulations that specify minimum construction and building standards to safeguard health, safety, and welfare of the public are known as*
   A. buffer zones.
   B. building codes.
   C. deed restrictions.
   D. property assessments.

8. *Tony works as a barber in the shop his grandfather built 50 years ago on the street in front of the family home. If the area was zoned residential 25 years ago, the barbershop is best described as a/an*
   A. conditional use.
   B. eyesore.
   C. nonconforming use.
   D. nuisance.

9. *Which of these statements is NOT true regarding deed restrictions?*
   A. Once established, they run with the land and are limitations on the use of future grantees.
   B. They are also called restrictive covenants.
   C. They are frequently encountered in residential subdivisions.
   D. They terminate upon the death of the grantor.

10. *Donna owns a small gas station in a residential area. She is allowed to have this zoning usage because there isn't another gas station within 10 miles. What type of permit does she have?*
    A. area variance
    B. conditional use special permit
    C. spot zoning
    D. use variance

Construction Basics

Key Terms

Amperage Amount of electricity going through electric wires, measured in amps.

Balloon Construction Type of framing with long studs going up the entire length of the house, from the foundation to the roof. No longer permitted as a construction method by most building codes. *Also called*: **Balloon Framing**.

Basement Part of the house or building partially or entirely below grade (ground level) and used to support the rest of the structure.

Beam A construction term for a long piece of wood, metal, concrete, etc.

Bearing Walls A wall that carries the load for the roof, ceiling, and/or floors.

Blueprint Detailed building plans used to evaluate design, determine feasibility, and guide a structure's construction.

British Thermal Unit (BTU) Amount of heat needed to raise the temperature of one pound of water by one degree Fahrenheit. Used as a measure of furnace or air conditioner capacity.

Building Codes The Uniform Fire Prevention and Building Code, as modified by local amendments. Governs the construction details of buildings and other structures in the interest of the safety of the occupants and public.

Building Envelope Sometimes called a building shell, the building envelope refers to the exterior elements—walls, windows, floor, roof, etc.—which enclose the interior.

Building Inspection The process whereby government authorities, usually state or local, are charged with ensuring compliance with prevailing building codes.

Circuit Breaker A device, usually located inside the electrical breaker panel or circuit breaker box, designed to break its electrical connection should an overload occur.

Concrete Slab A foundation made from a layer of poured concrete reinforced with steel rods.

Crawl Space Unfinished space below the first floor of a house or other structure that is less than a full story in height.

Eave The lowest sections of the roof, which project beyond the side walls.

Fascia A panel or board facing the outer edge of the soffit.

Flashing Material used to cover joints where two or more types of materials join together for the purpose of preventing water from penetrating the joint (e.g., metal over the seam between a brick chimney and a shingle roof).

(continued on next page)

Key Terms - continued

Flitch Beams Two or more timbers cut lengthwise and bundled together to provide additional support for the ceiling and roof.

Footer The underground base, usually concrete, that supports a foundation.

Foundation The basic structure on which the rest of the house will sit. A foundation can be concrete slab, pier and beams, crawl space, or basement.

Foundation Walls The side walls that support a structure, typically made of poured concrete, concrete block, or brick.

Fuse A protective device for a wiring system that contains a wire designed to melt and open the circuit when overheating occurs.

Girder The main support beam of a structure, spanning the foundation walls.

Headers In construction, reinforcements made of wood for door and window placement. *Also called*: **Lintels.**

Joists Long beams of wood or steel that span the piers of a foundation (floor joists) or the load-bearing walls of a roof (ceiling joists).

Lally™ Columns Steel support columns filled with concrete.

Percolation Rate The rate at which water moves through soil.

Permits System used by state and local governments to monitor compliance with and enforce building codes and other regulations.

Pitch A roof's vertical rise in inches, divided by its horizontal span in feet.

Plaster Board Gypsum plaster sandwiched in-between two layers of coarse paper. It is commonly used in homes as a wall covering. *Also called*: **Wall Board**, **Dry Wall**, or **Gypsum Board**.

Platform Framing A type of framing used to build a house or building one story at a time, with each story serving as a platform for the next. *Also called*: **Platform Construction.**

Post and Beam Framing A type of framing with the floor for higher stories (and the roof) supported by beams that sit on top of posts and the outside wall perimeter. *Also called*: **Post and Beam Construction.**

Rafter Sloped support beams that follow the pitch of the roof and serve to hold the outer roof covering.

R-Factor A way to measure the insulating value or resistance to heat flow through a material or an object. The more effective the insulation, the higher the R-Value it will have.

R-Value Insulation's R-Factor multiplied by the amount of material.

Septic System A type of private sewage disposal system used in areas that do not have public sewers.

Sheathing A structural covering, often made of plywood, placed over a building frame's exterior wall studs or roof rafters.

Siding The outer covering for a home's exterior walls, designed to shed water and protect the home from outdoor elements.

Sill Plate Bottom piece of a frame that is anchored to the foundation horizontally, and provides a nailing surface for the floor or wall system.

Slab-on-grade Construction A concrete foundation that is built directly on the ground level. A slab-on-grade house or building doesn't have a basement.

Soffit The underside of an arch, beam, overhang, or eave.

Studs The vertical beams that serve to frame the house. Drywall and/or siding are attached to studs.

Voltage A measure of the force that pushes electricity through a wire.

Starting the Construction Process

- Develop specifications
- Once the lot or parcel is chosen, a **blueprint** is used to obtain quotes from prospective builders
- Get approval of the building specifications and blueprints from local authorities
- Obtain the necessary **permits** to begin construction

Building Codes

Building codes set minimum standards and require builders to use certain construction standards, methods, and materials. Standards vary by the type of work being done and the type of structure, but common codes include:

- Uniform Building Code
- National Electric Code
- Uniform Plumbing Code
- New York City's International Building Code
- New York State Energy Conservation Construction Code, which provides minimum standards concerning energy efficiencies in new commercial and residential buildings in order to save energy and make New York's air cleaner

After a building is completed, a **building inspection** takes place, whereby government authorities, usually state or local, ensure compliance with prevailing building codes. After all inspections have been made and the property is deemed fit for occupancy, a **certificate of occupancy** is issued.

New York Site Requirements

- The State of New York regulates water supply and sewage disposal systems serving subdivisions (under Article 11, Title II of the Public Health Law and Article 17, Title 15 of the Environmental Conservation Law).
- The **New York State Department of Health** has regulations for sanitary and safe water that act as guidelines for well water.
  - Specific standards are set for **well location and construction** to protect well waters from contamination.
- On-site **sanitary waste system requirements** are detailed in Section 75-A of the New York Public Health Law.

Site Use

Several factors determine the best use of a site. These factors must be considered before beginning a construction project or before someone purchases a property:

- **Drainage** – the natural or artificial movement of water from a given area; a site must have proper drainage and be properly graded so that rainwater is directed away from the property
- **Landscaping** – improving property or land by adding plantings, trees, bushes, etc.
- **Appurtenances** – rights that go with real property ownership; affect how a site can best be used

- **Shading** – the amount of shade property receives depends on how a structure is situated on it; it can reduce energy bills by reducing the overall temperature of a building
- **Walkways** – the Fair Housing Act sets minimum standards for walkways. Buildings must be accessible by those with disabilities
- **Zoning** – zoning and other regulated limitations on land usage may limit development and affect property values

Structure

Foundation
- Basic structure on which the rest of the house sits
- Either concrete slab (called *slab-on-grade*), pier and beams, crawl space (the result of pier and beam foundation), or basement
- **Foundation walls** support the structure and are typically made of poured concrete, concrete block, or brick
- A **footer** (or footing) is the underground base, usually concrete, that supports the foundation; local building codes dictate how footers must be built
- Footers go below the **frost line** (the deepest depth that ground freezes in winter)

Framing
The building envelope, sometimes called a building shell, refers to exterior elements (walls, windows, floor, roof, etc.) that enclose the interior. Framing is the basic load-bearing skeleton of a structure. Three basic types of framing are:

- **Platform** – commonly used type of framing in which the house or building is constructed one story at a time
- **Post and beam** – type of framing with the floor for higher stories and the roof supported by beams that sit on top of posts and outside the wall perimeter
- **Balloon** – type of framing with long studs going up the entire length of the house; no longer permitted because of its poor fire-resistant design and the high cost of the long studs

Beams, Wood Framing Members, and Flooring
- **Beams** – long piece of wood, metal, concrete, etc.
- **Studs** – vertical beam used to frame a structure (also called wood-framing member)
- **Girders** – large, main carrying beam that usually runs horizontally and supports the vertical loads
- **Joists** – long, horizontal beams of wood or steel that span the piers of a foundation (floor joists) or load-bearing walls of a roof (ceiling joists)
- **Lally™ columns** – steel support columns filled with concrete; used only for interior
- **Sill plate** – bottom piece of a frame that is anchored horizontally to the foundation and provides a nailing surface for the floor or wall system; first layer of wood that starts construction of a house

Structural Tie-Ins

- Wall development begins with **bearing walls**, which carry the load for the roof, ceiling, and/or floors.

- Reinforcements made of wood for door and window placement are called **headers** or lintels.

- Flitch beams, made of two or more timbers cut lengthwise and bundled together, provide additional support for the ceiling and roof.

Roof Framing

- A **roof rafter** is a sloped support beam that follows the pitch of the roof and holds the outer roof covering

- Rafters are fastened to the roof ridge beam, a horizontal beam at the top of the roof

- The **pitch** is the slope of a roof; its vertical rise in inches, divided by its horizontal span in feet

- The **eave** is the lowest section of the roof that projects beyond the side walls

- The **soffit** is the underside of an arch, beam, overhang, or eave; often ventilated to provide air flow to the attic

- The **fascia** is a panel or board facing the outer edge of the soffit

- **Flashing** is added to cover joints where two or more types of materials join together

Common Roof Styles

- Hip (square or rectangular)
- Gable (pitched)
- Mansard
- Gambrel
- Flat
- Saltbox
- Shed

Finish Work

Exterior

- Protects exposed surfaces from the elements

- **Sheathing** – structural covering, is placed over a building frame's exterior wall studs or roof rafters

- **Siding** – which is often made of vinyl, wood, steel, or aluminum; may be added to the exterior to shed water and protect the building from the elements

Interior

- **Rough-ins** – items hidden later by finished walls, but are vital to the operation of the house (wiring, plumbing, heating, air-conditioning)

- **Wallboard** – gypsum plaster sandwiched between two layers of coarse paper (also called drywall, plasterboard, or sheetrock); mold resistant

- Wall and floor coverings, light fixtures, cabinetry, etc.

Energy Efficiencies: Insulation

- Necessary to keep property warm in winter and cool in summer
- Parts of a structure that need to be insulated include floor, walls, and ceilings
- Rated by **R-Factor**, a way to measure the insulating value or resistance to heat flow through a material or object
- **R-Value** is R-Factor multiplied by the amount of material; the more effective the insulation, the higher its R-Value
- New York State regulates insulation requirements through the New York Energy Code, which dictates where insulation is to be installed and what materials are used, among other regulations

Types Of Insulation

- **Blanket** – made of a mineral fiber, such as fiberglass, enclosed in paper covering
  - Often comes in a pre-measured width to pair with standard stud, joist, or rafter spacing
- **Foamed-in** – starts as a liquid, but expands into a plastic solid
  - Works well for insulating irregularly shaped spaces
- **Loose-fill or blown-in** – made of fiber pellets or loose fibers
  - Good at filling small, tight areas
  - Typically blown into an area, often the attic
- **Rigid** – made of a fibrous material like fiberglass or polyurethane
  - Commonly used on basement walls and comes in a variety of thicknesses
- **Reflective** – has a reflective surface that either contains or resists heat to keep a space warm or cool
  - Used between roof rafters, joists, or wall studs

Major Systems

Heating

Elements of heating systems include boilers, registers, radiators, furnaces, or heat pumps, flues, thermostats, ducts, and ductwork. The **British Thermal Unit (BTU)** is used to measure heating capacity. **Solar** and **radiant** heating are becoming popular, but the three most common heating systems are:

- **Hot water** – consists of a boiler, pipes, and convectors or radiators. It relies on a process of heating and cooling liquid to heat a home
- **Steam** – needs a boiler, pipes, and convectors or radiators; steam is produced in the boiler and moves through the pipes to convectors or radiators that release steam into the room; often found in older buildings
- **Forced warm air** – most commonly used today; includes a furnace with a blower, a heat source (i.e., **gas, oil, electricity**), distribution ducts, and return air ducts
- **Heat pump** – uses energy more efficiently than a furnace that burns fuel

Ventilation

Interior air can contain high levels of pollutants and irritants. Effective ventilation means both a controlled ventilation rate and a means of distributing the fresh air to habitable spaces. To ensure proper ventilation, the ventilation rate should be 15 cubic feet per minute (CFM) per person. Types of ventilation include:

- **Natural ventilation** – relies on windows and natural airflow through cracks in the building for ventilation
- **Spot or source point ventilation** – uses exhaust fans (bathroom and kitchen)
- **Balanced ventilation** – requires the use of two fans: One to remove moist and polluted air and a second to replace the air being vented with fresh air
- **Exhaust ventilation** – uses an exhaust fan to remove air from the property; an equal amount of fresh air enters either by way of intentional openings or specially designed windows
- **Supply ventilation** – uses either a supply fan or a forced-air heating/cooling fan to deliver fresh air and, in some cases, can pressurize the property

Air Conditioning

- Components of an air conditioner include the condenser, condenser fan, compressor, evaporator and blower, and liquid refrigerant
- Cooled by either air or water, or a combination referred to as evaporative cooled condensing units, which are typically used in commercial construction
- Rely on expelling heat outside and are most often used in residential construction

Plumbing

- Requires a system of pipes for water supply and drainage and includes piping, sinks, drains, toilets, tubs, vents, showers, valves, hot water tanks (gas or electric), and faucets
- Piping includes cold water lines, hot water lines, and waste water lines (sewer lines)
- Gas lines often included as part of the plumbing system
- Pipe size affects water pressure; building codes offer standards for maximum and minimum water pressure
- Types of piping include:
  - Cast iron
  - Galvanized
  - Copper
  - Brass
  - PVC
  - PEX
- Lead pipes an extreme health hazard and can contaminate drinking water; always explain to clients that lead pipes should eventually be replaced
- Vent system is a system of pipes that provide airflow through wastewater piping
- Drain traps (P-traps or older S-traps) keep some water in the elbow of a pipe so fumes or gases from the sewer do not escape back into the drain
- Tank-type heaters in which water is continually kept heated and ready for use most common in New York

- **Tankless water heaters** do not retain water in a traditional tank; heating coil is installed in the boiler or furnace through which water flows; more energy efficient since they do not heat water continuously, only when hot water is needed

Electrical

- **Service lateral** is underground power supply line; **service drop** are aboveground wire lines going from the service pole to a building
- A building's electrical system composed of wiring distribution box, the circuit breaker box and circuit breakers, fuses, lighting, and wall outlets
- **Voltage** – measure of the force that pushes electricity through a wire
- **Amperage** – amount of electricity going through the wire measured in amps
- Standard electric service in New York requires a minimum of **200 amps** for new construction
- Amperage capacity can usually be found on the main disconnect switch
- Most building codes require kitchens and bathrooms to have specially grounded outlets, called **ground fault interrupters (GFI)**, which turn off power at the outlet instantly if the device or appliance plugged into it gets wet, shorts out, or malfunctions
- Power consumption is measured in **watts** or kilowatts
- Two kinds of circuit protectors to reduce risk from overloading a wire's capacity:
    - **Circuit breaker** – device usually located inside the electrical breaker panel or circuit breaker box, designed to break its electrical connection should an overload occur
    - **Fuses** – protective devices for a wiring system that contain a wire designed to melt and open the circuit when overheating occurs

Wiring Materials

Aluminum and **copper** are common wiring materials. Aluminum wire is less expensive than copper wire and weighs less. Copper conducts better than aluminum and is easy to bend. Other types of wiring include:

- **BX cable** – a type of armored cable, which is a grouping of wires wrapped in a metallic covering
- **Romex** – cable wrapped in plastic that contains two or more conductors; is relatively easy to install and cost effective
- **Conduit** – electric wiring enclosed in a metal or plastic pipe; can be flexible or rigid
- **Greenfield** – a type of flexible conduit; not designed to be used in wet areas

National Electric Code

The National Electric Code® (NEC®) provides for the safe installation of electrical equipment and wiring. As of 1962, the NEC® required that new 120-volt household receptacle outlets for general purpose use be both grounded and polarized.

- A **grounded circuit** is connected to the ground for safety, limiting voltage buildup and providing an alternate route for electrical current flow

- **Polarized outlets** have one slot larger than the other so items can be plugged in only one way. One side is hot (or live), the other side is neutral. By limiting the path of the electrical current, the risk of electrocution is reduced

Mandated Warranties And Guarantees

New York General Business Law 36-A and B provides regulations that home improvement contractors must follow and warranties that home builders must extend to buyers.

Home Improvement

A few important points of this law indicate that home improvement contracts exceeding $500 should contain the following:

- The approximate dates when the work will begin and end and a description of the work to be performed

- A notice to the owner from the contractor about mechanic's liens

- A schedule of progress payment, if needed

- A notice to the owner that the owner has until midnight of the third business day after the contract has been signed to cancel the contract

The General Business Law 36-A Home Improvement also provides information on penalty for fraud, including:

- An owner who signed a contract with fraudulent terms or statements may sue a contractor for a penalty of $500 plus attorney's fees, in addition to other damages

- Contractors who do not deposit funds into an escrow account (or provide a bond of contract of indemnity or irrevocable letter of credit) will be subject to a civil penalty not to exceed $250 per violation or 5 percent of the contract price (the total penalty will not exceed $2,500 per contract)

New Home Construction

New York's General Business Law 36-B provides information on laws governing a new home. The warranties include:

- One year for workmanship

- Two years for plumbing, heating, electrical, cooling, and ventilation systems

- Six years for material defects

NOTE: New York State law requires the installation of a functioning smoke detector and carbon monoxide detector in all one- and two-family residential properties as well as residential condominiums and cooperatives.

QUIZ

1. *Standard electric service in New York requires a minimum of how many amps for new construction?*
    A. 50
    B. 150
    C. 200
    D. 400

2. *Vertical wood beams that serve to frame a structure are called*
    A. joists.
    B. lally columns.
    C. rafters.
    D. studs.

3. *_____ is used to measure the insulating value or resistance to heat flow through a material or object.*
    A. BTU
    B. CFM
    C. R-Factor
    D. R-Value

4. *The rate at which water moves through soil is called*
    A. condensation rate.
    B. flow rate.
    C. percolation rate.
    D. soil density rate.

5. *After all of the inspections have been made and a property has been deemed fit, what is issued to builders?*
    A. builder's certificate
    B. certificate of occupancy
    C. permit
    D. specification

6. *The common measurement of heating capacity is the _____, or the amount of heat needed to raise the temperature of one pound of water by one degree Fahrenheit.*
    A. amperage
    B. BTU
    C. CFM
    D. voltage

7. *In order to provide enough water to an average household, wells are expected to produce at least*
    A. 5 gallons of water per minute.
    B. 5 gallons of water per hour.
    C. 10 gallons of water per minute.
    D. 10 gallons of water per hour.

8. *What is the minimum warranty required by law for workmanship of the builder?*
    A. 1 year
    B. 3 years
    C. 6 years
    D. 12 years

9. *Home improvement laws apply when the*
    A. goods and services exceed $500.
    B. goods and services exceed $1,000.
    C. home improvement contractor is licensed.
    D. homeowner and contractor sign an agreement.

10. *In construction, the right of rescission law allows the homeowner*
    A. three days to back out of the contract.
    B. to bring suit for unsatisfactory work.
    C. to file a mechanic's lien against the contractor.
    D. to refinance his loan in order to pay for the work.

Environmental Issues and Property Concerns

13

Key Terms

Asbestos Fibrous material derived from a naturally occurring group of minerals commonly used in insulation. Asbestos fibers released into the air are toxic.

Carbon Monoxide (CO) Colorless, odorless gas that is a natural byproduct of fuel combustion.

Chlorofluorocarbons (CFCs) Chemical compounds containing chlorine, fluorine, and carbon atoms. Sold under the trademarked name of Freon for many years and used as a coolant in refrigerators, air conditioners, and dehumidifiers. Now known to contribute to the depletion of the ozone.

Due Diligence Investigation to discover facts or liabilities about a property prior to its purchase.

Electromagnetic Fields (EMFs) Invisible fields produced by electrically charged objects.

Environmental Hazard A situation that exists with potential for harm to persons or property from conditions that exist outside or within a property.

Environmental Impact Statement (EIS) Study required by the National Environmental Policy Act for all federal and federally related projects, which details a development project's impact on energy use, sewage systems, drainage, water facilities, schools, and other environmental, economic, and social areas.

External Environmental Hazards Concerns that exist outside the boundaries of a property, which can have a significant impact on its value.

External Obsolescence Any influence that falls outside the actual property site and negatively affects a property's value.

Freon The brand name for the chemical compound CFC used as a coolant in refrigerators, air conditioners, and dehumidifiers; now known as a contributor to the depletion of the ozone.

Friable Characteristic of asbestos in which it can crumble easily or become powdery when manipulated by hand, releasing toxic particles into the air.

Groundwater Naturally occurring water found in subterranean crevices or spaces.

High-tension Power Lines Large transmission cables carrying electrical energy.

Internal Environmental Hazards An environmental hazard that occurs within a property.

(continued on next page)

Environmental Law

The **Environmental Protection Agency (EPA)** was founded in December 1970 as an independent agency, it is responsible for creating and enforcing environmental protection standards, and providing support and research on environmental issues.

Federal Environmental Protection Laws

- **National Environmental Policy Act (NEPA)** – promotes methods to prevent or eliminate damage to the environment and educate the public of the importance of our natural resources and ecological system
  - NEPA requires an **environmental impact statement** (EIS)
- **Clean Air Act (CAA)** – requires the EPA to develop air quality standards for existing pollutants and to establish air standards for new pollution sources
  - States are required to prepare a state implementation plan (SIP)
- **Clean Water Act (CWA)** – requires that the EPA set national water quality standards and penalties for water pollution violations
- **Comprehensive Environmental Response, Compensation, and Liability Act (CERCLA)** – creates requirements for closed or abandoned waste sites, and establishes taxes and fines that provide money for the Superfund
  - Two types of response actions authorized: short-term and long-term
  - Liability for contaminated property must be transferred to new owners, forcing potential buyers and lenders to conduct **due diligence** (an environmental assessment, which consists of four phases, of the property to determine potential liability)

Key Terms - continued

Methamphetamine An illegal, man-made drug that is extremely addictive. Residues left in a residence from the manufacturing process can be toxic.

Mold A fungus that can release toxins into the environment causing various levels of allergic reaction in some people.

Mycotoxin A toxic substance produced by some molds.

Nuisance Interference with the right of quiet enjoyment of property.

Radon Gas A naturally occurring radioactive gas that emanates from rocks, soil, and water because of the decay of uranium.

Residential Lead-based Paint Hazard Reduction Act Requires sellers and landlords to disclose known lead paint hazards for homes built before 1978.

Sick Building Syndrome When poor air quality in a building causes symptoms of headache, fatigue, nausea, sore throat, nose and eye irritation, etc., among its occupants.

Stachybotrys A type of mold known as "black mold" that produces mycotoxins.

Stigmatized Property Properties that do not have any physical defects but have become less marketable because they were the scene of a crime, suicide, or other undesirable event.

Transformers Transfer power from one circuit to another.

Underground Storage Tanks (USTs) Holding tanks that can used to store chemicals, fuels, toxic wastes, and other substances. Regulated by the EPA.

Urea-Formaldehyde A clear chemical that is used in manufacturing including particle board, plywood paneling, carpeting, and insulation.

Urea-Formaldehyde Foam Insulation (UFFI) A type of housing insulation used in the 1970's. It was banned because of the formaldehyde fumes it released that caused a myriad of symptoms among homeowners who had it.

Wetlands Ecosystems where the land is permeated with water, which either lies on or near the surface of the land.

- **Superfund Amendments and Reauthorization Act (SARA)** – amended CERCLA and increased the monetary size of the Superfund
- **The Resource Conservation and Recovery Act (RCRA)** – gave EPA the authority to control hazardous waste throughout its entire life cycle (generation, transportation, treatment, storage, and disposal)

State Environmental Protection Laws

- **Safe Drinking Water Act (SDWA)** – established by the EPA and sets standards for water intended for human consumption. The New York State Department of Health (NYSDOH) regulates drinking water in New York State and sets standards for private water supplies and septic systems
- Installation and approval of individual residential on-site wastewater treatment systems in New York are controlled by the following:
  - New York State Department of Health (NYSDOH) for systems of less than 1,000 gallons per day
  - New York State Department of Environmental Conservation (NYSDEC) for systems of 1,000 gallons or more per day
- **New York Environmental Law** – when a person, entity, or government agency wants to initiate a project in New York State, the project must undergo an environmental impact assessment. The process for review is directed by the **State Environmental Quality Review Act (SEQRA)** that mandates local governments consider the impact on the environment, as well as the social and economic benefits, when determining whether to proceed. Some minor construction projects do not require an assessment

Environmental Concerns

- **Wetlands.** Ecosystems where the land is permeated with water, which either lies on or near the surface. They provide a habitat for aquatic plants and wildlife, act as a flood barrier, and naturally filter water.
  - In New York State, a protected wetland must cover an area of at least **12.4 acres** or have unusual **significant importance**. To conform to the standards set by the Freshwater Wetlands Act, the NYSDEC maintains maps showing all protected wetlands. These maps may be obtained at the NYSDEC regional office and other local government offices.
  - NYSDEC has established the **Freshwater Wetlands Act** and **Statewide Minimum Land-Use Regulations for Freshwater Wetlands**.
- **Nuisance.** Anything that interferes with right of quiet enjoyment (e.g., airport noise, farm stench); permanent nuisance can be external obsolescence
- **Environmental hazards.** Situations of potential harm to persons or property from conditions that exist in property or external to it; examples of **external hazards** are toxic waste dumps, nuclear power plants, and high-tension power lines
- **Internal environmental hazards.** Hazard within a property, can be as dangerous or more dangerous than external hazards
- **Stigmatized property.** Property that people think is undesirable because of a past event or because of its proximity to an undesirable situation; perception of risk may persist among buyers, even after the danger is removed
- **Pesticides.** Application limited to those who are licensed by the NYSDEC

Man-Made Hazards

- **Asbestos.** A fibrous heat-resistant material once used as insulation.

  - *Issues:* Airborne asbestos particles breathed into a person's lungs can cause asbestosis, mesothelioma, and lung and other cancers; debate over whether it is best to remove or leave since removal can cause more contamination if done improperly; removal is expensive and requires a licensed contractor.

  - *Remedies:* If asbestos is loose or coming off, it needs to be encapsulated, enclosed, or removed, which is regulated by the **New York State Department of Labor** (NYSDOL).

- **Carbon monoxide.** A natural byproduct of fuel combustion; it's a colorless, odorless gas that is released as fuel sources are broken down to produce heat.

  - *Issues:* Overexposure to CO can cause dizziness, nausea, and death; difficult to detect and can easily be absorbed into the body.

  - *Remedies:* The most effective method to keep track of CO is to use a CO detector. **In New York, CO detectors, as well as smoke detectors, are required by law in all homes and rental properties.** All appliances that produce CO and ventilation should routinely be checked to ensure nothing is malfunctioning.

- **Chlorofluorocarbons (CFCs).** Chemical compounds containing chlorine, fluorine, and carbon atoms; used as a coolant in refrigerators, air conditioners, dehumidifiers, Styrofoam, aerosols, and cleaning agents.

  - *Issues:* Detrimental to the earth's atmosphere.

  - *Remedies*: Proper disposal procedures must be followed for old appliances containing these compounds and owners must maintain equipment to prevent coolant leaks.

  - *Note*: Hydrofluorocarbons (HFCs) may be used in current refrigerant/cooling systems and are less of a threat to the atmosphere since they do not contain chlorine.

- **Electromagnetic fields (EMFs).** Invisible fields creating electrically charged objects.

  - *Issues:* High-tension power lines, transformers, and secondary distribution lines create large electromagnetic fields; suspected cause of hormonal changes, cancer, and abnormalities in behavior.

  - *Remedies:* Evidence is controversial and no remedies have been established.

- **Lead.** A bluish-white metal added to exterior and interior paint as a drying agent and for pigmentation. Also used in pipes and solder in plumbing systems in homes and businesses.

  - *Issues:* Digesting or inhaling lead or lead dust causes neurological disorders and learning disabilities; can contaminate soil; corroded lead water pipes can result in dangerous levels of lead in the water.

  - *Law:* Residential Lead-based Paint Hazard Reduction Act of 1992, or Title X.

  - *Requirements:* For houses built before 1978, lead paint brochure must be given to buyers and tenants; known lead paint hazards must be disclosed; buyers must be given time to conduct lead tests (usually a 10-day period) if they desire.

  - *Penalty for noncompliance*: Up to $10,000

- **Methamphetamine.** Illegal, man-made drug that is extremely addictive. It can be powder or chunks. It can be swallowed, snorted, smoked, or injected. The street names include speed, meth, chalk, glass, crank, ice, and crystal.

  - *Issues:* Residue from meth lab permeates throughout property, contaminating floors, ceiling, walls, carpeting, vents, blinds, and personal property; toxic by-products can contaminate water supply and soil; health problems include serious respiratory problems, burning in the hands and feet, nausea, headaches, liver damage, and death; currently, there are no federal disclosure laws, but some states are passing laws.

  - *Remedies:* House must be professionally cleaned to remove residue and to keep new owners/tenants from getting sick.

- **Urea-formaldehyde.** A clear chemical used in adhesive for household materials (particleboard, plywood paneling, carpeting, ceiling tiles) and blown-in foam insulation.

  - *Issues:* When first installed, insulation releases toxic fumes and high concentrations of formaldehyde; health risks include shortness of breath, wheezing, asthma, and skin and eye irritation; suspected to cause cancer.

  - *Remedies:* Use safe alternatives.

- **Uncapped gas wells.** In 2007, Section 242 of the Real Property Law was amended to require sellers to inform buyers prior to a sale of the existence of any uncapped natural gas wells of which the seller has actual knowledge.

- **Polychlorinated biphenyls (PCBs).** Colorless, odorless, organic compounds used as cooling and insulating agents for transformers and capacitors; found in many other products.

  - *Issues:* Contaminate soil and runoff leaches into streams and rivers. Are carcinogens; suspected to affect the immune, reproductive, nervous, and endocrine systems.

  - *Remedies:* Public water suppliers must regularly test for PCB levels. PCBs can be destroyed physically by incineration, irradiation, ultrasound, and microorganisms.

- **Poor air quality.** Can create problems and discomfort for those who must spend time inside.

  - Issues: Can cause Legionnaires Disease and sick building syndrome.

  - Remedies: Improve airflow throughout a structure.

- **Underground storage tanks.** Buried tanks that store heating oil, gasoline, chemicals, and hazardous waste.

  - *Issues:* Can corrode, spill, leak, and overfill, contaminating soil and water supplies; emit toxic substances.

  - *Remedies:* Install leak detection, catch basins, and automatic shut-offs; some tanks exempt.

Naturally Occurring Hazards

Environmental concerns are not necessarily man-made. They can also be found in nature. Common naturally occurring internal hazards include:

- **Mold.** Fungus that has many varieties; dangerous mold is black mold (stachybotrys), a greenish-black mold that grows on materials with high cellulose content.

- *Issues:* Produces allergens, which can trigger allergic reactions (wheezing, eye and skin irritation, stuffy nose, asthma attacks), rashes, and immune system problems (affecting the lymphoid tissue and bone marrow); evidence controversial; litigation is including sellers, brokers, management companies, and agents.
    - *Remedies:* Repair moisture problems and remove mold.
- **Pests.** Bees, termites, carpenter ants, rodents, etc.
    - *Issues:* Can cause major physical damage to a property.
    - *Remedies:* Advise clients to contact a reputable termite or pest control professional. Counsel sellers to dispose of problems before marketing the home.
- **Radon gas.** A naturally occurring, odorless, colorless, and tasteless radioactive gas that emanates from rocks.
    - *Issues:* Can build up to dangerous level in home due to inadequate ventilation; causes cancer and other health issues.
    - *Remedies:* Readings of 4 picoCuries/liter or more generally trigger some sort of remediation: sealing cracks; installing fan or blower to bring in fresh air and keep air moving through the house.
- **Ground Water Contamination.** Water found in subterranean crevices or spaces. New York does require the seller to disclose the source of the water supply (whether a well, private, or municipal).
    - *Issues:* Dumping of toxic waste into soil, faulty septic tanks, leaky underground storage tanks, and toxic surface spills can contaminate ground water; pollution of private wells and public water systems.
    - *Remedies:* Enforce and monitor pollutant sources to stop contamination.

Liability

Real estate agents must take steps to protect themselves. They need to know the current laws and keep up-to-date on new laws and trends. It is wise for agents to be informed on environmental issues and to know what to look for as they walk through homes. They need to remind sellers to be honest on disclosure forms. Improper disclosure can result in trouble for everyone.

 Note: As of August, 2010, New York City landlords must let prospective tenants know in writing if an apartment has suffered a bedbug infestation within the past year, or if there has been a bedbug problem in the building during that time. The proper form is the DBB-N - Owner's Notice to Tenant Disclosure of Bedbug Infestation History.

QUIZ

1. **Which federal environmental law, known as the Superfund, creates requirements for closed and abandoned waste sites?**
   A. CAA
   B. CERCLA
   C. SDWA
   D. SARA

2. **Based on the requirements for the Residential Lead-Based Paint Hazard Reduction Act, which statement is FALSE?**
   A. A seller must pay for a lead-based test if the buyer requests it.
   B. Buyers must be given time to conduct lead-based tests; this is usually 10 days.
   C. Sellers must disclose any known lead-based paint hazard.
   D. Sellers must present any prospective buyer with a pamphlet prior to accepting a contract.

3. **Which statement about asbestos is TRUE?**
   A. It can contaminate a house further when removed improperly since the airborne particles are the issue.
   B. It is dangerous only when it is wet and thus it should be encapsulated in waterproof material.
   C. It is inexpensive to remove.
   D. It is required to be removed if found in a residential property.

4. **Radon gas**
   A. can present a problem if high concentrations are found, since it indicates the presence of a toxic uranium dump close to the property.
   B. can present a problem indoors if allowed to build up to dangerous levels.
   C. is a man-made waste by-product.
   D. makes a house worthless because it must be condemned by the EPA.

5. **Wetlands are protected under what federal act?**
   A. Clean Water Act
   B. Federal Wetlands Protection and Wildlife Act
   C. SARA
   D. U.S. Army Corps Act

6. **What can homeowners do for protection against carbon monoxide (CO) poisoning?**
   A. Since CO is a radioactive gas emitted from rock, they need to make sure there is adequate ventilation.
   B. They should remove all appliances that emit CO.
   C. They should routinely clean their houses since CO can leave a residue that is toxic.
   D. They should routinely have furnaces and other heat-producing appliances checked.

7. **If a licensee is aware of an insect infestation in a home she is going to list, she should**
   A. disclose the information to potential buyers and try to negotiate around the problem.
   B. hire an exterminator, keep the records, and disclose the information to potential buyers.
   C. keep quiet until the transaction is closed.
   D. put out bait and not mention the problem to anyone.

8. **Which statement about mold is FALSE?**
   A. Not all molds are toxic.
   B. Research on the health effects of mold is inconclusive and controversial.
   C. Some insurance companies have stopped offering homeowners insurance in some states because of their mold laws.
   D. The federal government has set standards for mold contamination and seller disclosure.

9. **The State of New York requires which of these items to be placed in all one- or two-family homes and condominiums?**
   A. radon detectors
   B. records from termite inspections
   C. lead-based paint property disclosure forms
   D. smoke detectors and carbon monoxide detectors

10. **Which statement about urea formaldehyde is TRUE?**
    A. The EPA banned urea formaldehyde foam insulation usage in homes.
    B. The EPA regulates emission from urea formaldehyde foam insulation, and any homeowner with unacceptable levels in the home must have it removed.
    C. Urea formaldehyde foam insulation installed in the 1970s would most likely not pose any health risk now.
    D. Urea formaldehyde foam insulation was banned because it can be used to create methamphetamine.

Human Rights & Fair Housing

Key Terms

Americans with Disabilities Act (ADA) Civil rights law that prohibits discrimination based on disability; creates consistent and enforceable standards regarding discrimination based on disability.

Blockbusting Illegal practice of inducing owners to sell their homes (often at a deflated price) by suggesting the ethnic or racial composition of the neighborhood is changing, with the implication that property values will decline as a result. *Also called*: **Panic Selling** or **Panic Peddling**.

Cease-and-Desist Zone Certain areas designated by the New York Department of State in which property owners can file notice indicating they do not want to sell, lease, or list their property.

Civil Rights Act of 1866 The first major legislation to directly affect equal rights to ownership of real property.

Department of Housing and Urban Development (HUD) The government agency charged with overseeing housing related issues and projects. Among other things, HUD sets minimum building standards for housing and is responsible for enforcing the federal Fair Housing Act.

Disability A physical or mental impairment that substantially limits or curtails one or more major life activity.

Discrimination Treating people unequally because of their race, religion, sex, national origin, age, or some other characteristic of a protected class.

Fair Housing Act of 1968 Common name for Title VIII of the Civil Rights Act of 1968.

Familial Status A protected group under the federal Fair Housing Act and New York State law, making it illegal to discriminate against a person because she is the parent or guardian of a child less than 18 years of age.

Filtering Down When one practice has negative residual effects. *See*: Redlining, Blockbusting.

New York State Human Rights Law Extends protected classes beyond those covered in the Fair Housing Act to include, age, creed, marital status, military status, and sexual orientation.

Non-solicitation Order Prohibits the solicitation of residential property listings, and applies to all real estate brokers and agents; ruled unconstitutional by the U.S. Court of Appeals.

Public Accommodation Title III of the Americans with Disabilities Act requiring all public and commercial facilities are100% accessible to the disabled.

(continued on next page)

Civil Rights Act of 1866

- First major legislation to directly affect equal rights to ownership of personal and real property, and to guarantee equal housing opportunities.
- Prohibited **racial** discrimination in the sale or rental of all real or personal property and gave all citizens the same rights with regard to property.
- This definition was later extended to include **color.**
- **There are no exceptions to the Civil Rights Act of 1866.**

Related Supreme Court Decisions

- *Plessy v. Ferguson (1896).* The Court ruled that separate but equal was legally acceptable; as long as separate housing or facilities for African-Americans and whites were deemed equal, they were legal.
- *Brown v. Board of Education (1954).* The Court reversed the ruling on *Plessy v. Ferguson*; finding that separate facilities were, by nature, unequal; the Board of Education was in Topeka, Kansas.
- *Jones v. Alfred H. Mayer Co. (1968).* In the ruling, the court held the Civil Rights Act of 1866 was applied, to prohibit any racially based discrimination in housing, private or public, in the sale of and rental of property.

Federal Fair Housing Act of 1968

- Also referred to as Title VIII of the Civil Rights Act of 1968.
- Prohibits discrimination in advertising, real estate brokerage, lending, and some other services associated with residential transactions based on membership in protected class:
  - Race
  - Color
  - National origin
  - Religion
  - Sex
  - Disability added in 1988 amendment to include any physical or mental impairment that substantially limits or curtails one or more major life activities; does not cover those addicted to illegal substances
  - Familial status added in 1988 amendment to include parent or guardian with custody of a child under 18 years old, pregnant women or any person in the process of obtaining legal custody of a child under the age of 18

Key Terms - continued

Reasonable Accommodation Make reasonable accommodations in rules, policies, practices, or services, if necessary, for the disabled person to use the housing on an equal basis with non-disabled persons.

Redlining When a lender refuses to make loans secured by property in a certain neighborhood because of the racial or ethnic composition of the neighborhood.

Steering Channeling prospective buyers or tenants to particular neighborhoods based on their race, religion, national origin, or ancestry.

Testers Person who poses as a customer or client attempting to secure real estate services to ensure fair housing is practiced. *Also called:* **Checker.**

Prohibited Acts

- Refusing to rent or sell residential property after receiving a good faith offer
- Refusing to negotiate for the sale or rental of residential property
- Taking any action that would otherwise make residential property unavailable or deny it to any person (this general clause prohibits steering, redlining, etc.)
- Discriminating in the terms or conditions of any sale or rental of residential property or in providing any services or facilities in connection with such property
- Using discriminatory advertising or any other notice that indicates a limitation or preference or intent to make any limitation, preference, or discrimination
- Making any representation that property is *not* available for inspection, sale, or rent when it is, in fact, available
- Inducing or attempting to induce, for profit, any person to sell or rent property based on representations made regarding entry into the neighborhood of persons of a particular race, color, religion, sex, or national origin (blockbusting; also called panic selling or panic peddling)
- Discriminating against anyone by a commercial lender in making a loan for buying, building, repairing, improving, or maintaining a dwelling or in the terms of such financing (includes redlining)
- Denying access to a multiple listing service or any similar real estate brokers' organization, or discriminating in terms or conditions for access to the organization
- Coercing, intimidating, threatening, or interfering with anyone because of his or her enjoyment, attempt to enjoy, or encouragement and assistance to others in their enjoyment of the rights granted by the federal Fair Housing Act

Exemptions

Assuming no real estate licensee is involved, the following may be exempt from the provisions of the Fair Housing Act:

- Single-family homes sold or rented by a private owner (with some restrictions)
- Room/unit rentals with no more than four units per dwelling
- Religious and non-profit organizations and private clubs
- Housing for older persons under some circumstances (e.g., 100% of residents are 62 or older)

These exemptions **never** apply to discrimination based on race or color.

Illegal Practices

These practices are illegal if based on protected classes:

- **Steering** – channeling prospective buyers or renters to or away from specific neighborhoods based on their race, religion, national origin, or other protected class to maintain or change the character of a neighborhood
- **Redlining** – discriminating against anyone by a commercial lender in making a loan or buying, building, repairing, improving, or maintaining a dwelling, or in terms of such financing
- **Blockbusting** – inducing or attempting to induce, for profit, any person to sell or rent property based on representations made regarding entry into the

neighborhood of persons of a particular race, color, religion, sex, or national origin (prohibited under federal and state law)

Reasonable Accommodations

If a tenant or someone associated with them has a disability, under the federal Fair Housing Act, the housing provider may *not* discriminate and must:

- Make *reasonable accommodations* in rules, policies, practices, or services, if necessary, for the disabled person to use the housing on an equal basis with non-disabled persons.

- Allow the tenant to make *reasonable* modifications to a dwelling or common use areas, at the tenant's expense, which would permit them to fully use the housing. Where reasonable, the housing provider can require the tenant to restore the property to its original condition upon moving.

Disclosure

Agents must provide written information to the client outlining the fair housing statement. All advertising of residential real estate for sale or rent and for real estate financing should contain a fair housing logo, statement, or slogan.

The Department of Housing and Urban Development (HUD)

- The federal Fair Housing Act is administered and enforced by HUD, through the Office of Fair Housing and Equal Opportunity (FHEO)
- HUD offers a variety of programs, including funding and grants to public and private organizations as well as state and local governments
- Through these programs, local agencies work with HUD to prevent, enforce, and eliminate discriminatory housing practices

Enforcement Authority

- HUD utilizes **testers** (agents posing as potential buyers or renters) to detect and combat discrimination of protected classes
- Agencies are encouraged to implement voluntary self-testing to check for compliance within their organizations

Filing a Complaint

- Fair housing complaints may be reported and investigated by HUD
- In states where there's a state fair housing law substantially equivalent to the federal law, HUD may refer complaints to the state or local agency that has similar responsibilities
- An individual can file a civil lawsuit in federal district court within one year of the incident
- The U.S. Attorney General may also bring a civil suit in federal district court
- When HUD is handling a dispute, if there is a violation, HUD will try to settle the dispute using negotiation and conciliation
- If HUD is unable to settle the dispute, the parties involved are referred to one of HUD's administrative law judges
- Almost anyone involved in a real estate transaction can be held liable for fair housing violations

Remedies

If the administrative law judge rules in favor of the complainant, the judge can:

- Issue an injunction against the respondent
- Award compensatory damages to the complainant
- Award punitive damages to the complainant not exceeding $10,000
- Impose civil penalties which include payment of monetary damages
- Order the respondent to pay the complainant's attorney's fees

Criminal Penalties

It is a felony to violate fair housing laws and obvious violators will be prosecuted and, if found guilty, a person could be sentenced to prison, pay fines, or both.

Treat all equally, let clients direct you, and keep good documentation to protect yourself from fair housing violations.

Americans with Disabilities Act

The **American with Disabilities Act (ADA)** gives civil rights protection to individuals with disabilities. It guarantees equal opportunity for individuals with disabilities in public accommodations, employment, transportation, state and local governments, and telecommunications. The greatest impact of the ADA may be in the area of **public accommodations**, which are privately owned or leased facilities such as restaurants, schools, theaters, hotels, museums, stores, offices, etc.

ADA Compliance

Existing buildings are required to comply based on what is easily accomplished without much difficulty or expense. This is also known as reasonable accommodation and includes such things as installing grab bars in showers, providing handicap parking spaces in parking lots, and widening doorways and hallways.

Penalties for Non-Compliance

The ADA prefers to work with entities toward compliance and utilizes alternative means of dispute resolution before enforcing penalties. In cases where resolution is not achievable, cases may be filed through state and federal courts. It is up to the individual to pursue legal enforcement of the ADA. Legal enforcement can include equitable relief, monetary damages, and civil action.

New York Human Rights Law

The **Division of Human Rights (DHR)** enforces the **New York State Human Rights Law**, which extends protected classes beyond those covered in the Fair Housing Act to include:

- Age (18 or older)
- Marital status
- Military status (United States or New York State)
- Sexual orientation

New York State Exceptions

Some exceptions to fair housing discrimination that are permitted under federal law may *not* be allowed under state civil rights laws. New York State Human Rights Law recognizes these exceptions:

* Rental of a room in an owner-occupied dwelling

* Rental of a unit in two-family owner-occupied dwelling

* Restrictions based on sex when all rooms in a housing accommodation are limited to those of the same sex (as in a dormitory)

* Restrictions based on age when all housing units are intended for occupancy by persons age 55 or older (and their spouses)

As with the federal laws, a real estate licensee is *never exempt* from following New York's Human Rights Law when involved in a real estate transaction either through employment or ownership. And, of course, **racial discrimination is never exempt**.

SONDA

New York State's Sexual Orientation Non-Discrimination Act (SONDA) prohibits discrimination on the basis of **actual or perceived sexual orientation** in employment, housing, public accommodations, education, credit, and the exercise of civil rights. SONDA defines sexual orientation as "heterosexuality, homosexuality, bisexuality, or asexuality, whether actual or perceived."

Cease-And-Desist Zones

To combat blockbusting, the Secretary of State has the authority to designate certain geographic areas as **cease-and-desist zones**, once it's determined that an area has been subjected to excessive illegal solicitation. Once property owners register on the cease-and-desist list, brokers and salespersons are prohibited from soliciting the property owner for listings via letters, phone calls, visits, flyers, etc. Violation of the cease-and-desist order is considered an act of untrustworthiness or incompetence on the part of the licensee and could result in disciplinary action.

New York City Human Rights Law

The New York City Human Rights Law, under the authority of the **New York City Commission on Human Rights**, is one of the most comprehensive civil rights laws in the country. It extends the definition of protected classes to include:

* Citizenship status

* Partnership status

* Lawful occupation and lawful source of income

SUMMARY

Licensees have an obligation to know and follow federal, state, and local fair housing and human rights laws. They must provide **equal service** to all, keep good records of their dealings with clients and customers, and **disclose** fair housing laws to their clients. When a real estate agent does not separate himself from a client's discriminatory behavior, the consequences can be serious for the agent *and* his broker.

Protected Classes

	Federally Protected Classes	State Protected Classes	NYC Protected Classes
Race	✓	✓	✓
Color	✓	✓	✓
Religion/Creed	✓	✓	✓
National Origin	✓	✓	✓
Familial Status	✓	✓	✓
Disability	✓	✓	✓
Gender	✓	✓	✓
Marital Status		✓	✓
Sexual Orientation		✓	✓
Age		✓	✓
Military Status		✓	✓
Citizenship Status			✓
Partnership Status			✓
Lawful Occupation/ Source of Income			✓

QUIZ

1. **Which of the following unlawful practices is also known as panic selling?**
   A. blockbusting
   B. coercion
   C. redlining
   D. steering

2. **Which was the first major legislation to directly affect equal rights to ownership of real property?**
   A. Americans with Disabilities Act
   B. Civil Rights Act
   C. The Emancipation Proclamation
   D. Fair Housing Act

3. **Which protected class was added to the federal Fair Housing Act by amendment in 1988?**
   A. color
   B. familial status
   C. gender
   D. religion

4. **Who would NOT be considered a disabled person as defined by the federal Fair Housing Act?**
   A. an amputee who must use a wheelchair
   B. a child with AIDS
   C. a man with mental illness who takes anti-psychotic drugs
   D. a woman addicted to methamphetamine

5. **A disabled individual applies to rent an apartment and states the property would need to be made handicapped accessible. Which action would NOT be lawful in this situation?**
   A. The landlord makes the renovations, but requires the tenant to pay the actual cost of the materials.
   B. The landlord makes the renovations to the property at the landlord's expense.
   C. The landlord refuses to allow the individual to make the renovations to the apartment.
   D. The landlord requires the tenant to make the renovations at the tenant's own expense and requires the tenant to return the property to its original condition at the end of tenancy.

6. **Which of the following is NOT a protected class according to the federal Fair Housing Act?**
   A. physical disability
   B. national origin
   C. religion
   D. sexual orientation

7. **An owner of an apartment complex may deny housing to children if**
   A. 80% of residents are over 62 years of age.
   B. 80% of the residents are over 65 years of age.
   C. 100% of the residents are over 62 years of age.
   D. 100% of the residents are over 65 years of age.

8. **Which is an example of steering?**
   A. Agent Tom tells homeowners that their property values will drop when a Puerto Rican family moves in.
   B. Mortgage banker Brad refuses to make loans for a particular inner city neighborhood.
   C. Property manager Amy suggests Jake would be happier in a more diverse building.
   D. Seller Oscar tells his listing agent to find only Caucasian buyer prospects.

9. **Todd, a real estate salesperson, has clients coming in from out of town. He is aware that his clients are from Mexico, so he prospects homes from the MLS in predominantly Hispanic areas. Since these areas were not selected at the clients' request, Todd will commit which violation if he shows just these particular homes?**
   A. diverting
   B. blockbusting
   C. redlining
   D. steering

10. **Who is NOT a member of a protected class according to New York State Human Rights Law?**
    A. Allison, who has a permit to breed snakes
    B. Eric and Jon, a gay couple
    C. Jack, a member of the National Guard
    D. Louann and Josh, an unmarried couple

Municipal Agencies

15

Key Terms

Architectural Review Board Determines the effects a proposed building or other structure, or alteration of an existing structure, will have on the desirability, property values, and development of surrounding areas.

Building Department Protects a municipality's residents by seeing that code restrictions are followed, and construction and renovation are done by licensed professionals.

City Council Municipal legislative body responsible for public policy including approving budgets, and passing laws, ordinances, and resolutions.

Conservation Advisory Council Studies matters affecting the environment, preservation, development, and use of a city's natural and physical features and conditions regarding ecologic integrity, aesthetic appeal, and quality.

County Health Department A human service and regulatory agency responsible for public health programs.

Historic Preservation Office Identifies, evaluates, preserves, and revitalizes any given city's historic, archaeological, and cultural resources.

Landmarks Preservation Commission (LPC) The New York City agency responsible for identifying and designating the city's landmarks.

Municipal Engineer's Office The municipal agency responsible for the planning, design, and construction of New York's public works facilities and projects.

Planning Board Holds public hearings, investigates solutions for the planning issues at hand, and makes recommendations to the appropriate legislative authority. In New York City, the planning board and the zoning board are one entity known as the Board of Standards and Appeals.

Planning Department An office of jurisdiction with employees who carry out administrative functions.

Real Estate Tax An annual tax levied on the value of real property. *Also called*: **Real Property Tax** or **General Real Estate Tax.**

Receiver of Taxes Municipal official responsible for managing the day-to-day operations of the Office of Receiver of Taxes, which collects local taxes. Other functions include tax billing and collection, banking, record maintenance, mail, and accounting functions.

(continued on next page)

Municipal Agencies

Real estate professionals need to have an understanding of the roles and responsibilities of their **local** municipal agencies.

- **City councils** typically set policies, approve budgets, and pass ordinances and resolutions that affect everything from land use to campaign finance. City councils usually partner with the mayor in governing the city. City council members are elected by constituents in the areas they serve for terms of varying lengths.

- In some areas of New York, a **village board of trustees** governs the village instead of a city council. The entities are similar in the fact that they both consist of elected officials whose main purpose is to the serve the constituents who elected them. A board of trustees usually includes a mayor, village administrator, or town supervisor, as well as several trustees. Trustees are responsible for the village's budget, programming, land use regulations, and services.

- In New York State, **real property tax** is based on the assessed value of real property. Cities, counties, villages, towns, school districts, and special districts all raise money through real property taxes. Money earned from taxes fund schools, police and fire protection, road maintenance, and other services enjoyed by residents. Property taxes are administered locally rather than by the state. Tax rates are determined by tax levies. In order to settle on a tax levy, a local budget must be adopted. Taxes are not the same as property assessments.

- Municipal **planning boards** hold public hearings, investigate solutions for planning issues at hand, and make recommendations to appropriate legislative bodies. Planning board members are appointed by the mayor, trustees, or equivalent, for terms of varying lengths. Planning board members are involved in creating a capital budget, creating and controlling the city's comprehensive plan, regulating plat, density, street, and traffic patterns, regulating subdivision development, reviewing site plans, and specific zoning actions.

- **Planning departments** focus on the day-to-day operations of a municipality. The overall mission of planning boards and planning departments is the same, which is to maintain and enhance the communities in which they serve through the organized and deliberate planning of how land is used.

- The **zoning board of appeals** hears and decides requests for variances and special use permits. Interpreting zoning laws is also a function of the zoning board of appeals. New York State statutes specifically give zoning boards of appeals the power to hear appeals seeking interpretations of provisions of local zoning ordinances.

- A local **architectural review board** determines the effects a proposed building or other structure, or alteration of an existing structure, will have on the desirability, property values, and development of surrounding areas. The purpose of local architectural review boards is to conserve the value of property and to encourage the most appropriate use of land within the community.

Key Terms - continued

Tax Assessor An official who evaluates property for the purpose of taxing it.

Village Board of Trustees Serve as the primary governing bodies of New York villages.

Zoning Board of Appeals By issuing variances, protects landowners from the unfair application of zoning laws in particular circumstances. Hears appeals from the decisions of zoning enforcement officers and building inspectors when interpretations of zoning ordinances are involved.

- **Conservation advisory councils** study matters affecting the environment, preservation, development, and use of a city's natural and physical features and conditions in regard to ecologic integrity, aesthetic appeal, and quality. A major function of the council is to ensure environmental issues prevalent in the community are handled according to municipal ordinances.

- The purpose of local **historic preservation offices** is to identify, evaluate, preserve, and revitalize the municipality's historic, archaeological, and cultural resources. Historic preservation offices provide advice and guidance regarding historic preservation in the community as well as recommend properties for preservation.

- **Building departments** issue building permits and see that code restrictions are followed, and construction and renovation is done by licensed professionals. Building codes are established locally and permits are issued through local government authorities. A building permit is issued only if the plans comply with codes.

- The **tax assessor's office** is mainly responsible for determining the assessed value of property on which property taxes are based. Assessors also process exemption applications and keep close watch on the local real estate market. The tax assessor's office does not determine property taxes.

- Tax departments in New York are called the **office of receiver of taxes**. The elected official who oversees this office is the receiver of taxes. This office is strictly administrative; it does not make policies. The office of receiver of taxes does not set taxes; it simply collects them.

- The planning, design, and construction of New York's public works facilities and projects are all within the scope of the **municipal engineer's office.** This office designs capital improvement projects, including roadways, sewer systems, and water connections.

- Each county in New York State has its own **health department**, which is a human service and regulatory agency that administers a number of public health programs and activities within the county. Health departments assess the health status of the community and then develop policies and plans to meet identified needs. This department is responsible for approving **septic and other sanitation systems**.

- New York City's Landmarks Law requires potential landmarks to be at least 30 years old and possess "a special character or special historical or aesthetic interest or value as part of the development, heritage, or cultural characteristics of the city, state, or nation" before it is designated a landmark. The **Landmarks Preservation Commission (LPC)** is the New York City agency responsible for identifying and designating the city's landmarks, which may include buildings, bridges, parks, cemeteries, fences, sidewalk clocks, building lobbies, and even trees. As long as it meets the Landmarks Law criteria, it may be considered for designation as a landmark. The commission also regulates changes to already designated landmarks.

QUIZ

1. *A group of New York City neighbors wants to get a theater on their block designated as a landmark. How old must that theater be?*
   - A. 25 years old
   - B. 30 years old
   - C. 50 years old
   - D. 75 years old

2. *A receiver of taxes*
   - A. collects taxes.
   - B. determines tax rates.
   - C. grants tax exemptions.
   - D. writes tax laws.

3. *Comprehensive municipal planning is the responsibility of the*
   - A. building department.
   - B. Historical Review Committee.
   - C. planning board.
   - D. planning department.

4. *The _____ board advises all other boards on land use matters and ensures the requirements of the State Environmental Quality Review Act are followed.*
   - A. advisory
   - B. building
   - C. planning
   - D. review

5. *Each _____ in New York has a health department.*
   - A. city
   - B. county
   - C. town
   - D. village

6. *An important function of the Zoning Board of Appeals is _____ zoning laws.*
   - A. enacting
   - B. interpreting
   - C. proposing
   - D. relinquishing

7. *Property tax rates are determined by tax*
   - A. brackets.
   - B. exemptions.
   - C. levies.
   - D. variances.

8. *As a tax assessor, Steve's job does NOT involve*
   - A. determining the assessed value of property.
   - B. keeping watch on the local real estate market.
   - C. processing exemption applications.
   - D. setting property taxes.

9. *In an area of New York designated as a village, what governs the village instead of a city council?*
   - A. administrative office
   - B. board of trustees
   - C. planning board
   - D. village planner

10. *Building permits are issued by*
    - A. fire department battalion chiefs.
    - B. local building departments.
    - C. planning boards.
    - D. village supervisors.

Property Insurance

Key Terms

Actual Cash Value (ACV) Calculated by determining the replacement cost of the damaged property at today's prices (not including the land) and then subtracting any depreciation, based on the property's age and its use over time.

Deductible A dollar amount the insured must pay on each loss. The insurance company pays the remainder of each covered loss up to the policy limits.

Direct Loss Referring to homeowner's insurance, a sudden loss due to a covered peril—such as fire, lightening, wind, hail, etc.

Indirect Loss A loss that occurs as a consequence of the direct loss. For example, regarding property insurance, on a dwelling policy, fire is covered as a direct loss. *Also called*: **Consequential Loss.**

Liability (Casualty) Coverage in case of a lawsuit filed by another person claiming bodily injury or damage to property.

Liability Insurance Insures the individual for financial losses that may arise out of the person's responsibilities to others imposed by law or contract.

Monoline Policy Insurance coverage designed to cover one specific area—*property*.

Mortgage Clause Clause that states in order to get a mortgage loan, property insurance must be obtained prior to closing. The mortgage clause covers the lender's interest in preservation and reconstruction of the property after a loss.

Package Policy Two or more lines of coverage combined into one insurance policy. A Homeowners policy is a true package policy because it combines property insurance with liability insurance.

Peril Anything that can cause a loss (i.e., fire, wind, hail).

Property Insurance Coverage that indemnifies a person with an interest in the property for a loss caused to the property by a covered peril.

Replacement Cost Basis The cost, for insurance purposes, of replacing property without deduction for depreciation.

Umbrella Policy Provides broad coverage for an insured's liability over and above liability covered by underlying contracts.

Overview of Insurance

Property insurance is almost always a requirement in order to get a mortgage loan from a lender.

- **Property insurance** – coverage that indemnifies a person with an interest in the property for a loss caused to the property by a covered peril
- **Fire insurance** – another name for property insurance, which can cover building structures (real property) or contents (personal property), or both on the same policy

Marketing of Insurance

Insurance companies market products in several ways:

- **Independent insurance agents** – sell insurance products from several companies and work for themselves or other agents
- **Exclusive** or **captive agents** – represent only one company and may be paid a salary or be compensated by commissions
- **Direct writing companies** – pay salaries to employees whose job function is to sell the company's insurance products
- **Insurance brokers** – do not represent any particular company nor are they employees of any insurance company

Types of Insurance Coverage

- **Monoline policy** – covers both real and personal property and can include liability (casualty) coverage
- **Liability insurance** – protects the individual for financial losses that may arise out of the person's responsibilities to others imposed by law or contract; there is usually no deductible for this coverage
- **Package policy** – combines two or more coverage parts in one policy
- **Umbrella policy** – provides high limits of liability and broad coverage for a very reasonable premium charge

Insurance Policies

Two policies most frequently used to protect a customer's property:

- **Dwelling**
- **Homeowners**

Dwelling Policy

- **Dwelling policy**:
  - Covers a **direct loss** to the physical property
  - Covers **indirect loss** that results because the insured cannot use the property after it is damaged
  - No theft coverage on contents
  - No liability coverage
- **Named peril policy** covers each listed peril in the policy, most policies provide coverage of these perils:
  - Riot or civil commotion

- ◆ Removal
- ◆ Explosion
- ◆ Volcanic action
- ◆ Vehicles (damage done by other than the insured)
- ◆ Fire
- ◆ Lightning
- ◆ Smoke, sinkhole collapse, and sprinkler leakage
- ◆ Wind or hail
- ◆ Aircraft (damage done by)
- **Open Peril, All Risk** policy covers for all direct risk of physical loss; therefore, everything is covered unless the peril is specifically excluded.

Dwelling Forms

All three Dwelling policy forms exclude ordinance or law, earth movement, water damage, power failure and neglect, war, nuclear hazard, and intentional loss.

- **DP-1 – Basic** form covers 11 named perils
- **DP-2 – Broad** form covers all perils from the basic form, plus four more
- **DP-3 – All Risk** form covers all perils unless specifically excluded somewhere in the contract (and except for contents coverage)

Selected endorsements to dwelling policies include broad theft coverage, limited theft endorsement, comprehensive personal liability, and premises liability.

Homeowners Policy

Homeowners policy has two parts:

- Section I, which covers property
- Section II, which covers liability

Homeowners Forms

When additional coverage is added to homeowners policies, the coverage is added to, or "stacks" on top of the others, providing increased coverage. Also when contents coverage is added, it "floats," meaning that articles are covered anywhere, even if not on the premises

- **HO-1 Basic** form is a Named Peril form on both dwelling structures and contents; vandalism and theft are included
- **HO-2 Broad** form is also a Named Peril form on both dwelling structures and contents; theft is included
- **HO-3 Special** form provides the best coverage for the money and is All Risk on the dwelling and other structures; contents are still named peril
- **HO-4 Renters** or **Tenants** form provides contents coverage for insureds who do not own the premises they inhabit; contains no structure coverage
- **HO-5 Comprehensive** form provides All Risk coverage on both the structure and contents
- **HO-6 Condominium Unit Owners** form is very similar to the HO-4, *except* it includes a small amount of coverage for the dwelling unit, which is the interior space owned by the insured

- **HO-8 Modified** form is named peril on structures and personal property; specially designed for older homes for which the replacement cost of the dwelling exceeds market value

Standard policies require the insured to carry at least 80 percent of the cost to replace the structure as the minimum amount of insurance on the property.

Claims

Claims can be filed for:

- **Partial loss** – cost to replace or repair the damage does not exceed the limit of insurance
- **Total loss** – cost to repair or replace exceeds the limit of insurance on the policy

Settlement of Claims

Claims can be settled in two ways:

- **ACV** or **Actual Cash Value** (Replacement Cost - Depreciation = ACV)
- **Replacement Cost** (better policies pay claims on a replacement cost basis and are the preferred form of coverage)

Most dwelling policies that contain replacement cost coverage require the insured to carry coverage for at least 80 percent of the replacement cost value.

Cost of Homeowners Insurance

Main factors that determine the cost of insurance:

- Location of property
- Construction materials
- Amount of insurance requested

A **deductible** is the dollar amount the insured must pay on each loss to which the deductible applies. The insurance company pays the remainder up to policy limits.

> **NOTE:** Deductibles can have an impact on the amount of the premium: The higher the deductible, the lower the premium.

Cancellation and Nonrenewal of Policies

- During the first 60 days a covered policy is in effect, a notice of cancellation must be accompanied by a statement of the **specific reason(s) for cancellation**.
- After the policy has been in effect for 60 days, or upon the effective date if the policy is a renewal, cancellation or nonrenewal can take effect only based on specific reasons, including nonpayment of premium.
- A **written notice** of nonrenewal must be sent at least 45-60 days prior to the nonrenewal date. The specific reason(s) for nonrenewal must be stated in the notice.

New York Property Insurance Underwriting Association (NYPIUA)

- Created in 1968 and designated a FAIR Plan (fair access to insurance requirements) to write certain types of property insurance
- Offers coverage for:
  - Fire
  - Extended coverage
  - Vandalism and malicious mischief
  - Sprinkler leakage
  - Time element coverage
- Insures:
  - Buildings (dwelling and commercial properties)
  - Contents of commercial premises
  - Household furnishings and personal property

Flood Insurance

- Property insurance does *not* cover damage caused by the peril of **flood.**
- Consumers who want this coverage need to purchase flood insurance from the **National Flood Insurance Program (NFIP)** or from an insurer participating in the Write Your Own program, which, in essence, provides the same coverage as the policy sold by the federal program.
- The **Coastal Market Assistance Program** (C-Map) was established by the State of New York Insurance Department and is administered by New York Property Insurance Underwriting Association (NYPIUA) to assist homeowners living in New York's coastal areas obtain insurance for their homes.

Commercial Property Insurance

- **Blanket property insurance** – provides a single amount of insurance that may apply to different types of property or to different locations
- **Specific property insurance** – provides a specific amount of insurance for specific types of property at a specific location

QUIZ

1. *On an All Risk policy, where would you look to determine if a loss is covered?*
    - A. conditions
    - B. declarations
    - C. exclusions
    - D. insuring agreement

2. *If a dwelling covered by the Basic Form suffered $5,000 in damages due to an explosion, a resulting fire that caused $10,000 in damage, and $1,000 in water damage from the water used to put out the fire, how much would the policy pay?*
    - A. $5,000
    - B. $10,000
    - C. $16,000
    - D. $26,000

3. *A program established by the New York Insurance Department to assist homeowners living in New York's coastal areas to obtain insurance for their homes is*
    - A. the Coastal Market Assistance Program (C-MAP).
    - B. the National Flood Insurance Program.
    - C. the NYPIUA.
    - D. Regulation 150 of the New York State Insurance Department.

4. *Homeowners who want flood coverage should*
    - A. not worry about it if they have an HO-3 policy, as it is included.
    - B. purchase Flood insurance as a rider on their existing Homeowners policy.
    - C. purchase Flood insurance from the National Flood Insurance Program.
    - D. wait and apply for Federal Disaster Insurance after damage is done.

5. *It is recommended that the buyer obtains property insurance that becomes effective*
    - A. after the closing.
    - B. at the closing.
    - C. at the time the sales contract is signed.
    - D. once the seller leaves the property.

6. *The actual cash value is determined by*
    - A. adding the deductible to the replacement cost.
    - B. adding the depreciation to the replacement cost.
    - C. factoring 60% of the replacement cost.
    - D. subtracting the depreciation from the replacement cost.

7. *The purpose of the deductible on a property policy is to*
    - A. cause the insured to think twice before submitting a claim.
    - B. eliminate small claims and control the cost of insurance.
    - C. make it harder for an insured to file a claim.
    - D. stop the premium from increasing after a loss.

8. *Replacement cost basis loss settlement is best described as the*
    - A. cost to replace the item minus depreciation.
    - B. cost to replace the item without depreciation.
    - C. market value of the item less sales tax.
    - D. repair costs minus depreciation.

9. *A type of policy that provides a very high limit of liability is a(n)*
    - A. All Risk policy.
    - B. Landlord policy.
    - C. Package policy.
    - D. Umbrella policy.

10. *A Dwelling policy does NOT cover loss from*
    - A. fire.
    - B. flood.
    - C. riots.
    - D. volcanoes.

Taxes and Assessments

Key Terms

Ad Valorem Taxes Tax based on the assessed value of property.

Administrative Review Initiated when a taxpayer files a grievance with his municipal assessing unit; prerequisite to judicial review.

Appropriation 1. The authorization of the expenditure of funds and the source of those funds. 2. Taking private property for public use, through the government's power of eminent domain. *Also called*: **Condemnation**.

Approved Assessing Unit An assessing unit certified by the New York State Board as having completed a revaluation program implementing a system of real property tax administration, which was or would be eligible, based upon the latest completed assessment roll, for state assistance.

Assessed Value Value placed on property to which a local tax rate is applied to calculate the amount of real property tax.

Assessing Unit City, town, or county department of assessment with the power to assess real property.

Assessment A percentage of a property's market value.

Assessment Review Board Local board that hears complaints regarding property assessments and property exemption determinations.

Assessment Roll Listing of the assessed value for all real property in a municipality.

Equalization Attempts to measure the relationship of locally assessed values to a fluid real estate market.

Equitable Right of Redemption The right of a debtor to save (redeem) property from foreclosure proceedings prior to confirmation of sale.

Homestead Dwellings of four or fewer units, owner-occupied mobile homes, residential condominiums, farms, and vacant land suitable for qualified buildings that may be eligible for a separate tax rate.

In Rem A lawsuit or legal action directed toward property, rather than toward a particular person. Judgments are binding to all persons who claim title to the property.

Judicial Review When a court considers whether a statute or regulation is constitutional.

Level of Assessment The ratio of total assessed value to the municipality's total market value.

(continued on next page)

Taxation Overview

Real property tax is an **ad valorem tax**, which refers to *taxes based on the assessed value of property*. This means two owners of real property of equal value should pay the same amount in property taxes. Or, the owner of more valuable property should pay more in taxes than the owner of less valuable property. Tax rates in New York State vary depending on the city, town, or county in which the land is located.

Purpose

- Relatively easy to administer because they are imposed on a known, stable tax base
- Municipalities can count on a predictable, steady stream of income from the time a property is assessed until it is reassessed
- Somewhat protected in slow economies when compared to other types of taxes
- Do not distinguish between resident and non-resident home and business owners – all land is taxed whether it is owned by resident or not, so no one is "missed" in the process
- The one single identifiable local revenue source for municipalities and schools, which makes local government directly accountable for executing operations and programs in a cost-effective manner

Who Administers Real Property Taxes?

Property taxes in New York State are administered locally to finance local governments and public schools. Entities who can raise money through real property tax includes:

- Counties
- Cities
- Towns

Key Terms - continued

Lien A non-possessory interest in property giving a lienholder the right to foreclose if the owner does not pay a debt owed the lienholder; a financial encumbrance on the owner's title.

Mill Rate The amount of tax paid per dollar of the assessed property value expressed in mills. One mill is 1/10th of a cent ($.001).

Non-homestead Property that consists of industrial and commercial parcels as well as vacant land.

Reassessment The new assessment of a percentage of a property's market value.

Special Assessment A tax or levy against real property for improvements; not imposed on all residents of a community, but only to owners who will benefit from the improvement.

Special Assessment Districts A geographic area designated to pay for infrastructure costs for a specific project. Properties within the district each pay a portion of the total project cost. Creates a **special assessment lien** (an involuntary lien).

Statutory Right of Redemption Allows a mortgagor to redeem property for a set period of time after a foreclosure sale, regardless of the timing of other events.

Tax Levy Determine tax rates by developing and adopting a budget, evaluating the revenue from all sources other than property taxes (state aid, sales tax, user fees, etc.), and then subtracting the revenues from the original budget.

Tentative Assessment Roll The public record listing assessed value for all real property in a municipality.

True Tax The amount that would be paid before any exemptions held by the present owner are subtracted.

- Villages
- School districts
- Special assessment districts

Who Pays Property Taxes?

Practically everyone who owns land is responsible for paying real property taxes.

Exemptions

Some entities, organizations, and even individuals are exempt from all or part of property taxes:

- Colleges and universities
- Schools
- Parks
- State and federal governments
- Religious corporations
- Hospitals
- Disabled – in New York, local governments and public school districts have the authority to grant a reduction in property taxes to qualifying persons with disabilities
- Veterans – qualified veterans may receive a partial exemption of 15 percent of the value of a primary residence, excluding cooperatives; does **not** apply to school taxes
- Elderly – homeowners who are 65 or older with modest incomes may be eligible for a partial exemption from property taxes on their primary residence (depending on income levels, exemptions can range from 10% to 50%)
- Farmers – in specific agricultural areas, exemptions may be offered to encourage the continuation of agricultural uses
- Gold Star parents – parents who have lost a child in combat may be eligible for a partial exemption
- STaR Program Homeowners – all homeowners are entitled to school tax relief (STaR), which permanently reduces school taxes on a main residence

Special Assessment Districts

- **Special assessment districts** – geographic areas designated to pay for infrastructure costs for a specific project
- **Special assessment taxes** – levied against real property for improvements, e.g. sidewalks, streetlights, curbs, sewers
- *Not* imposed on all residents of a community, but only to the owners of the properties who will benefit from the improvement

Calculating Real Property Taxes

Unlike income taxes and sales taxes, property taxes do not depend on how much money a person earns or spends; instead, property taxes depend solely on how much the property is worth. **Market value** – the price most people would pay for the property in its current condition – is used as the basis for property assessments.

The Tax Assessment

- **Tax assessor** – a local government official who estimates the value of real property within a city, town, or village's boundaries
- **Market value** – New York State law obligates assessors to maintain assessments at a uniform percentage of market value each year
- **Assessment rolls** – public record that lists the assessed value of each property

Assessed Value

- **Assessment** – a government's valuation of property for tax purposes
- **Assessed value** – the value placed on land and buildings by a city, town, or county assessor for use in levying annual real estate taxes; determined by an assessor as a percentage of a property's market value
- **Approved assessing unit** – an assessing unit certified by the New York State Board as having completed a revaluation program implementing a system of real property tax administration, which has or would be eligible, based upon the latest completed assessment roll, for state assistance
- **Reassessments** – assessments change because of new construction, fires, demolition, and periodic community-wide assessment updates necessary to maintain an equitable assessment roll

Assessment Rolls

An **assessment roll** is a public record that lists the assessed value of each property. Every municipality sets a specific date for the following milestones:

- **Tentative assessment roll** – contains **level of assessment** (*the percentage at which the properties are assessed relative to market value*) and the proposed assessed values for each property in the assessing unit
- **Grievance day** – the day on which the local Board of Assessment Review hears complaints from property owners seeking reductions in their tentative assessments (after the public is given time to review it)
- **Final assessment roll** – signed and filed by the assessor to show final assessments, including all changes

Property Tax Equity

According to the New York State Office of Real Property Services (ORPS), to achieve assessment equity, assessments must be:

- Arrived at fairly.
- Measured annually.
- Based on an accurate inventory of properties.

For all constituents, assessment processes must be:

- Simple.
- Widely accessible.
- Understandable.
- Perceived as fair.
- Open to review.

Assessments in New York

According to New York State law:

- All property in municipality must be assessed at the same uniform percentage of value.

- Real property is assessed **annually** in New York.

- Assessors are required to add value to the property for most new construction that increases the value of the property.

- New York State and many local laws require assessment of all improvements to residential and commercial property that increase livable and useable space and become a party of the realty.

- Undeclared improvements are possible significant improvements that could be made to a property and then go undiscovered for several months, or even years.

- **Selective reassessments** occur when a municipality is not in the midst of a municipal-wide reassessment, yet specific parcels, various portions of an assessing unit, or certain types of property are reassessed without regard to the relative uniformity within the municipality. Selective reassessments are mostly illegal.

- **Equalization** attempts to measure the relationship of locally assessed values to a fluid real estate market. The New York State Office of Real Property Services is obligated by law to administer an equalization program to ensure equitable property tax allocation among all the taxing jurisdictions in New York.

  - **Level of assessment (LOA)** – an equalization rate is the state's measure of a municipality's LOA, which is the ratio of total assessed value (AV) to the municipality's total market value (MV):

    Total Assessed Value (AV) ÷ Total Market Value (MV) = Equalization Rate

Homestead and Non-Homestead Property

Allows approved assessing units to apply separate levels of assessment to different categories of property.

- **Homestead properties** – dwellings of four units or less, owner-occupied mobile homes, residential condominiums, farms, and vacant land suitable for qualified buildings

- **Non-homestead properties** – consist of industrial and commercial parcels and most vacant land

Determining Tax Rates

A municipality's tax rate is a direct result of the tax levy. A **tax levy** is the formal action taken to impose a tax. There are several steps involved in establishing the tax levy:

1. Develop and adopt a budget.
2. Evaluate the revenue from all sources other than property taxes (state aid, sales tax, etc.).
3. Subtract the revenues from the original budget.

- Before a tax levy can be introduced to the community at large, **appropriation** occurs, which authorizes the expenditure of funds and provides for the sources of money

- Tax rates are calculated by dividing the total amount of money raised from the tax levy by the taxable assessed value of taxable real property in a municipality

Disputing Assessments

If homeowners believe their property has been assessed incorrectly, they may voice their concerns and request adjustments by contacting their local **Assessment Review Board**. The amount of a tax bill is not sufficient grounds for challenging an assessment.

Tax Assessment Review Grounds

Taxpayers in New York have four grounds on which to challenge a tax assessment:

1. **Excessive assessment** – the property's assessment exceeds its full market value or some portion of an exemption is denied or accidentally overlooked.
2. **Unequal assessment** – a property is assessed at a higher percentage than other properties.
3. **Unlawful assessment** – often a technicality, for example, the property is not really within the boundaries of its designated assessing unit.
4. **Misclassified assessment** – the real property is misclassified; for example, residential classified as industrial.

Residential Disputes

There are two types of review proceedings for taxpayers with grievances concerning their property assessments:

- **Administrative review** – a prerequisite to judicial review and initiated when a taxpayer files a grievance with the assessing unit
- **Judicial review** – allows taxpayers who are still dissatisfied with the decision of the Assessment Review Board to seek judicial review by commencing a tax certiorari (legal action challenging an assessment) proceeding in the New York State Supreme Court or by filing a Small Claims Assessment Review (SCAR)

If a taxpayer has exhausted his options and is still dissatisfied, he may continue to appeal by commencing an **Article 78 proceeding** in New York State Supreme Court.

Commercial Disputes

Commercial property owners may also take assessment disagreements to the Assessment Review Board. The procedure used is the same as residential property owners, including the four grounds on which to challenge a tax assessment. Commercial property owners may not request a SCAR if they disagree with a property assessment—they must seek judicial review.

Tax Liens

A **lien** is a non-possessory interest in property giving a lienholder the right to foreclose if the owner does not pay a debt owed to the lienholder. Taxes are actually liens on property titles and always have a higher priority over other previously recorded liens.

Enforcing Tax Liens

- **Tax foreclosure** – tax foreclosures are **in rem**, which are lawsuits or legal actions directed toward property, rather than toward a particular person. Judgments are binding to all persons who claim title to the property

- **Tax sale** – occurs when a mortgagor defaults on his mortgage loan

  - **Equitable right of redemption** – the owner, and delinquent taxpayer, may **redeem** the property prior to the sale by paying the delinquent taxes plus interest as well as any penalties associated with the delinquency

  - Statutory **right of redemption** – New York State laws also grant a period of redemption after a tax sale if the delinquent taxpayer pays the amount owed at the tax sale along with interest and penalties

QUIZ

1. *All of these have the authority to levy property taxes EXCEPT*
   - A. a county.
   - B. a local school district.
   - C. a special assessment district.
   - D. the state.

2. *Anita lost her job and has not paid her mortgage, credit card debt, or property taxes for nine months. She also owes money to a contractor who did some remodeling. The mortgage lien was recorded first, then a general lien for non-payment of the credit card, then the mechanic's lien. When the property is sold at foreclosure, which lien will be paid first?*
   - A. general lien for credit card default
   - B. mechanic's lien
   - C. mortgage lien
   - D. property tax lien

3. *Ad valorem refers to a tax that is*
   - A. based on the assessed value of property.
   - B. charged by the county to transfer a deed when property sells.
   - C. a percentage of a property's sale price.
   - D. a percentage of someone's income.

4. *Which is an example of an administrative review related to property tax assessments?*
   - A. Abigail files for a Small Claims Assessment Review (SCAR).
   - B. Charles challenges his assessment on grievance day.
   - C. Mary refuses to pay her property tax and requests a review by the IRS.
   - D. Thomas commences a tax certiorari proceeding.

5. *Which is NOT a legitimate reason why a homeowner may challenge his assessment?*
   - A. The assessment exceeds full market value.
   - B. The property is in a neighboring assessing unit.
   - C. The single-family home is classified as commercial.
   - D. The tax rate is too high.

6. *The value placed on land and buildings by a city, town, or county assessor for use in levying annual real estate taxes is a property's*
   - A. appraised value.
   - B. assessed value.
   - C. market value.
   - D. sale price.

7. *Which of these improvements would be LEAST LIKELY to require re-assessment?*
   - A. brick patio
   - B. enclosed porch
   - C. finished basement
   - D. storm windows

8. *All of these are examples of things that might be paid for with a special assessment tax EXCEPT*
   - A. ornamental street lights.
   - B. school operating costs.
   - C. sewer repair.
   - D. sidewalk replacement.

9. *Which property could NOT be considered a homestead property?*
   - A. condop
   - B. four-unit apartment building
   - C. owner-occupied mobile home
   - D. vacant land less than 10 acres zoned for single-family homes

10. *In New York State, real property is assessed*
    - A. annually.
    - B. bi-annually.
    - C. monthly.
    - D. quarterly.

Income Tax Issues in Real Estate

Key Terms

Active Income Earnings received from any of the following: wages, salaries, commissions, bonuses, and other payments for services rendered; profit from a trade or business where the taxpayer is an active participant; gain on sale or disposition of assets used in an active trade or business; income from intangible property if the taxpayer played a significant role in creating the property.

Adjusted Basis Original cost of property, plus gains and minus losses.

Appreciation The increase in value of an asset over time.

Basis Accounting procedure used to determine the capital gain or loss after the sale of property. It is equal to purchase price, plus capital improvements, less depreciation.

Boot Extra, non-like-kind property that can be a part of a like-kind exchange to make up for pricing disparity between like-kind properties.

Capital Gain Profit made from an investment.

Capital Loss Monetary loss resulting from an investment's decrease in value.

Cash Flow Money available after subtracting all expenses. Positive cash flow means more money is coming in than going out. Negative cash flow is the converse.

Debt Service Amount of money needed to meet the periodic payments of principal and interest on an amortized loan or debt. If the periodic payments are constant and equal, then a portion will pay off accrued interest with the remainder reducing principal.

Depreciation A loss in value for any reason.

Double Declining Balance An accelerated method of deprecation.

Home Acquisition Debt A mortgage a taxpayer takes out to buy, build, or substantially improve a qualified home.

Home Equity Debt A loan that does not qualify as home acquisition debt but is secured by a qualified home.

Passive Income Defined in Section 469 as earnings derived from any trade, business, or income-producing activity in which the taxpayer does not materially participate.

Portfolio Income 1. Earnings from interest, dividends, annuities, and royalties *not* derived from the ordinary course of business. 2. Gain or loss from the disposition of property that produces portfolio income or held for investment purposes.

(continued on next page)

Benefits of Home Ownership

Home ownership comes with many benefits, including tax deductionsfor:

- Paid property taxes
- Interest paid on a mortgage
- Interest paid on home equity loans
- Individual Retirement Account (IRA)

Tax benefits of owning a second home: As long as the home is not rented for more than 14 days during the year, any rental income can be excluded and taxes and interest can be deducted.

Sale of a Principal Residence

Gains from the sale of a principal residence are normally taxable as portfolio income. The **Taxpayer Relief Act of 1997** created a provision for this with Section 121 of the Internal Revenue Code. Section 121 provides some relief to taxpayers by exempting most, if not all, of the gain. Section 121 conditions include that the taxpayer must have owned and used the property as a principal residence for at least two of the last five years prior to the date of sale. Special circumstances that allow the provisions include:

- Change in place of employment
- Health considerations
- Unforeseen circumstances

There are limits on the total allowable exclusions under Section 121:

- A single person cannot exceed **$250,000.**
- A married couple filing joint tax returns cannot exceed **$500,000.**

Calculating the Realized Gain

- **Adjusted basis** – to calculate the realized gain, you must subtract the adjusted basis (the original cost plus capital improvements) from the amount realized (the sale price minus selling expenses)
- **Appreciation** – increase in the value of the property
- **Recaptured depreciation** most commonly occurs on a personal asset used for business purposes when that asset is sold

Key Terms - continued

Progressive Tax A tax that takes a larger percentage from the income of high-income people than it does from low-income people, such as the federal income tax.

Recaptured Depreciation Occurs on a personal asset used for business purposes when the asset is sold.

Straight Line Depreciation Simple depreciation method that takes the total cost of a building and divides that by the number of years the building is expected to be useful.

Tax-Deferred Exchange Exchanges where taxable gain is deferred until a later date.

Tax Depreciation Calculating depreciation that can be used to determine any expense that can be deducted from income to determine net profit.

Tax Shelter Any method used to reduce taxable income, thereby reducing the amount of tax paid to a government.

Home Acquisition Debt vs. Home Equity Debt

The following types of debt can provide loan-related tax deductions:

- **Home acquisition debt** – a mortgage a taxpayer took out to buy, build, or substantially improve a qualified home. The loan must be secured by the home. The amount of the mortgage used to calculate qualified interest is limited to the value of the home *plus* any substantial improvements. The debt is limited to $1,000,000.

- **Home equity debt** – a loan that does not qualify as home acquisition debt but is secured by a qualified home. The amount of debt is limited to the smaller of $100,000 or the home's fair market value, reduced by the amount of home acquisition debt and grandfathered debt.

- **Points** (discount points) – a type of prepaid interest that mortgage borrowers can purchase to lower the amount of interest they will have to pay in subsequent payments (each discount point is generally 1% of the total loan amount).

  - Points must meet certain IRS criteria
  - The points paid to **refinance** a mortgage are not fully deductible in the year paid

Capital Gains and Losses

A **capital asset** is something that is owned long-term (such as land, buildings, and machinery). Other examples include stocks and bonds, real property, and collectibles. Capital gains and losses are generated when a capital asset is sold. They are categorized as short-term (held for 12 months or less) or long-term (held for more than 12 months):

- **Capital gain** – the profit made from an investment
- **Capital loss** – occurs when an investment decreases in value

Depreciation

Depreciation is the *recovery of the cost of a capital asset over time by expensing a set portion of it each year*. Depreciation, instead of expensing, is done to make expenses even over time. **Straight-line depreciation** assumes an equal amount of an asset's price will be expensed each year of its useful life.

- Residential rental real property is depreciated over **27.5 years**.
- Nonresidential (commercial) real property is depreciated over **39 years**.

Only the improvements on property held for business and investment purposes can be depreciated. Land is *never* depreciable, so any property value attributable to the land must be deducted from the price paid to determine its **depreciable basis**.

Like-Kind Exchanges

The Internal Revenue Code **Section 1031** allows a taxpayer to sell an investment property and purchase another investment property in its place **without paying taxes on the proceeds** from the sale. These like-kind exchanges are nontaxable exchanges of property, provided certain conditions are met:

- The transaction must be an exchange and not a sale (i.e., actual property must be exchanged not solely for cash)

- Transactions are structured as **tax-deferred exchanges** or exchanges where taxable gain is deferred until a later date
- Property received and property transferred must be held either for use in a trade or business or for investment
- Properties must be similar or like-kind

A **reverse exchange** is another way in which a taxpayer might defer tax. The replacement property is acquired prior to transferring the relinquished property.

Exclusions, Exceptions, and Restrictions

- Livestock of different sexes
- Personal property for real property (and vice versa)
- Realty in the United States for realty in a foreign country
- Related parties
- Depreciable tangible personal property
- Time limits

Possible Taxable Realized Gain

Occasionally, property that is not like-kind can be a part of a like-kind exchange to make up for a pricing disparity between the like-kind properties. This extra, non-like-kind property is called **boot**.

Determining Basis

Basis is the price paid for the property, including any expenses or gains. When the property is exchanged, the basis must be adjusted to reflect any postponed gain or loss.

Adjusted Basis of Surrendered Like-Kind Property

+ Adjusted Basis of Boot Given

+ Gain Recognized

- Fair Market Value of Boot Received

- Loss Recognized
_____

Basis of Like-Kind Property Received

This approach uses the *recovery of capital doctrine* (any amount taxed in the exchange is added to the basis of the new property since that amount has already been taxed and should not be taxed in a future transaction).

Holding Period and Qualified Intermediaries

The **holding period** of new property includes the holding period of old property. Assistance from a **qualified intermediary** is required for Section 1031 exchanges.

Low-Income Housing Incentives

The federal government offers incentives for the development of low-income housing. The major incentive to building and maintaining housing for low-income individuals and families in the **low-income housing tax credit (LIHTC)**, which provides a credit against tax liability (a dollar-for-dollar reduction in tax liability). Low-income housing is defined by the IRS as a project where at least **20% of the units** have rents affordable to, and are occupied by, households with incomes no greater than 50% of the area's gross median income, or at least 40% of the units are affordable to, and occupied by, families with incomes no greater than 60% of the area's gross median income.

QUIZ

1. **Which is allowed under the Internal Revenue Service Code?**
    A. deducting a loss on the sale of a primary residence
    B. deducting credit card interest
    C. deducting mortgage interest
    D. reducing income by the amount paid to rehabilitate a home

2. **What may be used for a like-kind exchange?**
    A. Boeing 737 and a tractor trailer
    B. delivery truck and a single office
    C. office building and an apartment building
    D. recreational vehicle and a stamping machine

3. **Which is a type of portfolio income?**
    A. capital gains on a rental property
    B. commission
    C. salary
    D. wages

4. **In order to deduct rental income from a second home, the home cannot be rented for more than _____ days during the year.**
    A. 10
    B. 14
    C. 20
    D. 30

5. **John is gathering up his paperwork to complete his income taxes. His home expenses include: mortgage interest per month = $520; property taxes = $3,280; new deck = $5,300. What is the total deduction John can take for the year?**
    A. $3,280
    B. $6,240
    C. $9,520
    D. $14,820

6. **The recovery of the cost of a capital asset over time by expensing a set portion of it each year is called**
    A. appreciation.
    B. capital decline.
    C. depreciation.
    D. negative cash flow.

7. **Commercial property can be depreciated over ___ years.**
    A. 15
    B. 27.5
    C. 30
    D. 39

8. **To qualify as a low-income housing project, the minimum number of units that must be designated for low-income is**
    A. 10%.
    B. 20%.
    C. 40%.
    D. 60%.

9. **Jack and Katherine purchased a home 15 years ago for $800,000 when they got married. They recently sold the property for $1,500,000. What amount will they have to pay capital gains taxes on?**
    A. $0
    B. $200,000
    C. $500,000
    D. $700,000

10. **Land can be depreciated**
    A. always.
    B. never.
    C. only for residential rental property.
    D. sometimes.

Condominiums and Cooperatives

19

Key Terms

80/20 Rule Rule that says in order for individual shareholders to continue to be able to write off yearly taxes and mortgage interest, no more than 20 percent of a co-op's yearly income can come from non-shareholder sources.

Alteration Agreement Written agreement, signed by co-op shareholder-tenants, before any renovations, modifications, repairs, or alterations can begin.

Assigning a Contract Assigning the purchase rights to property or a condominium unit to another buyer before that property or unit is closed.

Board Package A package presented to the co-op (or sometimes condo) board of managers/directors from a potential shareholder or buyer. It often includes financial qualifications, employment verification, letters of reference, and other material requested by the board.

Bylaws Rules and regulations that govern the activities of the condominium and cooperative associations. These include the purpose of the building, rules for elections and voting, and frequency of board of directors or shareholders meetings.

Common Areas Land and improvements in a condominium, planned unit development, or cooperative all residents use and own as tenants in common, such as the parking lot, hallways, and recreational facilities; individual apartment units or homes are not included. *Also called*: **Common Elements.**

Condominium Property developed for co-ownership, with each co-owner having a separate interest in an individual unit, combined with an undivided interest in the common areas of the property.

Condominium Act New York State law governing the establishment of condominiums.

Condominium Declaration Document filed for record when property is developed as, or converted to, a condominium.

Condop A building that has been divided into at least two condominiums. The first is the co-op residential units considered one condominium unit. The second unit is the professional and commercial units.

Cooperative A building owned by a corporation, where residents are shareholders in the corporation; each shareholder receives a proprietary lease on an individual unit and the right to use the common areas. *Also called*: **Co-op** or **Stock Cooperative**.

(continued on next page)

Condominiums

A condominium is a **property** developed for co-ownership, with each co-owner having a separate interest in an individual unit, combined with an undivided interest in the common areas.

- The Condominium Act, Article 9-B of the Real Property Law, is New York State's law governing the establishment of condominiums.
- Condominium owners own **fee simple absolute** title to the airspace within their units.
- Condominium unit owners own **real property**, documented in a unit deed.
- Condominium owners also own an undivided interest in a specified percentage of the **common elements** as **tenants in common**.
- Some condominium unit owners have exclusive use of **limited common areas** owned by all but used by only one owner (i.e., assigned parking spaces, a unit balcony).

Key Terms - continued

Cooperative Policy Statement #1 (CPS-1) Applicable to cooperatives, condominiums, and homeowners associations and is used to test the market, explore the venture, and determine the needs to meet a variety of conditions.

Covenants, Conditions, and Restrictions (CC&Rs) A declaration of covenants, conditions, and restrictions, usually recorded by a developer to create a general plan of private restrictions for a subdivision.

Flip Tax A fee, imposed by the co-op board, for the transfer of ownership during the sale of the unit.

Flipping 1. Purchasing a property and immediately reselling it for a profit. 2. When a condominium owner assigns his purchase rights to another buyer before the sale of that property or unit has closed. *Also called*: **Assigning a Contract**.

Horizontal Property Acts Laws that create the legal framework for creating a condominium form of ownership and make it possible to define actual ownership rights.

House Rules The rules and requirements established for condo or co-op tenants. These could include rules for common areas, parking, noise, pets, use of recreation room, etc.

Letter of Intent Signifies two or more parties agree to do business together.

Limited Common Areas Areas in a condominium or co-up owned by all but used by only one owner (i.e., a designated parking space).

Maintenance Fees Monthly fees paid by condominium owners or co-op shareholders for common area expenses like utilities, building maintenance, and upkeep. *Also called*: **Common Area Expenses** or **Maintenance**.

Offering Plan A document provided by the sponsor (of a condominium or co-op) that offers detailed information regarding the property. *Also called*: **Offering Statement**.

Proprietary Lease Exclusive, longer term lease given to a person who lives in a cooperative and owns stock in the cooperative.

Recognition Agreement An agreement between three parties—the lender, the coop, and the shareholder—that recognizes the rights of lenders who finance the shareholder.

Right of First Refusal A right to have the first chance to buy or lease property if the owner decides to sell or lease it. *Also called*: **Right of Pre-emption**.

Share Loan A type of co-op loan signifying a buyer is purchasing shares in a corporation, rather than a mortgage for ownership of property.

Simultaneous Closing A seller financing technique used when an investor or seller creates a private mortgage note and then simultaneously closes with the buyer on the same day.

Sponsor Also known as the developer, a sponsor is the person, corporation, or other entity that is part of the sale and development of a condo or co-op property.

Timeshare An ownership interest that gives the owner a right to possession of the property only for a specific, limited period each year.

- Condominiums may be residential, commercial, retail, recreational, or a combination.
- Condominium owners' associations enforce bylaws of the development, assess fees, and arrange for the maintenance of the common areas.
- The cost of maintaining and insuring common areas is covered by the collection of **maintenance fees** from each unit owner.
- Each unit is taxed and assessed independently.

Condo Considerations

- A **sponsor** is a condo developer and is the person, corporation, or other entity that is part of the sale and development of the condo or co-op.
- **Bylaws** are the rules and regulations that govern the activities of the condominium association.
- **Covenants, Conditions, and Restrictions (CC&Rs)** create a general plan of private restrictions for a subdivision.
- CC&Rs are binding to all unit owners and are usually enforced by a condo association.
- A condo's owners' association is made up all unit owners.
- The condo association elects a board of directors to make decisions on behalf of the condo owners.

New Condo Development

- A **condominium declaration** is the document that must be filed for record when a property is developed as, or converted to, a condominium.
- When a property is developed or converted as a condo, an **offering plan** must be provided by the sponsor that details information regarding the property to be developed.
- Offering plans are regulated by New York State's Attorney General, thus amendments to the plans are also regulated.
- The **Martin Act**, Article 23 of the General Business Law, requires a full description of the property in the offering plan.

Cooperative Policy Statement #1

A **CPS-1** is applicable to cooperatives, condominiums, and homeowners associations and is used to test the market, explore the venture, and determine the needs to meet a variety of conditions.

Certificate of Occupancy

There are two types of **certificates of occupancy**, which is a permit issued to builders or developers after all inspections have been made and the property is deemed fit for occupancy:

- A final certificate of occupancy
- A temporary certificate of occupancy (TCO)

A certificate of occupancy can be issued only after:

- The construction matches submitted plans.
- All applicable laws, ordinances, and regulations have been followed and approvals obtained.

- Necessary paperwork has been completed.

- Department fees have been paid.

Nearly all lenders require a certificate of occupancy before approving a mortgage loan.

Purchasing a Condominium

A developer may ask a buyer to sign a **letter of intent**, which signifies two or more parties agree to do business together. The buyer will probably put down an initial deposit as well (as low as $1,000). A **non-binding letter of intent** most likely signifies the parties' intent to move forward with a transaction and is not meant to be enforceable. A **binding contract** is a valid contract that is enforceable.

Cooperatives

- Cooperatives, or **co-ops**, are buildings owned in severalty by non-profit corporations formed for that purpose.

- Co-op residents are **shareholders** in the corporation.

- Owners have a **proprietary lease**, which is an exclusive, longer-term lease given to a person who lives in and owns stock in a cooperative.

- Co-op owners do not actually own real property; their ownership interest is considered **personal property.**

- Owners pay a prorated share of the building's expenses and property taxes to the corporation.

- An owner who does not pay the assessment can be evicted by the co-op corporation.

- A cooperative is governed by its Articles of Incorporation, bylaws, CC&Rs, and other rules and regulations.

- Co-ops are taxed as though they are real property (real estate taxes/mortgage interest).

- Cooperative shareholders have the authority to vote whether or not to allow a particular person to buy into the cooperative.

- Rather than a mortgage loan, co-op shareholders have a **share loan.**

- Co-ops often include a **flip tax**, which is a fee imposed by the co-op board on the seller for the transfer of ownership during the sale of the unit.

Co-op Sale and Purchase Documents

Several documents are needed for the sale and purchase of cooperatives, including:

- Stock certificates and proprietary leases

- Co-op lien search

- Lender/co-op recognition agreements

- Offering plan

- House rules

- Alteration agreement

Cooperative Board Package

A **board package** is presented to the co-op board of directors, including:

- Purchase application form
- Employment verification letter
- Fully executed contract of sale
- Business letters of reference
- Financial statement
- Tax returns
- Letters of personal reference
- Authorization to perform a credit search
- Appropriate NY State disclosure forms

Once complete, the board package is submitted to the co-op's **managing agent** (who directly oversees building activities, building staff, and maintenance issues) who confirms it is complete and does the necessary fact checking. Then the package is forwarded to the board of directors for review.

The Board Interview

Licensees must prepare clients who are buying co-ops for their board interview. Most boards expect to meet everyone who will be living in the co-op, including children.

Primary Residence vs. Sublet

Some co-ops allow subletting. For those that do, common requirements include:

- A shareholder must occupy a unit for a specific number of years before subletting is allowed.
- An apartment can be sublet for only a certain number of years.
- Only a certain number of units in the building can be sublet at one time.
- There must be specific reasons for subletting (i.e., financial hardship).

In addition to meeting the requirements in place for subletting, many buildings require the following fees also be paid:

- Move-in and move-out fees
- Sublet fees
- Application fees

Sponsors must give up control of the board after five years or after 50% of the shares in the building are sold.

Holder of Unsold Shares

A **holder of unsold shares** is an investor in a co-op building who is not using it as a primary residence. He or she is usually exempt from fees such as flip taxes and subletting fees.

Condo and Co-op Eviction Plans

When a building is converted into a condo or co-op, sponsors offer existing tenants either an **eviction plan** or a **non-eviction plan**. In New York, effective plans meet the following criteria:

- For an **eviction plan** to be declared effective, **51%** of the bona fide tenants in the occupancy (excluded from the calculation are eligible senior citizens and disabled tenants) of all the dwelling units on the date the Attorney General accepts the offering plan for filing **must sign purchase agreements**.

- For a **non-eviction plan** to be declared effective, at least **15%** of the dwelling units **must be sold** to bona fide tenants or non-tenant purchasers who intend, or whose family members intend, to live in the unit.

Condops

- A condop is a building that has been divided into at least two condos:
    - Residential unit(s)
    - Professional/commercial unit(s)
- Owners purchase shares in a corporation rather than real property.
- The **80/20 rule** says that no more than 20% of the co-op's yearly income can come from non-shareholder sources, in order for individual shareholders to continue to be able to write off yearly taxes and mortgage interest.

QUIZ

1. **Which type of ownership has separate mortgages and taxes for each unit?**
   - A. apartments
   - B. condominiums
   - C. cooperatives
   - D. syndicates

2. **The rules and regulations that govern the activities of the condominium and cooperative association are called the**
   - A. board package.
   - B. bylaws.
   - C. deed.
   - D. offering plan.

3. **Who does NOT own real property?**
   - A. Amy, who has a house in a planned unit development
   - B. Gary, who has a unit in a condominium complex
   - C. Lori, who has a unit in a cooperative
   - D. Will, who has a vacant lot

4. **John owns fee simple title to Unit 30 and 5% of the common elements. What does John own?**
   - A. a condominium
   - B. a cooperative
   - C. a land trust
   - D. a timeshare

5. **An amount of money imposed by the co-op board for the transfer of ownership during the sale of a unit is a**
   - A. flip tax.
   - B. maintenance fee.
   - C. move-in/move-out fee.
   - D. tax abatement.

6. **Who typically pays the condo's New York City and State Transfer Tax unless the purchase is made directly from the sponsor?**
   - A. board
   - B. buyer
   - C. managing agent
   - D. seller

7. **According to most condo offering plans, sponsors must give up control of the board of managers/directors after _____ year(s) or _____ % of the building is sold, whichever comes first.**
   - A. one, 10
   - B. two, 20
   - C. five, 50
   - D. 10, 100

8. **The Smiths purchase a cooperative on the Gold Coast. What will they receive at closing?**
   - A. a deed and limited common area usage
   - B. a deed and title insurance policy
   - C. shares of stock and a deed
   - D. shares of stock and a proprietary lease

9. **A _____ is is a policy statement used to examine the marketability of a condominium development.**
   - A. CC&R
   - B. CPS-1
   - C. condon
   - D. offering plan

10. **An area in a condominium complex that is owned by all but only used by one person is a**
    - A. common area.
    - B. declaration.
    - C. limited common area.
    - D. proprietary lease.

Commercial and Investment Properties

20

Key Terms

After Tax Cash Flow Cash flow from income-producing property, less income taxes, if any, attributable to the property's income. If a tax loss provides a tax savings from the shelter of income earned outside the property, that savings is added to the property's earned cash flow.

Amenity Purchaser Person who values a property based on its ability to fulfill his specific business needs, unlike investors who value a property based primarily on its investment return.

Anchor Tenant Major department or chain store strategically located at shopping centers to give maximum exposure to smaller satellite stores. A center may have several anchor tenants.

Before Tax Cash Flow Gross amount of income available before considering taxes.

Capital Gain Profit made from an investment.

Capitalization Rate Rate of interest considered a reasonable return on investment; commonly used in the process of determining value based on net income. *Also called*: **Rate**.

Cash Flow Measure of cash available from an investment after subtracting all expenses. Positive cash flow means more money is coming in than going out. Negative cash flow is the converse.

Cash on Cash Return The bottom line of any investment expressed as a percentage by dividing the investment's cash flow by the deposit and settlement costs.

Clear Span Open distance between inside faces of support members.

Common Area Maintenance Land and improvements in a condominium, planned unit development, or cooperative all residents use and own as tenants in common, such as the parking lot, hallways, and recreational facilities; individual apartment units or homes are not included. *Also called*: **Common Elements.**

Consumer Price Index (CPI) An index published monthly by the United States Bureau of Labor Standards (BLS) considered by many to be the basic indicator of inflation in the U.S.

Debt Service Amount of money needed to meet the periodic payments of principal and interest on an amortized loan or debt. If the periodic payments are constant and equal, then a portion will pay off accrued interest with the remainder reducing principal.

(continued on next page)

Key Terms - continued

Depreciation A loss in value for any reason.

Effective Gross Income Potential gross income minus vacancy and collection losses.

Escalation Clause Lease clause that allows an increase in rent for increases in expenses paid by the landlord, such as real estate taxes, operating costs, and cost of living expenses.

Fixed Expenses Occur on a regular basis and have regular payment amounts; occur whether the property is vacant or fully leased, and generally do not vary in response to changing levels of occupancy.

Gross Income Total income, both cash and non-cash, received from an investment or business, before expenses are paid.

Lease Escalation Clause Clause that allows landlords to raise rent to protect their margin of profit and, in some cases, prevent the erosion of their expected return due to inflation.

Leverage The use of borrowed funds to purchase property with the anticipation of a return on the funds invested, such that the investor sees a profit not only on his own investment, but also on the borrowed funds.

Liquidity The ability to convert an asset into cash quickly without the loss of principal.

Loft Characterized by the fact that most of the building's interior is left unfinished, or minimally finished.

Loss Factor The difference between rentable square footage and usable square footage. *Also called*: **Load**.

Market Value The theoretical price a property is most likely to bring in a typical transaction.

Market Price The price a buyer actually paid for a property.

Net Lease Lease for which a tenant pays all taxes, insurance, etc., plus utilities and rent.

Net Operating Income (NOI) Income left after all operating costs are paid.

Operating Statement Document that illustrates total revenues generated for a given period based on rent rolls and management style.

Pass-Through Many leases allow landlords to pass along unexpected increases in operating costs to tenants.

Porter's Wage Escalation Formula Ties rent escalation to the wages of a building's cleaning and maintenance personnel (called "porters"). The formula provides tenant's rent will increase a specific amount per square foot for a specified increase in the porter's hourly wages.

Pro Forma Statement A schedule of the projected income and expenses for a real estate investment over a given period.

Pro-rata Share A proportionate share.

Rate of Return The rate at which an investor recaptures his investment in income-producing property.

Rentable Square Footage/Gross Square Footage The amount of space used in calculating a lease payment; rentable square footage is larger than the actual space tenants occupy because it includes their share of the property's service areas like the lobby, corridors, and other common areas.

Retail Investment Property Where a specific type of business activity occurs—retail sales and related business activities.

Return on Investment A saver/investor's expectation that he will eventually get back the interest paid while the equity was invested.

Risk The probability that events will not occur as expected.

Tax Shelter Any method used to reduce taxable income, thereby reducing the amount of tax paid to a government.

Usable Square Footage/Net Square Footage The amount of actual space within the perimeter of the tenant's premises, including walls, columns, and airshafts; the floor area where tenants can actually lay carpet and place furniture.

Value Amount of goods or services offered in the marketplace in exchange for something.

Variable Expense Expenses that are not consistent and regular amounts, and depend on issues including the type, size, age, and condition of a property.

Commercial Investment Property Overview

Commercial real estate is property used for investment purposes. It may also be referred to as **investment real estate**.

Owning vs. Leasing

An investor may **own** or **lease** commercial property. A **user-client** refers to an investor who either lives in or runs his business out of a commercial real estate property. An investor who is a **leaseholder** *does not* own the commercial property. An **amenity purchaser** is most likely an owner/user who is motivated to find a location from which to house and operate a business, and an **investor** desires to place money where it will earn more money.

Owning

Advantages	Disadvantages
• Tax savings	• Initial capital outlay
• Appreciation	• Liability
• Income	• Financing
• Control of the property	• Management requirements
	• Inflexibility

Leasing

Advantages	Disadvantages
• Flexibility	• Loss of appreciation
• Lower up-front cash requirement	• Lack of control over property
• Tax relief	• Lack of operational control and changes
• Lower risk of obsolescence	• Limited tax relief
• Stability of costs	• Contractual penalties
• Mobility	• Actual cost of leasing is often more expensive per square foot than owning
• Fewer management distractions	
• Better return on inventory turnover	

Sale-and-Leaseback vs. Ground Lease

Sale-and-Leaseback

- A company constructs a building that suits its needs, and then sells the building to an investor, who becomes the landlord
- Allows lessee to have more **liquid assets** to invest in product or other resources
- Provides some tax advantages for both parties

Ground Lease

- Also referred to as a **land lease**
- Enables tenants to lease *only the land,* but not any structures or improvements on the land
- Separates ownership of land from ownership of the buildings and improvements

Commercial Real Estate Licensing

Practicing commercial real estate does **not** require a special license. The real estate issued by New York State is all-encompassing, which means licensees may conduct residential and commercial transactions.

Commercial Commissions

Sales

The commission rate paid on the sale of commercial property is negotiated between the client and the broker at the time a listing agreement is made. There are no fixed or established commission schedules; in fact, any attempt to create an acceptable commission schedule is a violation of **antitrust laws**. Licensees may calculate commercial commissions using one of these four methods:

Fixed Percentage Method

The agreed upon percentage is multiplied by the actual sale price of the property to arrive at the amount of the commission.

Sale Price x Commission Percentage = Commission

Graduated Percentage

Typically used on higher priced properties or large properties split into several parcels using a scale such as:

- 7% on the first $500,000
- 6% on the next $500,000
- 5% on everything above $1 million

Fixed Fee

A fixed dollar amount is paid for the performance of specific real estate services. To be paid, the fee arrangement generally requires the successful completion of the transaction.

Retainer or Hourly Fee

A retainer (in advance) or a fee based on hours worked to perform specified tasks may be paid even when transactions do not close.

Leases

The commission paid for procuring leases is based on the schedule and arrangement between the participating parties. Licensees may calculate commercial commissions for leasing property using one of these four methods:

Lump Sum

Often based on a percentage of the total rent value of the lease (i.e., the aggregate lease amount).

Square Footage x Rent Rate x Lease Term x Commission Rate = Commission

Per Square Foot Fee

Commission is based on a dollar amount per square foot of leased space.

Flat Fee

Commission is based on a fixed dollar amount for leasing the space regardless of square footage.

Procurement Fee

Typically paid when a licensee is working with a tenant representative and is paid a fee for finding space for the tenant. Procurement fees are often fixed fees but can be percentage based.

Investing In Real Estate

The broad goals for investing in real estate include:

- **Preservation** of capital (return *of* investment or recapture)
- Reasonable **profit** on invested capital (return *on* investment)

Investors are motivated by:

- Receiving a **continuing stream of income** (cash flow model).
- Creating a **tax shelter**, which gives owners certain income tax advantages, such as deductions for property taxes, mortgage interest, and depreciation.
- Earning a **return on investment** when the property is sold (capital growth).

Investment Characteristics

- **Liquidity** – the ability to convert an asset into cash quickly without the loss of principal (real estate is traditionally one of the more **non-liquid** or **illiquid** of the various investment alternatives)
- **Marketability** – the ability to convert an asset to cash quickly, at any price
- **Leverage** – the use of borrowed funds to finance a portion of a property's purchase price
  - **Negative Leverage**: Occurs when borrowed funds are invested at a rate of return lower than the cost of funds to the borrower
  - **Positive Leverage**: Occurs when borrowed funds are invested at a rate of return higher than the cost of funds to the borrower
- **Tax Impact** – the effect of federal, state, and local income laws on the income, profit, and losses from an investment
- **Rate of Return** – a measure of investment performance
- **Risk** – the degree of probability the actual rate of return earned will differ from the return expected when the investment was made; types of risk include:
  - **Space Market** – demand for space will affect rents, vacancy rates, and NOI
  - **Capital Market** – changes in the market for capital will affect the value of real estate
  - **Financial** – exists when debt is used to finance an investment
  - **Liquidity** – difficulty of converting an investment into cash at market value quickly without the loss of principal

- ◆ **Environmental** – the value of a property will be influenced by environmental factors that affect the owner's ability to develop or lease the space
- ◆ **Inflation** – unexpected inflation will affect future income and purchasing power
- ◆ **Legislative** – changes in laws, building codes, zoning, and other regulations will affect the market value
- ◆ **Management** – property management issues may affect the performance of a property
- ◆ **Technology** – ever-changing technology creates obsolescence among businesses

Investment Property

Single-Family Residential

Readily available and have smaller management requirements. Many real estate professionals start their commercial careers selling single-family investment properties. The market value of single-family investment property tends to be influenced by general market conditions and comparable single-family property sales.

Multi-Family Residential

These types of properties range from small apartment buildings consisting of two to four units to large apartment complexes with hundreds of units. Smaller multi-family residential property may attract investors who are interested in income generated from renting the proprty to tenants. Typical investors in large multi-family units are often larger companies adept at acquiring and managing these properties.

Office Buildings

Office space may:

- Include former single-family homes converted into commercial space, insurance, or doctor's offices, as well as small, medium, and large office buildings located in the suburbs, and downtown high rises.

- Be located in mixed-use buildings or loft buildings. Investors in commercial office buildings are interested in the rental income received from leasing the space to tenants.

- Be of a variety of size/design; e.g., skyscraper. high-rise, mid-rise, low-rise, garden/subterranean.

Class Categories

Usually based on characteristics such as age, architectural design, location, building amenities and services, lease rates, occupancy levels, tenant profiles, and building management. There are four classes of buildings in most markets:

- **Class A.** The most desirable and new buildings in a particular market with the best design, superior construction and amenities, and features that attract the highest quality tenants

- **Class B.** An excellent building, just not the best around; it is usually older and/or less modern in its architecture or may have lost status since a new Class A office space opened nearby; still desirable, but not quite the top of the market, primarily due to age

- **Class C.** Properties are older and still functionally viable, but not as favorably located or maintained; may be found in what are now considered secondary locations and attract secondary market tenants who are price driven
- **Class D.** Older, functionally obsolete buildings that need extensive renovations or major repairs; prime candidates for rehabilitation projects or teardown

Valuation Considerations

The value of office property, like any commercial property, is dependent upon its ability to produce income. Considerations related to investment in office property are:

- Location
- Accessibility – ingress and egress; compliance with ADA
- Visibility – building and signage
- Adequacy of parking
- General market conditions and rent levels
- Common areas and facilities
- Tenant profile; ease of tenant improvements
- Type/adequacy of mechanical systems; special maintenance requirements
- Security and lighting in common areas
- Staffing and management requirements
- Appearance and market appeal
- Ancillary services (vending, cafeteria, child care, etc.)
- Technology issues (cable lines, satellite, fiber optics, etc.)

Retail

Retail properties are diverse and unique when compared to all other types of real estate investments. In the retail market, the ability of the property to produce an acceptable income stream will depend upon factors that are unique to retailing. A wide range of property types is available to buyers interested in purchasing investment property for retail purposes. Typical examples include:

- Strip shopping centers (minimum of 3 stores; up to 30,000 square feet)
- Neighborhood centers (often built around supermarket anchor; 30,000-100,000 square feet)
- Community shopping centers (multiple anchors; 100,000-300,000 square feet)
- Regional malls (broad range of retail and services; 250,000-900,000 square feet)
- Super regional or mega malls (every imaginable retail and services; 500,000-1.5 million square feet)
- Specialty shopping centers (no traditional anchor client)
- Power centers (multiple "big box" retailers)
- Outlet centers

Valuation Considerations

The **value** of retail property is based on its ability to generate income for the investor. The ability of a property to produce an acceptable income stream depends on a number of factors unique to retail sales. An **anchor tenant** is a magnet store strategically located in shopping centers to generate traffic for smaller stores. **Considerations** for the retail investor and the retail tenant are similar. They will both ask questions about:

- Market appeal.
- Access to public transportation.
- Location.
- Parking.
- Signage.
- Traffic flow.
- Visibility.
- Tenant mix.
- Anchor tenants.
- Competition.

Industrial

Often purchased by an investor who will use the property for a special purpose. Commercial industrial investment represents a broad category and includes investment in:

- Factories (light or heavy assembly, high tech)
- Warehouses
- Distribution/transit warehouse
- Wholesale trade
- Service center
- Research and development facilities

Industrial properties may be larger plants that house factories or assembly lines or smaller buildings that function as service centers or research and development facilities. Unlike office space, this type of property is often purchased by an investor who will use the property since it often has highly specialized features.

Valuation Considerations

Considerations related to investment in industrial property are:

- **Foundation and Floor Load Capacity.** Floor capacity, or weight that the floor can hold per square foot, is important because equipment used for industrial purposes has enormous weight and there are requirements related to floor load
- **Ceiling Height.** How many feet there are from the floor to the steel girders
- **Clear Span.** A measurement of the open distance between inside faces of support members or columns
- **Loading Docks/Shipping and Receiving.** What types of docks are available within the property as well as the features related to shipping and receiving requirements
- **Accessibility.** The ease of getting to and from the property
- **Type/Adequacy of Mechanical Systems.** The investor will be interested in the available mechanical systems that are part of the property

- **Environmental Assessment.** An environmental assessment of the site will be required and any concerns discovered must be addressed

Unimproved Land

Land is another type of commercial investment property that can be acquired by investors. As with most categories of real estate, location is usually the first item on the list of considerations with regard to what can be done with property. Additionally, there is a long list of site considerations to address as well, including zoning, condition of title, and characteristics of the land itself. All of these can impact the investor's decision whether to purchase the property.

Evaluating an Investment's Performance

Cash Flow Model / Operating Statements

Since a **return of/on the investment** is often not realized until the real estate is sold, it is necessary to analyze the ability of a property to produce an acceptable return to the investor during the entire ownership period. An **operating statement** consists of income and expense items associated with operating the property. The ultimate goal of an operating statement is to find the **cash flow**:

	Gross Potential Income
-	Vacancy/Credit Loss
+	Other Income (Misc.)
=	Effective Gross Income
-	Total Expenses
=	Net Operating Income (NOI)
-	Annual Debt Service (Interest and Principal)
=	Cash Flow Before Taxes

Expenses

- **Fixed expenses** occur on a regular basis and have regular payment amounts, such as ad valorem property taxes and insurance
- **Variable expenses** are expenses that are necessary to maintain the income stream of the property and provide services to the tenants
- **Capital Improvements**, e.g., a new furnace or new roof, do **not** appear as expenses on an operating statement, but are capitalized and gradually expensed over the **useful life.**

Valuation Overview via Capitalization

The capitalization rate, or cap rate, is determined by dividing what was made from the investment by what was paid for the investment. The bottom line of any investment expressed as a percentage by dividing the investment's cash flow by the deposit and settlement costs is the property owner's **cash-on-cash return**.

The IRV Formula

The capitalization approach to value calculates the value (V) of an investment by comparing the net operating income (I) to the rate of return (R) necessary to attract an investor. The calculation is the IRV formula:

Income = Rate x Value or I = R x V

As long as you know two of the factors, you can calculate the third:

Value = Income ÷ Rate

Rate = Income ÷ Value

Cash-On-Cash Return

The ratio of income generated by the cash investment is calculated as:

Before Tax Cash Flow ÷ Purchase Costs = Cash-on-Cash Return

Taxable Income

The amount of income on which an investor must pay taxes is calculated as:

	Before Tax Cash Flow
-	**Depreciation**
+	**Principal Payments**
	Taxable Income

Depreciation

Sources of depreciation are categorized as:

- **Physical deterioration** – the building physically wears out, decays, or experiences a loss of physical soundness
- **Functional obsolescence** (inside property lines) – the building becomes outdated and obsolete; it experiences functional deficiencies
- **External obsolescence** (outside property lines) – the property location experiences reversals, changes in the population or laws, or extraneous conditions which lower property value and utility

IRS Straight Line Depreciation for Investment Property

- Residential income property – **27.5 years**
- Non-residential income property – **39 years**

Pro Forma vs. Operating Statement

Operating Statement	Pro Forma
Used by property owners to illustrate total revenues generated and expenses for a given period as a means of evaluating the property's performance.	Also called the annual property operating data (APOD), it shows the hypothetical projection of income and expenses for the first full year of ownership.
Shows contract rent (rent currently being charged).	Shows economic rent (rent that would be possible to charge in the market).
Shows vacancy loss either as: • Specific number, if known. • Calculated as % of gross annual income.	Shows anticipated vacancy loss using data from: • Historical data from existing operating statements. • Projections based on current market conditions in the area, such as unemployment, etc. • A market analysis to determine the vacancy losses of comparable properties.

Square Footage

Rentable Square Footage
- Total floor area of a building, including all tenant space as well as common areas (lobbies, corridors, etc.)
- Most often used for calculating the **lease payment** for commercial properties
- Tenant pays for their specific space and then a pro rated share of the identified common areas
- Also called **gross square footage**

Useable Square Footage
- Amount of actual space within the perimeter of the defined space occupied by a specific tenant, including walls, columns, and airshafts
- Also called **net square footage** or **carpetable square footage**

Loss Factor and Building Efficiency
The difference between rentable square footage and usable square footage is the **loss** or **load factor**. To determine the efficiency of space leased, it is necessary to know what the loss factor is. To calculate the loss factor:

(Rentable Sq. Ft. - Usable Sq. Ft.) ÷ Rentable Sq. Ft. = Loss Factor

The flip side of the loss factor is **building efficiency**, which is the ratio of unstable square footage to rentable square footage. To calculate building efficiency:

Usable Sq. Ft. ÷ Rentable Sq. Ft. = Building Efficiency

Commercial Leases

Net Leases

- The tenant pays some or all of the costs of ownership, except mortgage interest and principal, in addition to the agreed upon rent, including:
  - Property taxes
  - Property insurance
  - Common area maintenance (CAM)
- Categorized by how many of these costs are covered in the lease:
  - Single net lease – tenant pays one of the ownership costs
  - Double net lease – tenant pays any two of the ownership costs
  - Triple net/absolute net lease – tenant pays all three of the ownership costs

Gross Leases

- A straightforward exchange of rent for occupancy
- Also called a **full service lease**
- Tenant pays a **fixed rent**
- Owner/landlord pays all ownership expenses (property taxes, mortgage payments, maintenance, insurance, etc., and sometimes, utilities)
- In a modified gross lease, tenant may be responsible for utilities, trash removal, and cleaning but the landlord pays the taxes, insurance, and maintenance

Typical Property Leases

Office Leases

- Typically quoted as price per gross square foot
- The **gross square footage** of a building, also called the *rentable square footage* or *payable square footage* includes common foyers, corridors, staircases, and elevators that lead to individual offices; this is the space the tenant pays for
- The **useable space**, also referred to as *net square footage*, is the space that the tenant uses
- **Office tenants** may have particular requirements for such things as parking, treatment of utilities, hours of operation, ancillary services, technology, and improvements

Retail Leases

- Are typically quoted as price per rentable square foot for base rent
- Percentage leases are often used, which means the tenant pays, in addition to their base rent, some percentage of their gross sales
- Office tenants are also responsible for their proportionate share of common area maintenance, taxes, and insurance, which are paid as additional rent
- Retail tenants who are part of a retail center or mall may contribute to a promotional fund for advertising and special events

Industrial Leases

- Are typically quoted in terms of dollars per square foot per year
- Industrial leases are usually quoted as **triple-net** leases, meaning the insurance, taxes, and common area maintenance charges are included

- Utilities are handled separately; this is referred to as **net plus utilities**

Rent Structures

Commercial leases are typically structured based on the way in which rent is calculated. Types of rent structures include:

- **Percentage** – tenant pays a fixed monthly base rent as well as a percentage of gross sales achieved by the tenant over and above a predetermined level of sales known as the "breakpoint"
- **Graduated** – step rent increases or decreases; generally paid in installments
- **Index** – the amount rent increase is tied to a common index, which is based on changes in the market place

Typical Lease Clauses

- **Use** – Specifically defines what type of business or use can be conducted by the tenant on the premises
- **Attornment** – establishes tenancy with a new owner and defends current tenants against claims for rent from the former property owner
- **Estoppel certificate** – a legal instrument that prevents a person from taking a position, denying a fact, or asserting a fact inconsistent with previous conduct or statements
- **Disposal of leased space options**
    - Close down the operation but continue to pay the obligated rental payment until the end of the current term and not exercise their renewal option
    - Approach the landlord with a "buyout" proposal, in the form of a lump sum paid to terminate the existing lease early
    - Sublease their space to another tenant, if the lease permits it
    - Assign their lease if they no longer wish to occupy the property (assumption agreement)
- **Subordination** – places the existing lease in an order junior to that of the new mortgage on the leased property
- **Nondisturbance** – requires lenders to sign a document agreeing to honor and not terminate the tenancies of lessees who are current with their rent and who are complying with all provisions and obligations of their leases
- **Utility Clauses** – details related to who is responsible for utility bills
- **Escape** – allows a tenant to get out of long-term lease under specified circumstances

Other Lease Options

A lease may be the beginning point of a future purchase:

- A **lease with option to buy** is a combination of a lease and an option to purchase (some or all of the rent paid may go toward the purchase price)
- A **lease purchase agreement** is a combination of a lease and a purchase agreement (some or all of the rent paid may go toward the purchase price; if the property is not transferred until settlement)
- **Right of first refusal** (also called a right of preemption):
    - Gives the tenant the right to have the **first opportunity** to buy or lease property if the owner decides to put it up for sale or lease

◆ Cannot be exercised until the owner gets a **bona fide offer** from a third party; the owner must then make the property available to the one holding the right at the **same terms** as the bona fide offer

Base Rent and Adjustments

• Commercial rent usually adds a proportionate share, or **pro-rata share**, of the direct operating expenses or common area maintenance on shared space and amenities to the rent per square foot to find the **base rent**

• If actual expenses exceed base rent, most leases allow the owner to pass excess charges back through the tenants (a **pass-through**)

• Leases may contain an **expense cap** or ceiling that limits the pass-through amount

• Leases may contain an **escalation clause** (or elevator) that allows rent to be adjusted during the lease term

• **Graduated leases** are when base rent is scheduled to step up or bump up at a predetermined negotiated percentage or pre-established dollar amount (no matter what happens to actual operating expenses)

• **Index leases** link an escalation clause to a readily available index such as:

 ◆ Porter's Wage Escalation Formula

 ◆ Consumer Price Index (CPI)

QUIZ

1. *Craig owns a warehouse and his property taxes were recently raised. In turn, Craig charged his tenant additional operating expenses. This is an example of a(n)*
   - A. loss factor.
   - B. pass-through.
   - C. pro rata share.
   - D. wage escalation.

2. *Leverage is*
   - A. the ability to covert an asset into cash quickly at any price.
   - B. the ability to convert an asset into cash quickly without the loss of principal.
   - C. the possibility of losing either the principal invested and/or the potential income from the investment.
   - D. the use of borrowed funds to finance a portion of the purchase price of an investment.

3. *What is the minimum license requirement to practice in commercial real estate in New York State?*
   - A. commercial broker license
   - B. commercial salesperson license
   - C. real estate broker license
   - D. real estate salesperson license

4. *Loss factor is calculated as the difference between*
   - A. commissions owed and commissions paid.
   - B. gross sales and net sales.
   - C. gross square footage and useable square footage.
   - D. rented units and rentable units

5. *George owns a bowling alley in a town that just voted to ban smoking in all public places. Consequently, he has lost a lot of customers and his receipts are down. George is experiencing*
   - A. capital market risk.
   - B. inflation risk.
   - C. legislative risk.
   - D. market space risk.

6. *The recovery of the cost of a capital asset over time by expensing a set portion of it each year is called*
   - A. appreciation.
   - B. capital decline.
   - C. depreciation.
   - D. negative cash flow.

7. *To find cash flow before taxes, subtract _____ from _____.*
   - A. annual debt service from net operating income.
   - B. net operating income from effective gross income.
   - C. total expenses from gross income.
   - D. vacancy loss from gross potential income.

8. *The ability to convert an asset into cash quickly without the loss of principal is*
   - A. leverage.
   - B. liquidity.
   - C. marketability.
   - D. utility.

9. *Which is NOT a factor you would need to know to find the capitalization rate?*
   - A. depreciation
   - B. market value
   - C. net operating income
   - D. vacancy loss

10. *Revenue generated from the investment property minus expenses required for operation is equal to*
    - A. cash flow.
    - B. leverage.
    - C. net operating income.
    - D. return.

Property Management

Key Terms

Actual Eviction Physically forcing someone off property, preventing someone from re-entering property, or using the legal process to make someone leave.

Anchor Tenant Major department or chain store strategically located at shopping centers to give maximum exposure to smaller satellite stores. A center may have several anchor tenants.

Building Manager Oversees the management of one building for a property owner.

Capital Expense An expense incurred to improve property.

Capital Reserve Budget A budget for expenses that are not fixed (variable).

Constructive Eviction When a landlord's act (or failure to act) interferes with the tenant's quiet enjoyment of the property, or makes the property unfit for its intended use, to such an extent the tenant is forced to move out.

Corrective Maintenance Repairing or restoring broken or failed equipment to a specified condition.

Cosmetic Maintenance Maintenance that increases a property's appeal.

Fiduciary Person in a position of trust held by law to high standards of good faith and loyalty.

General Agent A person authorized to handle a principal's affairs in one area or in specified areas.

Lessee Person who leases property; a tenant.

Lessor Person who leases property to another; a landlord.

Management Agreement A written agreement that governs the relationship between a property owner/investor and the property manager and outlines the duties of the property manager. *Also called*: **Property Management Employee Contract**.

Management Proposal A plan created by the property manager for overseeing the property, including market analysis, and developing a variety of financial reports including the operating budget.

Operating Budget A budget created to project the income and expenses for a property over a one-year period.

Planned Unit Development (PUD) A special type of subdivision that may combine nonresidential uses with residential uses, or otherwise depart from ordinary zoning and subdivision regulations; some PUD lot owners co-own recreational facilities or open spaces as tenants in common.

(continued on next page)

Overview

Property management is the leasing or renting, or the offering to lease or rent, of real property of others for a fee, commission, compensation, or other valuable consideration pursuant to a property management employee contract.

Property Manager

A **property manager** is a person hired by a real property owner to administer, market, and maintain property – especially rental property. To become a property manager in the state of New York, one must have a real estate salesperson or broker license. Most states require that anyone who takes or publishes a listing, negotiates a lease, or interacts with potential tenants have a real estate license. Property managers may be responsible for collecting rents, selecting tenants, renting and leasing units, maintaining and repairing buildings, supervising building personnel, maintaining tenant relationships, and accounting for income and expenditures.

Functions

The different property manager roles include:

- **Property manager** – usually oversees the management of a number of properties for various owners
- **Building manager** – manager of just one building
- **Resident manager** – represents a property management firm and may live on the premises of the building being managed

Everyone in the property management field must:

- Have an understanding of leasing regulations to collect rents, and basic construction knowledge to ensure routine maintenance is performed

Key Terms - continued

Preventive Maintenance Routine maintenance and inspections that keep equipment and the property in good working order.

Principal A person who grants another person (an agent) authority to represent him in dealings with third parties.

Property Management Leasing or renting, or offering to lease or rent real property of others for a fee, commission, compensation, or other valuable consideration pursuant to a property management employee contract.

Property Management Report A report prepared by property managers to inform owners of the status of their property, often including income, expenses, and disbursements information.

Property Manager A person hired by a real property owner to administer, market, merchandise, and maintain property, especially rental property.

Rent Roll Spreadsheet or listing of key information about a property (i.e., total number of units, tenant names and apartment numbers, lease dates, rent each tenant pays).

Resident Manager Represents a property management firm and may live on the premises of the building she manages.

Risk Management Identifying, managing, and minimizing the potential risks on a property.

Stabilized Budget A property's income and expenses averaged over a five year period.

Tenancy (or Estate) for Years Leasehold estate set to last for a definite period (e.g., one week, three years), after which it automatically terminates. *Also called*: **Term Tenancy**.

Variable Expenses Expenses that are not consistent and regular amounts, and depend on issues including the type, size, age, and condition of a property.

- Know how to develop a management proposal
- Create and manage several reports and budgets for property owners
- Possess exceptional communication skills
- Understand basic marketing principals

Relationship with Owner

A property management company is in an *agency relationship* with a property owner, and owes the property owner the same fiduciary duties of obedience, loyalty, disclosure, confidentiality, accountability, and reasonable care owed to all clients. Typically, a property manager is in a principal-agent relationship, with the principal being the owner and the agent being the property manager. A property manager or property management company is a general agent because of the broad range of duties performed. A **general agent** is an agent authorized to handle all of the principal's affairs in one area or in specified areas.

A property manager's three main jobs are to:

- Fulfill the goals and objectives of the owners.
- Create income for the owners.
- Maintain or increase the property's value.

The Management Agreement

Property owners and property managers should spell out the details of their relationship in a written **property management agreement** (also called the **property management employee contract**); this establishes the agency relationship. The contract contains some or all of these components:

- Property description – an exact address and, sometimes, a full legal description
- Length of agreement – negotiated between the property manager and owner
- Management authority – outlines what a property manager is authorized to handle in regard to all aspects of leasing property
- Management fee – may be a fixed (flat) or percentage fee
- Accounting responsibilities and reports – **property management reports** are prepared by property managers to inform owners of the status of the property, often including income, expenses, and disbursement information
- Insurance and risk management – **risk management** is identifying, managing, and minimizing the potential risks on a property
- Owner's responsibilities and objectives – vary and should be listed in the property management agreement
- Management agreement termination – details about the termination of the owner-manager relationship

Property Management Responsibilities

A property manager should have some knowledge of appraisal, finance, money markets, depreciation techniques, financial trends, and local market conditions to produce useful reports and accomplish the owner's overall objectives and goals.

Management Proposal

A **management proposal** is a plan created by the property manager for overseeing the property. It includes an analysis of the market and a variety of financial reports, including an operating budget. The proposal should include a one-year operating budget, a five-year plan, and a market analysis.

Reporting

In order to develop a one-year and five-year plan for the management proposal *and* to complete the regular financial reporting to the owner, the following reports must be generated and pertinent information analyzed:

Operating Budget

This statement projects the income and expenses for the property over a **one-year period** and includes:

- **Total income** – gross rental income and other income are listed and added together
- **Expenses** – fixed expenses are ongoing operating expenses that do not vary based on occupancy levels of the property. Variable expenses are operating expenses necessary to the property, but dependent on the property's occupancy level
- **Net operating income** – income after expenses are deducted

Other Financial Reports and Statements

- **Capital expenses** – used to improve the property and increase its value
- **Capital reserve budget** – budget for capital expenses that are not fixed (variable expenses)
- **Stabilized budget** – the income and expenses averaged over a **five-year period**
- **Budget comparison statements** – compare the actual working budget with the budget developed at the beginning of the year
- **Profit and loss statements** – a brief statement issued at regular intervals,

Gross Receipts - Operating Expenses - Total Mortgage Payment + Mortgage Loan Principal = Net Profit

- **Cash flow reports** – usually issued on a monthly basis and gives the owner a detailed financial picture of the property

After all reports have been generated, the property manager should be able to develop the management proposal and make recommendations to the owner about the property.

Management Office Operations

Whether managing a property that is industrial, retail, or residential, a property management office is often necessary. The following tasks may be included as part of operations management:

- **Maintaining accounts** – the property manager owes his or her fiduciary duty to the property owner, and must maintain a property management account that is separate from all other accounts

- **Supervision** – a property manager might manage an assistant property manager, tenant services coordinator, or administrative assistant, as well as contractual employees
- **Rent roll** – a spreadsheet or listing of key information about a property such as the number of units, tenant names with apartment numbers, lease dates, and the rent each tenant pays on a unit

Building Systems and Construction

Property managers should have knowledge of major building systems, such as:

- Electrical
- Structural engineering
- Gas
- Maintenance
- HVAC (heating, ventilation, and air conditioning)
- Elevators
- Security
- Waterproofing
- Plumbing

Maintenance

Maintenance costs should be carefully scheduled and controlled because they represent a relatively large part of a property's operating budget:

- **Preventative maintenance** – routine maintenance and inspections to keep equipment and the property in good working order.
- **Corrective maintenance** – restores broken or failed equipment to a specified condition.
- **Cosmetic maintenance** – increases a property's appeal.

Appraisal

An **appraisal** is an opinion of the value of property, as of a specific date, supported by objective data. When a building is appraised, the property manager is the one who interacts with the appraiser. Therefore, it is important to have an understanding of the appraisal process.

Landlord-Tenant Relationships

Creating good relationships with tenants is a key aspect of a property manager's work. Often, property managers who maintain good relationships with tenants have fewer problems and lower turnover.

Leasing Space

The **lessee** is a person who leases property—a tenant, and a **lessor** is a person who lease property to another—a landlord. A lease is a binding document and should include:

- Names and signatures
- Occupancy date
- Description of the space

- Terms of the lease
- Valuable consideration
- Escalation clauses
- All parties' rights and obligations
- Any restrictions on use of rental space
- Stipulation that illegal activities on the premises are grounds for immediate termination

A **tenancy (or estate) for years** is a leasehold estate set to last for a definite period (i.e., one week, three years), which is automatically terminated when the lease is up.

Eviction

Property managers may find they have to evict a tenant who does not pay the rent, breaks the rules, or is involved in criminal behavior.

- **Actual eviction** is using the legal process to make someone leave
- **Constructive eviction** is when a landlord's act (or failure to act) interferes with the tenant's quiet enjoyment of the property or makes the property unfit for its intended use, to such an extent that the tenant is forced to move out
- **Self-help eviction** (sometimes called a **lock-out** or a **freeze-out**) is when a landlord uses physical force or other means to get rid of a tenant instead of going though the legal process

Advertising And Marketing

A solid marketing and promotional plan is needed to attract tenants. There are several routes a property manager can take to advertise a property available for rent:

- Word of mouth
- Advertisement
- Signage
- Brochures
- Direct mail
- Online
- Press release

By tracking how prospective tenants heard about an open unit, property managers can get an idea for what methods of advertisements are working.

Codes and Regulations

A critical law for property owners is the **New York Multiple Dwelling Law (MDL)**. This series of laws dictates the specific responsibilities of property owners related to required maintenance, building codes, services, tenant protection, landlord liability, etc.

In addition to the New York State law, landlords must comply with:

- Federal Fair Housing laws and the Americans with Disabilities Act
- New York Human Rights Law
- Local occupancy laws
- Environmental laws that spell out requirements for trash disposal

- Health and building department laws
- Zoning regulations

Other Responsibilities

A property manager may be involved in many aspects as the owner's agent, including:

- **Union negotiations.** As a property manager in the State of New York, it is important to be aware of and have an understanding of union contractors.
- **Purchasing**. It is not unusual for property managers to be responsible for purchasing supplies, writing purchase orders, and paying a wide variety of contractors.
- **Environmental awareness.** Depending on the market and the specific property you are assigned to, it is important to be aware of ways you can save energy and/or money on electric, gas, water, and landscaping.

Types of Properties Managed

No matter what type of tenant occupies the space in a building, property managers have the same mission—market and rent space effectively, maintain the property in good condition, comply with government regulations, and keep operating costs low.

Office Buildings

Property managers should familiarize themselves with competing office spaces throughout the area, so they can establish appropriate rental rates and standards for design and structural elements. Negotiating an office lease is more complex than negotiating other kinds of leases. Before starting negotiations, a property manager should be very clear about the owner's priorities. Property managers also often prepare emergency plans for office buildings.

Retail

Retail outlets include everything from grocery stores to plaza shopping centers and sprawling outlet malls.

- An **anchor tenant** is a major department or chain store strategically located within a shopping center to give maximum exposure to smaller satellite stores.
- Percentage leases are often used with retail spaces.
- Liability for accidents is complicated in shopping malls; if there is an accident, property managers should notify the insurance company immediately.

Residential Property

Residential property includes single-family homes, apartments, condominiums and cooperatives, mobile home parks, and retirement communities. Pricing and marketing are key elements in successfully renting residential housing.

Condos and Cooperatives

Managing a condo is similar to managing multi-family residential properties. Tenants should purchase their own insurance and condo owners should also be insured. Property managers of subsidized housing funded through HUD need to follow

HUD's rules and standards. Both condos and co-ops have an owners association and a property manager would likely have to work with those boards.

Special Purpose Properties

Property managers may have the opportunity to manage special purpose properties, including:

- Hotels and motels
- Theaters
- Schools
- Places of worship
- Housing for the elderly – includes independent living, assisted living, and nursing homes
- Planned Unit Developments (PUDs) – special types of subdivisions that may combine non-residential uses with residential uses, or otherwise depart from ordinary zoning and subdivision regulations

Industrial Property

Industrial property includes manufacturing facilities and warehouses. Industrial properties usually have net leases, requiring tenants to pay a greater percentage of property expenses than most leases do. Industrial tenants usually pay for and perform their own maintenance.

QUIZ

1. **In the property owner/property manager relationship, the property owner is the _____ and the property manager is the _____.**
   - A. agent / broker
   - B. agent / principal
   - C. broker / agent
   - D. principal / agent

2. **Mary, who is in a wheelchair, wants to install a ramp in her rented apartment. Property owner Jack**
   - A. can ask Mary to find a more appropriate place to live.
   - B. can refuse to allow the ramp since it's on the outside of the unit.
   - C. must allow Mary to install the ramp at her expense.
   - D. must install the ramp for Mary at his expense.

3. **A _____ has a fiduciary obligation to a _____.**
   - A. property manager / property owner
   - B. property manager / tenant
   - C. property owner / property manager
   - D. tenant / property owner

4. **Tenant Tom has often complained to his landlord about the terrible conditions of his apartment. There are holes in the windows, leaks in the ceiling, and an infestation of roaches. When things become unbearable, Tom moves out and quits paying rent, even though he has five months left on his lease. This is an example of**
   - A. actual eviction.
   - B. constructive eviction.
   - C. retaliatory eviction.
   - D. self-help eviction.

5. **Property manager Phyllis manages a building for property owner Lowell. A written agreement that governs the relationship between Lowell and Phyllis and outlines her duties as property manager is called a**
   - A. management agreement.
   - B. management proposal.
   - C. planned unit development.
   - D. property management report.

6. **For the purposes of an operating budget, property taxes and insurance are examples of what type of expenses?**
   - A. capital
   - B. fixed
   - C. net
   - D. variable

7. **A property manager is what type of agent?**
   - A. dual
   - B. general
   - C. special
   - D. universal

8. **In a retail development, a large store intended to lure customers to the smaller stores is known as a(n) _____ store.**
   - A. anchor
   - B. magnet
   - C. planned unit
   - D. target

9. **A stabilized budget is created for what time period?**
   - A. 6 months
   - B. 1 year
   - C. 5 years
   - D. 7 years

10. **Bart manages a building with 30 units. No one has moved in about five years. What should Bart, as property manager, recommend to the owner?**
    - A. enhance the apartments
    - B. make no changes
    - C. raise the rent
    - D. reduce the rent

Math Review

INDEX

The Circle Equation

The first "formula" (aid) we are going to learn is the circle, or pie, equation. The pie can be used for a large portion of the problems and is an aid to tell you when to divide or multiply. Some of the problem types include interest, rate of return on an income property, percentage of appreciation or depreciation, and many more.

The Basics

The circle equation is made up of the part, the total, and the percent. What the pie tells us is:

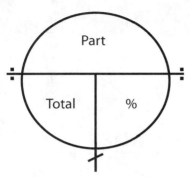

a. Part equates total times percent
part = total x %

b. Total equals part divided by percent
total = part ÷ %

c. Percent equals part divided by total
% = part ÷ total

The part is usually the smallest number in a problem, but not always. Usually, we are dealing with percentages smaller than 100%. If the percentage is greater than 100%, then the part is larger than the total, as we will explain later. The part can be obtained by multiplying % times total.

The total is usually the largest number, with the same exceptions as the part defined above. The total can be calculated by dividing the part by %.

The % can be calculated by dividing the part by the total. In most problems, it is less than 100%, but not always as we'll see in appreciation problems.

The % box can also be in the form of a fraction or decimal. Maybe we should say if the problem is in the form of a fraction or decimal, you can convert that to percent.

Breaking Problems Down For The Pie

The challenge of each problem is to know when to multiply and when to divide. These are the only possible steps to solving problems other than adding and subtracting. There are only three slots in the pie and the problem must give us two of the three numbers.

Key word — **"of"** (means multiply)

Example 1: One-half of a dollar is how much?

	%	x	Total	=	Part
or	_	x	$1.00	=	Part
or	0.5	x	$1.00	=	Part
or	50%	x	$1.00	=	Part

Convert fractions to decimal equivalents.

1/2 is (1 ÷ 2) and equals 0.5

3 1/2 is 3 + (1 ÷ 2) and equals 3.5

Convert decimals to percentages.

Move the decimal point two places to the right (multiply by 100).

Example 2: $400 is 2 1/2% of what amount? $400 ÷ 2.5% = $16,000

0.5	is 5.0%	fifty percent
0.505	is 50.5%	fifty and a half percent
3.5	is 350.0%	three hundred and fifty percent

Note: You can add zeros to the end of decimal numbers without changing its value

Example 3: A commission on a $35,000 home sale was $2,200. What was the commission rate?

(a)   We want to know commission which is a %

(b)   Therefore, the problem must give us the total and the part.

(c)   The commission ($2,200) is obviously only a part of the selling price ($35,000)

(d) $$\% = \frac{\text{Part}}{\text{Total}} \quad \text{or} \quad \text{Part} \div \text{Total} = \text{Percentage}$$

(e)

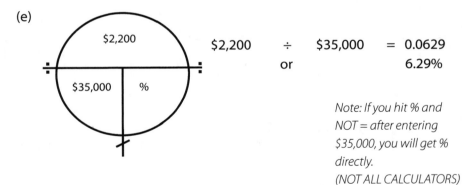

$2,200 ÷ $35,000 = 0.0629
or   6.29%

Note: If you hit % and NOT = after entering $35,000, you will get % directly.
(NOT ALL CALCULATORS)

Complex Problems (More Than One Calculation)

Sometimes the problem will require two calculations to get the answer. Relax, read the question, and write down the givens. Two out of three pieces of the secondary pie will be given—solve to get the second of the three parts needed for the primary pie.

Mr. Smith gets two-thirds of the seven percent commission on a $79,000 home sale. How much was Mr. Smith's commission?

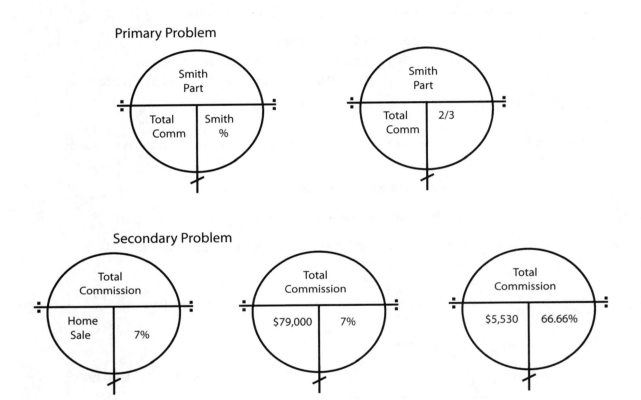

Answer: $79,000 x 7% = $5,530
            $5,530 x 66.66% = $3,686.298 = $3,686.30

Interest Problems– Amortizing Loans

An amortizing loan is our typical home mortgage loan where the payment stays the same over the life of the loan, but the principal in each payment varies. We are not bankers and do not need to calculate principal. We do need to compute interest and, once we learn how easy it is, we can subtract the interest from the total payment to determine how much of the payment is being applied to the principal (or tell us what the principal is). Let's do some basic interest problems!

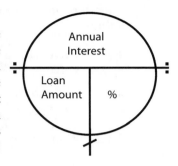

(a) What is the annual interest rate on a $73,000 loan with monthly interest payments of $821.25?

1. 11.25%
2. 13.5%
3. 15.0%
4. 10.5%

First: What are we looking for?
Answer: % (we can also see that all the answers are %.)

Second: What formula can I use?
Answer: The circle—it's an interest problem.

$73,000 ==>

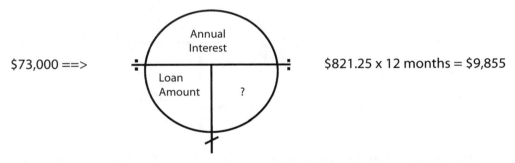

$821.25 x 12 months = $9,855

Remember: The "PART" must always be an "ANNUAL AMOUNT." That is why we multiplied the monthly interest by 12.

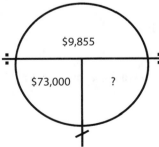

Now, put it into your calculator just how you read it—$9,855 ÷ $73,000 = 0.135—OOPS! But all the answers are in %. Remember: Convert a decimal to a %, just multiply by 100, or move the decimal 2 places to the right.

Answer: #2 (13.5%)

(b) A quarterly interest expense of $650 represents an 11% rate on what amount?

1. $5,909.10
2. $70,909.09
3. $11,818.20
4. $23,636.36

First: What are we looking for?

Answer: The loan amount (THE TOTAL)

<==$650 x 4 = $2,600*

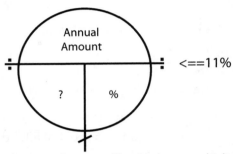

<==11%

Remember: The "PART" must always be annual amount. That is why we multiplied the quarterly interest payments by 4.

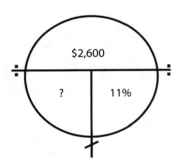

Now, put it into your calculator just how you read it: 2,600 ÷ 11% is $23,636.36.

Remember: To enter % for 11%. Do not hit the = sign. After you hit %, the # on your calculator is the answer. (NOT ALL CALCULATORS)

Answer: #4 ($23,636.36)

(c) What is the monthly interest on a mortgage of $54,600 at annual interest rate of 13.25%?

1. $ 723.40
2. $ 602.88
3. $7,234.50
4. $ 816.00

First: What are we looking for?

Answer: Monthly interest (the "PART" ÷ 12 months)

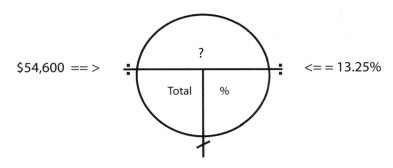

Now, put it into your calculator like this: $54,600 x 13.25% is $7,234.50*

Again, you do not need to hit the = key. After you press %, the number on your calculator is the answer for that step.

Remember: The "PART" is an annual amount. You must divide by 12 to get monthly interest.

$7,234.50 ÷ 12 mos. = $602.88/month

$54,600 x 13.25% is $7,234.50*

Answer: #2 ($602.88)

(d) Walt Fisher and his wife Betty, obtain a 30-year, $78,000 loan to buy a house. If loan payments are $698.98 per month, including 10 1/4% interest per year, and the second monthly payment includes $665.97 in interest, what will be the amount of interest paid over the life of the loan?

1. $125,813
2. $173,850
3. $239,850
4. $251,626

The total monthly payment including principal and interest is $698.98. How many total payments are we going to make over the life of the loan?

(30-year mortgage) x (12 months per year) = 360 total monthly payments
$698.98 x 360 months = $251,632.80 total paid over the life of the loan including principal and interest.

How much of that is principal over the life of the loan? That's right! The amount of the mortgage is $78,000.

$251,632.80	total principal and interest
Less - $ 78,000.00	loan amount
$173,632.80	interest

Answer: #2 ($173,626 the closest)

Capitalization Problems – Rate of Return on Investment

Now let's try some capitalization problems. It's almost the same as interest but the circle looks like this:

Remember: Net income is gross income minus expenses.

(a) An apartment building has a rate of return of 9%. The monthly net rental is $850. What is the market value of the property?

1. $94,444.44
2. $113,333.33
3. $102,000.00
4. $116,000.00

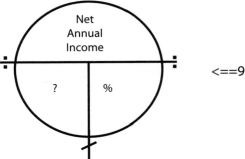

$850 x 12 months = $10,200 annual income

Note: This problem gives us monthly net income. We only have to make it an annual amount.

$850 x 12 months = $10,200/annual
$10,200 ÷ 9% = $113,333.33

Answer: #2 ($113,333.33)

(b) An office building has a gross annual income of $64,000. Expenses are $3,230 per month. If the building is valued at $252,400, what is the owner's rate of return?

1. 25.36%
2. 10.00%
3. 15.36%
4. 24.07%

First: What are we looking for?

Answer: Rate of Return or %

Remember: The "PART" must always be net annual income. They give us gross annual income and monthly expenses so we must multiply monthly expenses by 12 months to get annual expenses. When we subtract the annual expenses from the gross annual income to get net annual income.

$3,230 x 12 months = $38,760 annual expenses

$64,000 (gross annual income) $38,760 = $25,240 net annual income

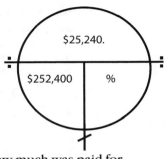

$25,240 net income ÷ $252,400 market value = 0.10 or 10%

Answer: #2 (10.00%)

(c) If a quarterly income of $1,250 yields an investor a 14% return, how much was paid for the property?

1. $ 8,928.57
2. $ 89,285.70
3. $ 35,714.29
4. $107,142.86

First: What are we looking for?

Answer: Value of the property/total

Remember: Quarterly income must be made into annual income.

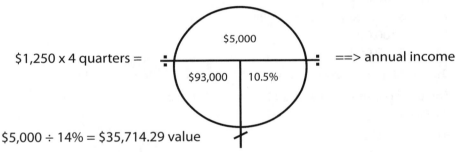

$1,250 x 4 quarters = ==> annual income

$5,000 ÷ 14% = $35,714.29 value

Answer: #3 ($35,714.29)

Commission Problems

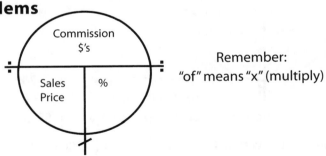

Remember:
"of" means "x" (multiply)

(a) The commission on the sale of a $102,000 house is 6%. How much is the commission?

1. $170,000
2. $ 17,000
3. $ 612
4. $ 6,120

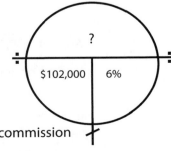

$102,000 sales price x 6% rate of commission = $6,120 total commission

Answer: #4 ($6,120)

(b) Your broker has agreed to pay you 40% of the company's share of the commission. The company received 3.5% of a $92,000 sale. What was your share of the commission?

1. $1,400
2. $1,288
3. $3,220
4. $3,680

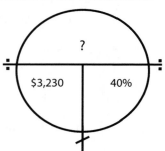

The company's portion: $92,000 x 3.5% = $3,220

Your portion: $ 3,220 x 40% = $1,288

Answer: #2 ($1,288)

(c) The agreed commission rate for selling an apartment building is 6% on the first $100,000 and 4% of anything over that amount. The total commission paid was $9,200. What was the sales price of the building?

1. $ 80,000
2. $100,000
3. $180,000
4. $150,000

This problem has several steps. Don't worry, each step is simple.

The total commission was $9,200. We know that 6% of $100,000 was part of it:

$100,000 x 6% = $6,000

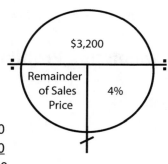

Total commission = $9,200
minus $100,000 x 6% = $6,000
Remainder of sales price x 4% = $3,200

We also know that 4% of something = $3,200 or said another way, $3,200 is equal to 4% of?

Answer: $80,000 ==>

You're not done, though.

Remember: "What am I looking for?"
The sales price of the building! So, $100,000 + $80,000 = $180,000

    Answer: #3 ($180,000)

(d) Sales associate Laura refers a listing on a $75,000 home and is to receive 15% of the total 7% commission if the property sells. Licensee Sam sells the property and Laura's 15% is deducted from Sam's 1/2 of the commission, how much will Sam receive?

    1. $ 5,250.00
    2. $ 787.50
    3. $ 4,462.50
    4. $ 1,837.50

Again, there are several steps to this problem. They're all easy, just take them one at a time. First, let's figure out the total commission.

The sales price was $75,000. The total commission was 7%.

$75,000 x 7% = $5,250 or

Laura is to receive 15% of $5,250 or $787.50

Sam receives 1/2 of the total commission minus Laura's portion.

Total commission $5,250 ÷ 2 = $2,625 (1/2 total commission)

$2,625 $787.50 (Laura's portion) = $1,837.50 Sam's commission

       Answer: #4 ($1,837.50)

(e) Broker Susan Harris of ABC Realty recently listed and sold Jack and Jill Smith's home for $43,500. Harris charged the Smith's a 6 1/2% commission and will pay 55% of that amount to the listing person and selling salesperson, on a ratio of 6 to 5, respectively. What amount of commission will the listing salesperson receive from the Smiths' sale?

    1. $1,555.13
    2. $1,272.38
    3. $ 848.25
    4. $ 706.88

First we must figure the total commission.

(Sales Price)	x	(Commission Rate)	=	Total Commission
$43,500	x	6.5%	=	$2,827.50

A portion of the commission is to be shared by two (2) salespeople which in this case is 55%.

Total Commission	$2,827.50
	x 55%
Salespeople's portion of the commission	$1,555.13

Listing person gets 6 parts out of a total 11 parts (6 to 5 ratio totals 11 parts).

Salesperson gets 5 parts of total 11 parts. The listing person gets 6/11 of $1,555.13.

$$\frac{6}{11} = 54.55\%$$

54.55% of salespeople portion of commission $1,555.13

$1,555.13 x 54.55% = $848.32

Answer: #3 ($848.25 is closest)

Net to Seller

A **seller's share**, or **net to seller**, is an *estimate of the money a seller should receive from a real estate transaction, based on a certain selling price after all costs and expenses have been paid.* This is *not* a guarantee but an approximation of what the seller should receive. The purpose of computing the net to seller is to let the seller know how much money he can expect to make from a transaction after everything has been paid. This is important information when considering both a listing price for the property and deciding whether to accept an offer.

Jane wants to sell her home. She must pay off her existing $35,000 mortgage and pay $3,200 in closing costs. She wants to have $40,000 left so she can buy another home. If she pays a 6.5% commission, what is the minimum offer she can accept?

First, subtract the known commission rate from the total sale price to find the percentage of the sale the seller will net:

100% - 6.5% = 93.5%

Total up the other known expenses:

$35,000 + $3,200 + $40,000 = $78,200

Finally, divide the total expenses by the net to seller percent:

$78,200 ÷ 0.935 (93.5%) = $83,636.36

Jane must sell her house for a minimum of $83,637

Answer : ($83,637)

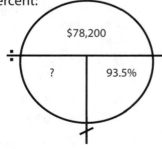

Appreciation and Depreciation

Appreciation "+"
("A" for addition to 100%)

Depreciation "-"
("D" for deduct from 100%)

Selling Price
or
Current Value

Original
Cost | 100%
+ or -

(a) If a building sold for $158,162 at a loss of 8%, what was the original cost of the building?

1. $145,509.04
2. $171,915.22
3. $170,814.96
4. $165,905.40

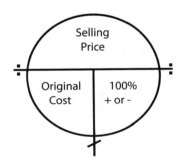

First: What are we looking for?

Right! Original Cost

Now, is it a depreciation or an appreciation problem? Did the building lose money? Yes, so it's a depreciation problem.

Next, we always start with 100%. If it's a depreciation problem, we subtract how much it depreciated from 100%. If it appreciates, we add to 100% how much it appreciated. Think of "A" for appreciate and "A" for add; "D" for depreciation and "D" for deduct. This problem says the building depreciated 8%, so...

100%
$-$ 8%
92%

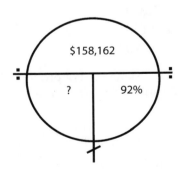

The selling price was $158,162. So...

$158,162 ÷ 92% = $171,915.22

Answer : #2 ($171,915.22)

(b) A property has depreciated annually 2 1/2% for 7 years. The current depreciated value of the property is $95,000. What was the original cost? (Use straight-line depreciation basis).

1. $166,250.00
2. $ 94,833.75
3. $ 78,375.00
4. $115,151.52

This question is meant to throw you off by saying "use straight-line depreciation basis." That's the only kind we use! There is one extra step to this problem. We must calculate the total amount of depreciation. That's easy: 7 years x 2 1/2% = 17 1/2% Now the problem is just like the previous one.

First: What are we looking for?

Original cost.   And it's a depreciation problem so, we know that we *subtract* from 100%.

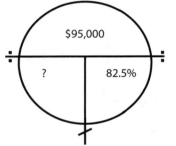

100.0%
− 17.5%
82.5%

$95,000 ÷ 82.5% = $115,151.52

Remember : Be careful to read your calculator correctly and select the correct answer.

Answer: #4 ($115,151.52)

(c) A house depreciated and is now worth $48,500, which is 82% of its original cost. What was the original cost of the property?

1. $39,770.00
2. $57,230.00
3. $59,146.34
4. $52,510.25

Again, it's the same kind of problem. We are looking for original cost. In this problem, we are already told what the house has depreciated to (we don't have to subtract from 100%).

$48,500 : 82% = $59,146.34

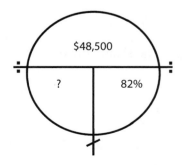

Answer: #3 ($59,146.34)

(d) A property that originally cost $93,500 has appreciated 25%. What is the property now worth?

1. $116,875.00
2. $ 70,125.00
3. $ 95,873.50
4. $110,250.25

This is an appreciation problem, so we'll add to 100% how much it appreciated.

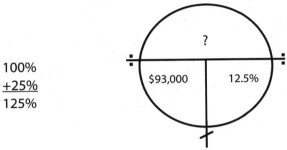

100%
+25%
125%

$93,500 x 125% = $116,875

Answer: #1 ($116,875)

Loan-to-Value Ratio (LTV)

Loan-to-value ratio is the % of the appraised value of the property that the bank will loan for a mortgage is the loan amount.

(a) If the LTV is 80%, and the house is appraised for $75,000 how much will the buyer be permitted to borrower?

1. $45,000
2. $15,000
3. $75,000
4. $60,000

$75,000 x 80% = $60,000 loan amount
$75,000 x 20% = $15,000 equity or down payment

Answer: #4 ($60,000)

Cash Flow on Income-Producing Property

It is important that we understand a basic cash flow statement for an income property—let's use a 10-unit apartment building—has a **potential gross income**. The potential gross income is the total amount of income a property could yield from rents, if all units were rented and all tenants paid their rent. This is typically not the case, so one must figure a vacancy as a collection loss. This is typically expressed as percentage of the potential gross income. The potential gross income less vacancy and collection loss is called the **effective gross income**. In determining the real rate of return on an income property, one must use the effective gross income as that amount represents the real dollars generated. After the effective gross income is determined, one subtracts the **annual operating expense"** to arrive at the **annual net operating income (NOI)**. The operating expenses include the fixed parts such as taxes, fire insurance, variable cost (i.e., utilities, maintenance, and replacement costs, appliances, carpet, etc.,) but do not include capital improvements, depreciation, or debt service. Once the annual NOI is determined, depreciation and debt service are deducted to arrive at the **internal rate of return (IRR)** before taxes or before cash flow. An investor would then consider their personal tax consequences to determine the internal rate of return after taxes. This is also referred to as the cash on cash return or after tax cash flow. The following is a basic cash flow summary: *(These are expenses in annual amounts.)*

		Potential Gross Income
(Less)	-	<u>Vacancy and Collection Loss</u>
		Effective Gross Income

		Effective Gross Income
(Less)	-	<u>Operating Expenses</u>
		Net Operating Income (NOI)

		Net Operating Income
(Less)	-	<u>Depreciation and Debt Service</u>
		Internal Rate of Return Before Taxes

		Internal Rate of Return Before Taxes
(Less)	-	<u>Personal Tax Consequence</u>
		Internal Rate of Return After Taxes
		(or Cash Flow After Taxes)

Now that we understand a basic cash flow for statements, let's look at capitalization problems. In our capitalization formula, we have annual net income; this is the same thing as net operating income.

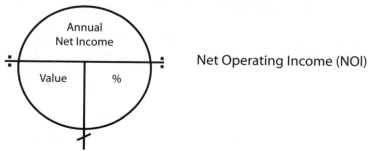

Net Operating Income (NOI)

1. The following information is available on a 10-unit apartment building with an annual gross potential rent of $57,500.

> Vacancy rate 5%
> Operating Expense $16,000
> Depreciation $8,500
> Debt Service $21,000

On the basis of the information above, what is the annual net operating income (NOI)?

   a. $54,625
   b. $38,625
   c. $57,500
   d. $16,000

Annual gross potential rent	$ 57,500	
Less vacancy rate	-$ 2,875	$57,500
		x 5%
Effective Gross Income	$54,625	$ 2,875
Effective Gross Income	$ 54,625	
Less Operating Expenses	-$ 16,000	
Annual Net Operating Income	$ 38,625	

Answer: B ($38,625)

2. An apartment building with 25 suites has a potential gross income of $97,500. The followinginformation is available:

> Vacancy and collection loss 6%
> Operating Expenses $31,000
> Depreciation $9,150
> Debt Service $46,500

Based on the above information, what is the cash flow before taxes?

   a. $60,650
   b. $51,500
   c. $5,850
   d. $5,000

Answer: D ($5,000)

% (Percent) of Profit

(a) A house that listed for $46,000 sold at 20% less than the list price. The buyer then turned around and sold for the list price. What was the % of profit?

1.   25%
2.   20%
3.   80%
4.   120%

The formula is: $\dfrac{\text{WHAT YOU MADE}}{\text{WHAT YOU PAID}} = \%\ \text{OF PROFIT}$

First: Let's figure out what he made.

The buyer bought the house for $46,000 less 20%:

$46,000 x 20% = $9,200

$46,000 - $9,200 = $36,800 (purchase price)

or, the buyer paid 80% of $46,000 = $36,800 (same answer)

The buyer then sold the house for $46,000:

   $46,000   sales price
- $36.800   paid
   $ 9,200   profit or what you made

$\dfrac{\text{What Was Made}}{\text{What You Paid}} = \dfrac{\$9,200}{\$36,800} = $ 25% profit

Answer: #1 (25%)

(b) Gallagher bought a parcel of land for $60,000. She subdivided the land into 8 lots of equal frontage and sold them for $30,000 each. What was the % of return on this original investment?

1.   3%
2.   300%
3.   30%
4.   3000%

First: Again, let's figure out what she made. She made 8 lots out of the parcel of land and sold them for $30,000 each.

8 lots x $30,000 = $240,000 gross revenue

She paid $60,000 for the parcel of land (her cost).

   $240,000 gross revenue
- $ 60,000 she paid
   $180,000 profit or what was made

$\dfrac{\text{What Was Made}}{\text{What Was Paid}} = \dfrac{\$180,000}{\$60,000} = $ 300% Profit

Points and Miscellaneous Financial Problems

1 Point = 1% of the loan amount, not the sales price! The seller must pay points on VA loans (on exam, real world all are negotiable), on other loans they (points) are negotiable.

1. In making a loan of $50,000, how much would the lender charge the seller at closing if the interest rate was 11 1/4% and three points were charged?

   a. $1,500.00
   b. $7,125.00
   c. $ 150.00
   d. $ 712.50

   First: We only care about the points.

   Remember, we don't need the interest rate information.

   1 point = 1% so, 3 points = 3%

   Answer: a (The loan amount $50,000 x 3% = $1,500)

2. Your buyer contracts to build an $80,000 home and is taking out a loan for $64,000. How much will a 1 1/2% loan origination fee cost him?

   a. $1,200
   b. $ 960
   c. $9,600
   d. $2,160

   $64,000 x 1 1/2% = $960

   Answer: b ($960) Trick: We don't care how much the house cost to build.

Taxes

The formula for taxes is x ÷ x. In New York, taxes are usually paid in advance. Don't worry about real life. With exam tax problems, they'll tell you what isn't paid.

   Step 1: x, appraised value by assessed rate

 * Step 2: ÷ assessed rate by 100

   Step 3: x that # by tax rate

*Taxes will usually be given as so many dollars per 100.

1. The tax rate in Revere County is $2.80 per $100 of assessed value. The assessed rate is 40%. What will the yearly tax be on a home valued at $98,000?

Step 1:	$98,000	x	40%	= $39,200
Step 2:	$39,200	÷	100	= 392
Step 3:	392	x	$2.80	= $1,097.60 yearly tax

Proration Problems

To prorate a cost such as taxes or insurance is to split that cost appropriately between buyer and seller. To avoid mistakes, and for consistency, we always figure the seller's portion. Assume 30 days per month, 365 days per year. Most proration problems can be figured bi-monthly, 1/3 of a month, etc.

Step 1: We make a timeline

Step 2: Mark closing date

Step 3: Count out time up to closing date

Step 4: Prorate

Step 5: Look at question and determine whose portion they are asking for

1. Taxes for the year were $570 and were paid in advance. If a house closes on August 15, how much would the buyer owe?

   (a) First make a timeline.

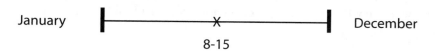

January ⊢————————×————————⊣ December

8-15

Now, mark the closing date under your timeline.

Now, count out how much time will elapse from closing to the end of the year. Count it on your fingers. Half of August. September, October, November, and December. That's 4.5 months.

All we have to do now is find out how much 1 month of taxes are.

One year taxes were $570 ÷ 12 months = $47.50 per month

($47.50 per month) x (4.5 months) = $213.75

The buyer's portion would be a credit to the seller.

Conveyance or Transfer Fees

The conveyance or transfer fee* (seller expense) is paid by the seller at closing. It is based on the selling price of the property. The formula is the tax rate multiplied by $1,000 of the purchase price. The transfer fee can be understood by looking at an example. Assume the tax rate is $4 per $1,000 of selling price.

Selling Price	Transfer Fee
53,300.00	213.20

One of the simplest ways to calculate the transfer fee is to multiply the selling price by .004.

53,401.00 x 0.004 = 213.20

Conveyance fee, transfer tax, auditors tax and state documentary stamps are synonymous terms.

Area Problems

 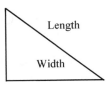 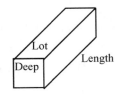 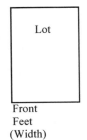

Square Feet:

Length
Width

Length
Width

Lot
Deep
Length

Lot

Front
Feet
(Width)

(w) x (l) = Sq. Ft.   [½(w)] x l   (w) x (l) x (d) = Cubic   Feet

There are 43,560 sq. ft. in an acre, so...

Total Sq. Ft. ÷ 43,560 = # of Acres $\dfrac{\$}{\text{Land}}$ = Cost per sq. ft. (etc.)

# of Acres x 43,560 = sq. ft.

1. A lot that is 200 ft. wide x 580 ft. long is how many acres?

    First: Figure total sq. footage (area = width x length)
             200' x 580' = 116,000 sq. ft.

    Next: Total area in sq. ft. ÷ 43,560 = # of acres
             116,000 sq. ft. ÷ 43,560 = 2.66 acres

2. Simon bought 8.2 acres. How many sq. ft. did he buy?

    First: (# of acres) x (43,560) = sq. ft.
             8.2 acres x 43,560 = 357,192 sq. ft.

3. A lot that measures 85' wide by 100' deep is what fraction of an acre?

    85' x 100' = 8,500 sq. ft.
    8,500 sq. ft. ÷ 43,560 = 0.195

    But all the answers are in fractions!

    Remember: A fraction has a decimal equivalent

    0.195 rounded up to 0.20 is 2/10 or 1/5.
    Hint: Convert all answers into decimals   (a) 1/4 = 0.25   (b) 3/5 = 0.60
                                                      (c) 2/3 = 0.66   (d) 1/5 = 0.20

    Now, which is the closest? That's right, "D"!

4. A buyer writes an offer to purchase some land 640' wide x 1,000' deep. His price is
    based on paying $1,500 per acre. How much is his offer for?

    640' x 1,000' = 640,000 sq. ft.
    640,000 ÷ 43,560 (sq. ft. in an acre) 14.69 acres
    14.69 acres x $1,500 per acre = $22,035.00

5. A lot is 80' wide by 225' deep and sells for $4,500. How much is the sales price per sq. ft.?

Remember the formula: $$\frac{\$}{Land} = \text{Cost per sq. ft. (etc.)}$$

Figure the total sq. footage 80' x 225' = 18,000 sq. ft.

$$\frac{\$4,500}{18,000 \text{ sq. ft.}} = 0.25 \text{ or 25 cents per sq. ft.}$$

6. A developer owns 15 lots each 100' wide by 185' deep. He wants to make $112,500 from selling the lots. How much per front foot will the sale price be?

Remember: $$\frac{\$}{Land} = \text{cost per sq. ft. (etc.)}$$

First: Figure how many total front feet you have to work with.

Remember, front feet is the width of the lot (the first dimension given unless stated otherwise).

15 lots x 100 front feet = 1, 500 total front feet

$$\frac{\$112,500}{1,500 \text{ front feet}} = \$75 \text{ per front foot}$$

7. A pool is 12' long, 8' wide, and 6' deep. The volume of the pool is:

12' x 8' x 6' = 576 cubic feet

To convert to cubic yards, you must divide by 27.

576 cubic feet ÷ 27 = 21.33 cubic yards

QUIZ

1. A sales associate has 1.65 acres of land listed at 20.5 cents per square foot. What is the selling price?
   a. $14,734.17
   b. $15,000.00
   c. $14,134.17
   d. $21,150.00

2. The taxes on a property were $345.00 and were paid in advance by the owner. What refund would the owner get from a purchaser if the owner sold the house, and the taxes were prorated on October 15? (Use 30-day month.)
   a. $77.28
   b. $71.88
   c. $70.15
   d. $273.12

3. A special tax levy is passed for 43 cents per 100. Clark owns property with a market value of $72,000. Property is assessed for tax purposes at 40% of its appraised value. What will the tax levy cost Clark yearly?
   a. $134.40
   b. $123.84
   c. $309.60
   d. $56.60

4. An investor purchased ten building lots for partial resale, each with a frontage of 75 feet, for $50,000. The investor wants to keep two lots for personal use and additionally make a profit of $25,000 on the resale. What must the sale price per front foot be on each lot sold?
   a. $225
   b. $125
   c. $100
   d. $720

5. A lender charged a 2% loan origination fee and 3 discount points to make a 95% conventional insured mortgage loan in the amount of $47,500. What was the cost of these charges to the borrower?
   a. $1,425
   b. $1,118
   c. $2,375
   d. $922

6. You, a sales associate, are to receive 60% of the brokerage fee from the sale of a property. The property sold for $52,000. The fee is 7% on the first $30,000 and 3.5% on the remaining amount. What commission will you receive?
   a. $1,925
   b. $1,148
   c. $2,870
   d. $1,722

7. A property has a gross annual income of $14,250 and monthly expenses of $300. It has been valued at $147,000. What is the capitalization rate?
   a. 7.2%
   b. 9.6%
   c. 6.1%
   d. 5.4%

8. A broker learns that his seller must net $24,000 from the sale of his property. There is an existing mortgage of $94,500, the agreed commission is 4.5%, and miscellaneous closing costs will be $4,350. What is the least amount that the property can sell for and return the seller's desired amount?
   a. $127,508
   b. $124,083
   c. $128,639
   d. $128,378

9. Chris wants to build a patio 60 feet x 20 feet and 4 inches thick. How many cubic yards of concrete will be needed?
   a. 14.8
   b. 12.4
   c. 120
   d. 400

10. A house sold for $35,550, which was 11% more than the original cost of the house. The original cost of the house was
    a. $33,000.
    b. $32,000.
    c. $32,027.
    d. $33,037.

Chapter Quiz Answer Key

Chapter 1: Real Estate License Law

1. **A.** A salesperson may accept compensation only from his employing broker.

2. **A.** Salesperson candidates are required to complete 75 hours of state-approved education but do not have an experience requirement.

3. **B.** An associate broker retains the right to have a broker's license as well. There is no separate commercial real estate license.

4. **C.** She must complete 22.5 hours of CE before she renews her license again.

5. **D.** The law requires the broker's business name and phone number appear on all advertising.

6. **B.** Of these, only Joe needs to be a real estate licensee since he works for a property management firm.

7. **A.** Joe has one broker's license, most likely a Class 31-Corporate Broker's license. Although the others have the education and experience and passed the broker's exam, they are associate brokers since they are employed by Joe. Only the broker's license is required to be displayed.

8. **A.** An office manager has an associate broker's license.

9. **C.** All advertising must be in the exact name under which the brokerage is licensed.

10. **C.** The money must be deposited as soon as it's practical to do so, which could reasonably be two days later.

Chapter 2: Law of Agency 1

1. **A.** If the broker made the decision to not disclose a material fact, he could be accused of actual fraud.

2. **C.** Where traditional agency is practiced in a brokerage, all affiliated licensees have the same agency relationship as the listing agent or seller's agent.

3. **D.** At this point, Howard and Owen do not have a fiduciary relationship. Howard is simply a customer. The seller of the home is Owen's client.

4. **D.** When an agent is authorized to do a variety of things in one area on behalf of the principal, the relationship is a general agency relationship.

5. **D.** By law, if either the seller or the broker dies, the listings are terminated. The listing is between the broker and the seller, not the agent, so the agent's death would have no effect upon the listing.

6. **B.** This is an example of subagency, since the broker enlisted a cooperating broker to show the property on the seller's behalf. The subagent must also act in the seller's best interest.

7. **A.** If an agent decides to take the listing at the price indicated by the seller, the agent must be loyal to the seller and not imply that the list price is unreasonable.

8. **B.** Each of the agents would be designated as a buyer's or seller's agent and the brokers would act as consensual dual agents.

9. **C.** An agent's duty of obedience applies only to lawful instructions. Latent defects must be disclosed.

10. **A.** An agent must follow all legal instructions of her client.

Chapter 3: Law of Agency 2

1. **C.** The disclosure form is simply a written description of the agency relationship.

2. **A.** Dual agency is not a conflict of interest if it is disclosed. Alex is obligated to remain completely neutral in this transaction.

3. **C.** The money must be deposited as soon as it's practical to do so, which could reasonably be two days later.

4. **C.** When a seller offers a commission to any broker who finds a buyer, it is as an open listing. The seller does not sign exclusively with one agency.

5. **D.** In an in-company transaction, the broker is a dual agent, as are all licensees.

6. **C.** You have to retain all documents for at least three years.

7. **D.** A net listing, which pays the agent the difference between the asking price and the selling price, is illegal in New York.

8. **B.** Only the exclusive right to sell listing agreement entitles a broker to a commission, no matter who brings the buyer.

9. **B.** Even the appearance of discussing fees could be considered an example of illegal price-fixing.

10. **A.** Under an exclusive agency agreement, the seller can still sell the property on her own and not owe a commission. In an exclusive agency listing, unlike an open listing, only the listing company can put a sign in the yard and advertise it.

Chapter 4: Being an Independent Contractor

1. **C.** New York law does not require brokers to record the number of hours an agent works on a transaction.

2. **B.** The term REALTOR® has nothing to do with the state license. It refers to a private trade organization; not all real estate salespersons are Realtors ®.

3. **B.** These are two possible IRS categories. If the salesperson is hired under a contract paid based on sales, and given an IRS 1099 at year end, he is an independent contractor. If he is paid a salary, required to put in a set number of hours in the office, has taxes taken out of his paycheck, and receives a W-2 at year end, he is an employee.

4. **D.** A real estate licensee who works for a supervising broker, yet maintains independence in his work schedule, is most likely a statutory non-employee.

5. **C.** An independent contractor must manage her taxes herself. Her employer does not withhold anything.

6. **C.** A real estate licensee would never be a statutory employee, but the other classifications are possible.

7. **A.** A real estate licensee has a fiduciary relationship with clients regardless of whether he is an employee of his broker or an independent contractor.

8. **C.** Using the term "broker" may imply that Sue is the broker in charge. If she lists her status as an associate broker, then it clearly indicates her status as a broker, but not as the principal broker of the office.

9. **B.** An independent contractor receives a 1099 MISC form detailing any commission-based income.

10. **B.** An independent contractor is paid commission for finding a ready, willing, and able buyer. It doesn't matter how many hours it took to do that.

Chapter 5: Estates, Interests, Liens, and Easements

1. **D.** Wheat is an annual crop and therefore, an emblement. Emblements are always considered personal property, even if included in the agreement of sale.

2. **D.** A fixture is personal property that has been attached to real property. The water faucet has not been attached so it is still personal property. The rest of the items are attached.

3. **C.** A lease that automatically renews is an estate from year to year, even if it is a month-to-month lease.

4. **D.** The shrub hanging over the property line is an encroachment, not an encumbrance. Liens and easements are encumbrances.

5. **A.** An appurtenant easement burdens one property, the servient tenement (Lin's property), for the benefit of another property, the dominant tenement (Darrell's property). Darrell is allowed to cross the property (nonencroachment). While the explanation with easement in gross is correct, here, the easement runs with the land and not a person.

6. **A.** An easement in gross gives a person or company the right to enter another person's property. It is often a right of utility companies to fix or repair equipment.

7. **C.** Joint tenancy allows co-owners to take ownership shares of a deceased co-owner automatically. Since Mark and Paula have unity of person, her interest is now 100%.

8. **D.** Tenancy in common is co-ownership with no right of survivorship. It is also the most common form of ownership.

9. **B.** Ownership in severalty is real property ownership by only one person. When that person dies, the property descends to his heirs.

10. **B.** In order to form a tenancy by the entirety, all five unities must be present.

Chapter 6: Sales and Lease Contracts

1. **B.** An executory contract is one in which the parties have agreed to the terms but some conditions still remain to be fulfilled. Once all of the conditions are met and all that remains is the closing, the contract is said to be complete, or executed.

2. **B.** No one but the offeree can accept an offer. The acceptance by the neighbor is not valid, no matter how or when it was communicated. It is, in fact, a new offer, which Walton now may or may not accept, as he chooses.

3. **A.** A voidable contract may be rescinded by an injured party. A void contract is not really a contract at all because it lacks one of the essential elements or is defective in some other way, and therefore is unenforceable.

4. **B.** An option is a unilateral contract, which is binding only on one party. The lease option is binding on the seller. If Larry exercises his option to buy, the seller must sell. However, Larry is under no obligation to buy.

5. **A.** Statute of Frauds requires all real estate contracts to be in writing to be enforceable.

6. **A.** A contract is discharged once an agreement has terminated. Ideally, this happens when all the terms of the contract have been carried out.

7. **D.** Besides the requirements listed, a valid contract must also have offer and capacity. Substantial performance is when the promisor doesn't perform all contractual obligations, but does enough so that the promisee is required to fulfill that part of the deal.

8. **D.** A novation is a new contract. One party of the contract withdrawals and a new one is substituted.

9. **A.** This type of contract is called a gross lease and is commonly used for residential space and for professionals renting commercial space. A disadvantage to this type of contract is the lease is subject to increases with inflation and taxes.

10. **B.** The original party remains secondarily liable under an assignment.

Chapter 7: The Valuation Process and Pricing Properties

1. **C.** Market value is the theoretical price a piece of real estate is most likely to bring in a typical transaction.

2. **C.** An appraisal is simply an estimate or opinion of value.

3. **C.** When an appraiser is looking for comparables, he or she will only look at homes that have sold recently.

4. **A.** The cost approach is an objective method to provide an accurate value for replacing or reproducing buildings, especially new or nearly new buildings with few comparable sales.

5. **D.** The principle of regression states that the value of the "best" home in a neighborhood is lower than what it might be in a comparable neighborhood.

6. **D.** Examples of external obsolescence include a declining neighborhood, a nearby landfill, or a new highway that creates noise or re-routes traffic.

7. **D.** The condition is curable because the cost of repair is less than the value that will be added to the property.

8. **B.** When making adjustments, subtract the value of an extra feature from the comp's value.

9. **B.** The estimated value using a GRM (Gross Rent Multiplier) is the monthly rent x GRM. In this case, $750 x 110 = $82,500.

10. **A.** Although a CMA is similar to an appraisal, it is never equal to an appraisal.

Chapter 8: Deeds and Real Estate Closings

1. **B.** The greatest protection for the buyer, the grantee, is with a general warranty deed with its five covenants.

2. **B.** The grantor must sign a deed for it to be valid. The grantee never signs the deed. Acknowledgement is only required for the deed to be recorded, the deed is valid without it.

7. **A.** Descent, devise, and escheat are all related to someone's estate after death.

4. **B.** Quitclaim deeds come with no warranties and provide the least amount of protection to the grantee.

5. **A.** An abstract of title is a chronological summary of the essential provisions of every recorded document pertaining to a particular parcel of land.

6. **B.** In New York, there must be open, continuous, notorious, and hostile possession for 10 years.

7. **B.** Title insurance does not cover known defects.

8. **B.** Remember that metes measure distance (like meters) and bounds indicate direction.

9. **A.** This clause describes the type of estate granted.

10. **B.** New York State requires the seller to pay the transfer tax, which is $2.00 for every $500 of the sale price.

Chapter 9: Overview of Real Estate Finance

1. B. The promissory note is the instrument of obligation secured by the mortgage with the homeowner pledging the real property as security for payment of the promissory note. A trustee's deed is used to transfer property a trustee is holding in a trust situation. A chattel mortgage uses personal property, not real property, as collateral.

2. A. The borrower is giving the mortgage to the lender so the borrower is the mortgagor. The lender is called the mortgagee.

3. A. When the lender loans money to a borrower and the borrower gives the lender a mortgage, it is called the primary mortgage market.

4. D. If the loan-to-value (LTV) ratio is 80%, the down payment is 20% of the purchase price: (85,000 x .20 = $17,000).

5. B. The alienation clause gives the lender certain stated rights when there is a transfer of ownership in the property.

6. C. A defeasance clause is a clause used to defeat or cancel a certain right upon the occurrence of a specific event. For example, upon final payment, the mortgage is thereby satisfied or cancelled or void, and the title is re-vested to the mortgagor.

7. B. He would pay $1,900 because $95,000 x 0.02 = $1,900. Discount points are paid on the mortgage amount. The down payment is separate.

8. A. The acceleration clause allows the lender, in the event of default or for violation of other contract provisions, to declare the entire balance remaining immediately due and payable.

9. B. A graduated payment plan is a type of buydown plan that has lower monthly payments in the early years with increases at specified intervals until the payment amounts are sufficient to amortize the loan over the remaining term.

10 D. The loan value is based on the appraised value or the sale price, whichever is lower. The appraised value is $86,500; 80% of that amount is $69,200. This would be considered the 80% loan-to-value ratio, the appraised value or the sale price, whichever is lower. The appraised value is $86,500.00; 80% of that amount is $69,200.00. This would be the maximum the purchaser would be permitted to borrow.

Chapter 10: Mortgage Basics

1. C. Statutory redemption occurs after the sale has been finalized, and is recognized only in those states which have extended the right of redemption to include the period after the sale. Equitable redemption occurs prior to the sale, when the homeowner avoids foreclosure by paying all past due payments, etc. Anticipatory repudiation is a breach of contract before it begins. A defeasance clause in a mortgage states that once the loan is paid in full, that mortgage is canceled.

2. D. Regulation Z of the Truth in Lending Act requires lenders to disclose all costs of obtaining a loan, including interest rate, costs of payments over the life of the loan, etc. This is referred to as the Truth in Lending letter, which must be given to the borrower within 10 days after the mortgage application. The Equal Credit Opportunity Act requires equal credit opportunity be given to persons regardless of race, religion, sex, etc. The Fair Credit Reporting Act requires creditors to truthfully record credit remarks on an individual's credit report.

3. C. A bridge mortgage (also referred to as a swing loan or gap loan) is a mortgage that occurs between the termination of one mortgage and the beginning of the next.

4. B. Pre-qualification of a buyer is not binding on the lender but it is a useful tool to help agents and prospects know what price range to look in.

5. D. Predatory lenders have been known to make loans to unqualified borrowers at high interest rates, regardless of repayment ability. Such loans often end in foreclosure. Requiring mortgage insurance is not considered predatory.

6. C. Interest rate adjustments are based on the upward and downward movements of the selected index.

7. B. The qualifying standard (set by the secondary market) states that 36% can be debt. This is considered the mortgage payment of PITI, car payments, credit cards, alimony, child support, and any other monthly revolving debt—not expenses such as car insurance, utilities, cable, and telephone.

8. D. Pre-qualification refers to the process of predetermining if a potential borrower is likely to get approved for a loan and for approximately how much money.

9. B. Total debt service ratio is calculated as: $3,000 (income) multiplied by (x) 0.36, which equals $1,080. From the $1,080, you must subtract his monthly debts ($350 +$50+ $50), which total $630.

10. **C.** Compared to conventional loan standards of 28%, FHA loans allow more of the borrower's income to be housing expense (31%). Housing expense is the principal, interest, taxes and insurance (PITI), which is the mortgage payment.

Chapter 11: Land Use Regulations

1. **D.** Setback requirements are usually dictated by subdivision regulations and restrictions put on the property by the original developer. It would be up to the neighbors to enforce these.

2. **A.** Appropriation or condemnation is the actual act of taking private land for public use. Eminent domain is the government's right to take private land.

3. **C.** The power to take private land for public use is known as eminent domain. The right to create regulations such as eminent domain is police power. The actual physical taking of the land is appropriation or condemnation.

4. **D.** The rights of property ownership are derived from the government, and so those rights revert to the state if they aren't assigned to someone else by the owner or if there are no heirs.

5. **D.** Spot zoning is an example of isolated zoning changes or rezoning that can be illegal because the law is not applied the same way to all landowners.

6. **A.** A deed restriction may be terminated only if it is in violation of a discriminatory act or impinges upon the owner's bundle of rights. Otherwise, a deed restriction stays with the property for the life of the property.

7. **B.** These are building codes.

8. **C.** Since the barbershop was built before the zoning laws were enacted, it is now a nonconforming use. If it had been built after the zoning laws were established, a conditional use zoning certificate or a variance may have been required. The barbershop may or may not be a nuisance and/or an eyesore.

9. **D.** These restrictions are appurtenant to the real property and thus run with the land. They do not terminate upon the death of the grantor or grantee.

10. **B.** A conditional special use permit may be granted to allow the use of property that is in the public's best interest.

Chapter 12: Construction Basics

1. **C.** Standard electric service in New York requires a minimum of 200 amps for new construction.

2. **D.** Vertical wood beams that frame a structure are called studs.

3. **C.** R-Factor is used to measure the insulating value or resistance to heat flow through a material or object. R-Value is its R-Factor multiplied by the amount of material.

4. **C.** The rate at which water moves through soil is called the percolation rate.

5. **B.** After all of the inspections have been made and a property has been deemed fit, a certificate of occupancy is issued.

6. **B.** The common measurement of heating capacity is the BTU, or the amount of heat needed to raise the temperature of one pound of water by one degree Fahrenheit.

7. **A.** To provide enough water to an average household, wells are expected to produce at least five gallons of water per minute.

8. **A.** New York State law requires a one-year warranty on the builder's workmanship.

9. **A.** New York State's home improvement laws take effect when the job is $500 or more. There are currently no licensing requirements for home improvement contractors or builders in New York State.

10. **A.** The right of rescission law applies to home improvement contracts and refinancing. It allows the homeowner three days to change his mind and back out of the contract.

Chapter 13: Environmental Issues and Property Conditions

1. **B.** It's the Comprehensive Environmental Response, Compensation, and Liability Act (CERCLA).

2. **A.** Sellers don't have to test, remove, or correct for lead-based paint hazards.

3. **A.** Since asbestos is dangerous when inhaled, its removal can contaminate the house if not done properly.

4. **B.** Radon gas is dangerous when it accumulates in the home because of inadequate ventilation.

5. **A.** Section 404 of the federal Clean Water Act deals with wetlands protection. The U.S. Army Corps of Engineers regulates and enforces Section 404, with the EPA having the ultimate authority.

6. D. CO is a by-product of combustion and produced by furnaces and other appliances that produce heat. Thus, these appliances should be checked regularly to make sure they aren't pumping more CO into the atmosphere than acceptable. Homeowners should also use a CO detector.

7. B. Unless you are a licensed exterminator, or the homeowner is willing to tackle the problem without a warranty for the repair, call a reputable professional and keep documentation and receipts.

8. D. There are currently no government regulations regarding mold or its disclosure.

9. D. The State of New York requires that carbon monoxide detectors and smoke alarms be placed inside all homes offered for sale that consist of one- to two-family units or condominiums.

10. C. The insulation emits levels of formaldehyde that dissipate over time, so old insulation would pose no current health risk.

Chapter 14: Human Rights and Fair Housing

1. A. Blockbusting is defined as inducing or attempting to induce, for profit, any person to sell or rent property based on representations made regarding entry into the neighborhood of persons of a particular race, color, religion, sex, or national origin.

2. B. The Civil Rights Act of 1866 prohibits racial discrimination in all property transactions in the United States, including real or personal, residential or commercial, or improved or unimproved.

3. B. In 1988, both familial status and disability were added as protected classes.

4. D. Someone illegally addicted to a controlled substance is not considered disabled and is not a member of that protected class.

5. C. The federal Fair Housing Act requires landlords/owners to make provisions for handicap accessibility, but it does not require the landlord to bear the expense of the renovations. The landlord is also allowed to require the property be returned to its original condition upon termination of occupancy.

6. D. As of today, the federal Fair Housing Act prohibits discrimination in housing based on "race, color, religion, sex, national origin, disability, or familial status in the sale or lease of residential property."

7. C. Exempt senior housing facilities and communities can lawfully refuse to sell or rent to families with minor children if the facility is intended for and solely occupied by persons 62 years or older.

8. C. Steering relates to buyers or renters and is defined as channeling prospective buyers or renters to or away from specific neighborhoods.

9. D. It is good practice to have buyers tell you the areas in which they prefer to live. As a licensed sales agent, it is steering if you channel home seekers to particular areas based on race, religion, country of origin, or other protected classes.

10. A. The New York State law does not recognize lawful occupation as a protected class.

Chapter 15: Municipal Agencies

1. B. According to New York's Landmarks Law, a potential landmark must be at least 30 years old in order to be designated as a landmark.

2. A. The primary function of the receiver of taxes is to collect taxes. Tax rates are determined by the taxing authority, such as a city; tax exemptions are considered by the assessor, and tax laws are written by the legislative body of the municipality.

3. D. The planning department is responsible for comprehensive municipal planning. Planning departments also help carry out plans once they are approved by the planning board.

4. C. The planning board advises other boards on land use and ensures compliance with the State Environmental Quality Review Act.

5. B. Each county has its own health department.

6. B. New York State statutes specifically give the zoning board of appeals the power to hear appeals seeking interpretation of provisions of local ordinances.

7. C. Property tax rates are determined by levies. Local entities establish where all sources of revenue come from, other than property taxes. These revenues are subtracted from the original budget and the remainder becomes the tax levy, which is raised through real property taxes.

8. D. Tax assessors do not determine property taxes. They determine the assessed value of property.

9. B. Villages are governed by a village board of trustees versus a city council.

10. B. Local building departments are responsible for issuing building permits and for seeing that code restrictions are followed.

Chapter 16: Property Insurance

1. **C.** On an All Risk policy, everything is covered unless specifically excluded.

2. **C.** All are covered losses. The explosion is the cause of the fire and water damage.

3. **A.** Homeowners applying for C-MAP must meet certain eligibility requirements.

4. **C.** Normal homeowners policies do not cover flood. Flood insurance can be purchased from the National Flood Insurance Program or an insurer participating in the Write Your Own Program.

5. **B.** The buyer should obtain insurance immediately at the closing. At this moment, the buyer becomes liable for any injury or property damage to others.

6. **D.** The formula for determining actual cash value is "Replacement cost – Depreciation = ACV."

7. **B.** Deductibles help reduce the overuse of the policy, thereby reducing insurance costs. The higher the deductible, the lower the premium.

8. **B.** In a replacement cost loss settlement, claims are paid in full without depreciation, up to the policy limits, less any deductible.

9. **D.** Umbrella policies provide high limits of liability and broad coverage for a reasonable premium.

10. **B.** Flood is not a covered peril.

Chapter 17: Taxes and Assessments

1. **D.** The state does not collect or receive any direct benefit from real property taxes.

2. **D.** Property tax liens always have a higher priority over other previously recorded liens.

3. **A.** An ad valorem tax refers to taxes based on the value of property.

4. **B.** An administrative review is a challenge brought to the Assessment Review Board on grievance day.

5. **D.** The assessment is just one factor that goes into the tax rate. An assessment cannot be challenged due to the tax rate.

6. **B.** The value placed on land and buildings by a city, town, or county assessor for use in levying annual real estate taxes is known as assessed value.

7. **D.** Storm windows would generally not involve the need to reassess.

8. **B.** Special assessments are primarily used to pay for infrastructure costs for a specific project, not for an operating budget.

9. **A.** Homestead properties are dwellings of four units or less, owner-occupied mobile homes, residential condominiums, farms, and vacant land less than 10 acres that are located in areas that are zoned for one- to three-family residential. A condop includes commercial space.

10. **A.** Property is assessed annually in New York State.

Chapter 18: Income Tax Issues in Real Estate

1. **C.** One of the biggest advantages to owning a home is that mortgage interest and property taxes are tax deductible.

2. **C.** Any real property can be exchanged for any other real property in a like-kind exchange, except for the exchange of property located outside of the U.S.

3. **A.** Capital gains on the sale of investment property as well as dividends and interest all qualify as portfolio income.

4. **B.** As long as the home is not rented for more than 14 days during the year, any rental income can be excluded and taxes and interest can be deducted.

5. **C.** John can deduct the entire interest paid on his mortgage. At $520 each month, he paid $6,240 in interest for the year. Add to that the property taxes that he paid, and John determines that he can deduct $9,520 on his income tax returns. The new deck is not deductible.

6. **C.** Typically, depreciation is calculated to deduct expenses from income.

7. **D.** The time requirement to depreciate residential rental property is 27.5 years; for commercial property it is 39 years.

8. **B.** The percentage rates required fluctuate depending on amount of income of the occupants, but 20% of the project is the minimum amount allowed to qualify for the low income housing tax credit.

9. **B.** They qualify for $500,000 exclusion, so they will pay capital gains taxes only on the amount above that – $200,000.

10. **B.** The appraised value of land is deducted from the price paid for property to determine its depreciable basis. Land itself is never depreciated.

Chapter 19: Condominiums and Cooperatives

1. **B.** Condo owners have a separate interest in their individual units, and therefore, they have individual mortgages and are taxed separately.

2. **B.** These rules and regulations are called bylaws.

3. **C.** A cooperative sells shares in the co-op, which are personal property.

4. **A.** John owns a condo. A condominium owner holds title fee simple to his or her unit and a specified share of the indivisible parts of the building and land, known as common elements.

5. **A.** Flip tax is imposed by the co-op board for the transfer of ownership during the sale of a unit.

6. **D.** The seller typically pays the condo's New York City and State Transfer Tax unless the purchase is made directly from the sponsor.

7. **C.** According to most plans, sponsors must give up control after five years or 50% of the building is sold, whichever comes first.

8. **D.** A cooperative is not real estate, but the purchase of stock shares in a corporation. With the stock comes a proprietary lease, or the right to occupy a specific unit.

9. **B.** A Cooperative Policy Statement #1 (CPS-1) is applicable to cooperatives, condominiums, and homeowners associations and is used to test the market, explore the venture, and determine the needs to meet a variety of conditions.

10. **C.** A common area is owned and used by all. A limited common area is owned by all but only used by one. An example would be a designated parking space.

Chapter 20: Commercial and Investment Properties

1. **B.** An example of pass through is when expenses are passed on to the tenant. Many contracts include an expense stop, which sets a maximum limit on the additional amount of expenses that can be passed through.

2. **D.** Leverage is the use of borrowed funds to finance a portion of the purchase price of an investment. The ability to convert an asset to cash quickly at any price is marketability. The ability to convert an asset into cash quickly without losing any principal is liquidity. And the possibility of losing principal invested or potential income from the investment is risk.

3. **D.** The New York State real estate broker's or salesperson's license is all-encompassing, which means the license permits an agent to conduct business in the brokerage of practically any type of real estate.

4. **C.** The difference between net (useable) square footage and rentable (gross) square footage is measured in percentage terms and is referred to as a loss factor, sometimes called the "load."

5. **C.** Changes in the law that affect the market value of George's property is an example of legislative risk.

6. **C.** Typically, depreciation is calculated to deduct expenses from income.

7. **A.** Cash flow is calculated by subtracting the annual debt service of principal and interest from the net operating income (NOI).

8. **B.** A liquid investment is one that can be converted to cash quickly without loss of principal.

9. **A.** The cap rate is calculated as value divided by NOI. Vacancy losses are needed to find NOI, but depreciation is not.

10. **C.** Effective gross income minus (-) operating costs is (=) net operating income (NOI).

Chapter 21: Property Management

1. **D.** The property owner is the principal in the property owner/property manager relationship. The property manager is an agent of the principal.

2. **C.** A landlord may not refuse to let a disabled renter make reasonable modifications to the apartment or common areas at the person's expense if such modifications are necessary for that person to use the housing.

3. **A.** A property manager has a fiduciary obligation to the property owner.

4. **B.** This is an example of constructive eviction.

5. **A.** A management agreement governs the relationship between a property owner and a property manager.

6. **B.** Property taxes and insurance are fixed expenses – ongoing operating expenses that do not vary based on occupancy levels of a property.

7. **B.** A property manager is a general agent because of the broad range of duties performed.

8. **A.** An **anchor tenant** is a major department or chain store strategically located within a shopping center to give maximum exposure to smaller satellite stores.

9. **C.** A stabilized budget documents the income and expenses averaged over a five-year period.

10. **C.** The rent for units in Bart's building may not be competitive if no one has moved in five years. It might be a good idea to raise the rent.

Chapter 22: Math Review

1. **A.** First, find the total square feet: 43,560 x 1.65 = 71,874. Then, multiply that by .205 dollars to find the selling price of $14,734.17.

2. **B.** There are a couple of ways to do this. Here's one: Divide the total taxes by 12 to find that the taxes are $28.75 per month. The owner paid for two and a half months that he did not use (half of October, all of November and December). Multiply 2.5 x $28.75 to find the amount of the refund: $71.88. You could have also figured it on a daily basis with the buyer owing the seller for 75 days.

3. **B.** First, find the assessed value: $72,000 x .40 = $28,800. Since the assessment is for each hundred dollars, divide by 100 to find $288. Multiply that by the rate to find the taxes: $288 x .43 = $123.84

4. **B.** The investor has 600 front feet to sell (75 front feet per lot x 8 lots to sell). If he wants to make $25,000 profit, he needs to sell all the land for $75,000 ($25,000 + $50,000). To find the price per front foot, divide the selling price by the number of front feet: $75,000 / 600 = $125

5. **C.** A point is 1% of the loan amount. There are a total of 5 points being charged on this loan. To find the dollar amount of the points, multiply 5% by the loan amount: $47,500 x .05 = $2,375

6. **D.** There's a 7% commission made on the first $30,000 ($30,000 x .07 = $2,100). On the remaining $22,000, the commission is 3.5% ($22,000 x .035 = $770). The total commission is $2,870. If you get 60% of that, your commission is $1,722 ($2,870 x .60 = $1,722).

7. **A.** You need to first find the annual net operating income by subtracting the annual expenses ($300 x 12 = $3,600) from the income: $14,250 - $3,600 = $10,650. Then use the IRV formula to find the capitalization rate: Income ($10,650) divided by Value ($147,000) to find the Rate: $10.650 / $147,000 = .0724 or 7.2%

8. **C.** First, add all the known costs of this transaction: $24,000 profit + $94,500 mortgage + $4,350 closing costs to find $122,850. To add in the 4.5% commission, you need to divide that dollar amount by 95.5% (100% - 4.5% = 95.5%): $122,850 / .955 = $128,639 (rounded)

9. **A.** First, note the depth is in inches, not feet, so you need to convert inches to feet (12 / 4 = .333). Then find the cubic square feet: 60 x 20 x .333 = 399.6. To find cubic yards, you need to divide that by 27: 399.6 / 27 = 14.8

10. **C.** The house sold for 111% of its original value, so divide $35,550 by 1.11 to find the original price of $32,027.